C000259293

The Seven Golden Rules For A Happy and Successful Life

A relevant but irreverent interpretation of the historical but hysterical facts of The Wars of The Roses, the reign of Henry VIII and the reigns of his three children; this book contains The Seven Golden Rules for a happy and successful life, greater fulfillment in everything you do, the two secrets to happiness, the purpose of life and what is probably the longest sub title in literary history.

By Philip Hesketh

First published 2010 by Philip Hesketh Ltd

ISBN 978-0-9567598-0-1

The Author

Philip Hesketh is a Psychology graduate from Newcastle University, a Sales graduate from Procter & Gamble and part of the Harvard Alumni.

In 1986 he was the creator, New Business Director and Managing Partner of an advertising agency, Advertising Principles. After 16 consecutive years of growth with the agency billing £48m, employing 143 people and with clients such as HSBC, Nestle, BBC and Disney he left to fulfil four dreams:

- To change the weather in February
- To be the best speaker on the planet
- To write a best selling book
- And to play live with Ralph McTell

Having spent his entire working life studying and practising influence and persuasion, he is now a professional speaker on 'The Psychology of Persuasion and Influence' and the author of the Amazon number one best selling book, 'How to Persuade and Influence People'

He speaks in a style that has been described as both 'enlightening and entertaining'. Philip is inspirational, insightful, motivational and thought provoking. Well - at least that's what his mother thinks.

He is also a Lancastrian who has been exiled in Yorkshire for over 25 years.

His qualifications to write this book are that he and his three sons have walked the Pennine Way and that he is a direct descendant of Edward III.

True, but unremarkable. There are millions of descendants of Edward III.

Contents:

Preface What Ifs, If Onlys, Maybes and The First Golden Rule

PART ONE - THE WARS OF THE ROSES

Chapter 1 1377 to 1413 ~ The French boy's Uncle and the Teddy Bear

Chapter 2 1413 to 1459 ~ 'Unsteadfast of wit'

Chapter 3 1459 to 1461 ~ 'When they were up they were up'

Chapter 4 1461 to 1485 ~ 'Short, violent and hairy'

Chapter 5 1485 to 1501 ~ The Battle of Bosworth and Turkeys at Christmas

Chapter 6 The Warbeck and Simnel Side Plots

Chapter 7 1501 to 1509 ~ 'Yikes, it's Katie' and The Second Golden Rule

PART TWO - THE REIGN OF HENRY VIII

Chapter 8 1509 to 1527 ~ The 4 minute mile and 'The Great Matter'

Chapter 9 1527 to 1536 ~ The Pot Bull, Aunty Dot and Lady Wallop

Chapter 10 1536 ~ The Musician, the Brother and the Bottom Wiper

Chapter 11 1536 to 1547 ~ Died, divorced, beheaded, survived

Chapter 12 The Third Golden Rule

PART THREE - THE REIGN OF EDWARD VI

Chapter 13 1547 to 1553 ~ Teddy's Uncles and The Nine Day Queen

Chapter 14 The Fourth Golden Rule

PART FOUR - THE REIGN OF MARY I

Chapter 15 1553 to 1558 ~ 'Make Mine A Bloody Mary'

Chapter 16 The Fifth Golden Rule

PART FIVE - THE REIGN OF ELIZABETH I

Chapter 17 1558 to 1559 ~ Elizabeth ~ CEO of England Ltd.

Chapter 18 1559 to 1566 ~ 'Someone to make me smile'

Chapter 19 1566 to 1570 ~ Darnley's Demise and Mary's imprisonment

Chapter 20 1570 to 1580 ~ Juggling balls, procrastination and succession

Chapter 21 Francis, Walter and William

Chapter 22 1580 to 1587 ~ Mary's boy child

Chapter 23 1587 to 1599 ~ 'Pass me something light'

Chapter 24 1599 to 1603 ~ Past pensionable age

Chapter 25 The Sixth Golden Rule

Postscript and The Final Golden Rule

Preface ~ What Ifs, If Onlys, Maybes and The First Golden Rule

If you could use just one word from the English language to sum up life and business, then for me that word would have to be unpredictable. Naturally, life can be many other things too. Like happy or sad, exhilarating or mundane, a breeze or a struggle. But the one thing you can be sure of is that things will happen when you least expect them. Plans will be dashed, rugs pulled from under your feet and doors slammed shut in our face. Just like the man who told the Beatles that they would never be successful, sometimes you just don't see it coming.

But there are Seven Golden Rules for you to be happier and more successful and make your life more predictable. And the rules and all the other lessons we could and should have learned from history keep repeating themselves over the years.

Rather like an award-winning BBC drama, allow me to transport you back in time to the summer of 1971 in Greater Manchester. I was standing outside the main hall in Ashton-under-Lyne Grammar School waiting for the invigilator to call us in to sit a Physics 'A' Level paper. Expectations were running high and confidence was flowing freely.

Earlier that term I had experienced a brief lunchtime meeting with the careers advisor. He was twice my age and sported long hair and a beard in the manner of George Best. Despite his tweed jacket, I felt I could trust him implicitly. Besides, he must have been good at his job because it took him only ten minutes to map out my entire future having learned just two things about me. Firstly, that I was studying Maths, Further Maths and Physics, and secondly that I was in the Scouts and so liked the outdoor life. From this he expertly concluded that I should apply to Bath University to study Civil Engineering.

I was to be a Civil Engineer, carving up the countryside, sculpting the landscape, wallowing in mud. It would be my job, nay, my destiny, to construct bridges and build roads for the good people of Britain. All I had to do was pass the Physics exam and my future was as good as sealed.

There was, however, one unforeseen problem on the horizon. Actually, it must have been slightly beyond the horizon because otherwise it would have been foreseen. You get the idea, anyway. Naturally, it came in the form of a woman. Well, almost a woman to be precise. You see, for the best part of the previous three years I had been completely and totally head over heels in love with a girl three years my junior.

Susan Garlick was unaware of my feelings for her. She barely knew I existed. But then at the age of 18 and about to leave school for a richly rewarding life as a road builder, I realised that if I didn't act soon I would be carrying a heavy heart under my bright yellow jacket. Beneath my hard, protective helmet my head would still be spinning for Susan. Nothing much would be happening to my feet but I would be wearing steel toe-capped boots just to be on the safe side. It's the law, apparently.

The problem was that I didn't have the courage to ask her out myself. Instead, I persuaded one of my fellow Physics students, Trevor 'Sid' Smith to ask her for me. He was instructed to ascertain whether or not she would be willing to meet me alone outside school and under no circumstances to embellish the offer with any fanciful notions that might lead to grass stains or other such undesirable marks on her school uniform. Sid could get carried away at times but I was relying on him to be delicate and discreet. The problem was that despite weeks of prodding and encouraging him to do the deed, he chose the morning of the Physics exam to actually approach her.

To make matters worse, Sid arrived at the hall at exactly the same time the invigilator opened the doors and ushered us in. I asked eagerly if he had spoken to her and he nodded. Just at this moment the invigilator ushered us into the hall and told us remain silent until the end of the exam. I silently mouthed the word 'well?' to Sid with my eyes widening manically to represent the question mark. But Sid remained silent. He even ignored my best Marcel Marceau impression for a quick thumbs up or down to signal Susan's answer.

And so that was it. My fate was sealed. I hardly wrote a thing, failed the Physics 'A' level exam, and never did get to Bath. The university town that is, not the ablution act. Sure I was down, but I still realised the value of good personal hygiene. I did a third year in the Sixth Form to make amends for my failure and during this time worked on the dustbins with Michael Bamforth who was reading Psychology at York. He got me interested in the subject and I eventually went on to Newcastle University to study for a BSc in it.

And the rest, as they say, is history. But actually it was also the beginning of a lifetime wondering what would have happened if Sid had not spoken to Susan Garlick on that particular day. If he had arrived at school either early enough to tell me her answer or too late for me to have questioned him at all. Perhaps I would have been in a different frame of mind, passed the exam and gone to Bath. Right now I could be standing in a field somewhere, up to my knees in mud and gazing expertly through a theodolite.

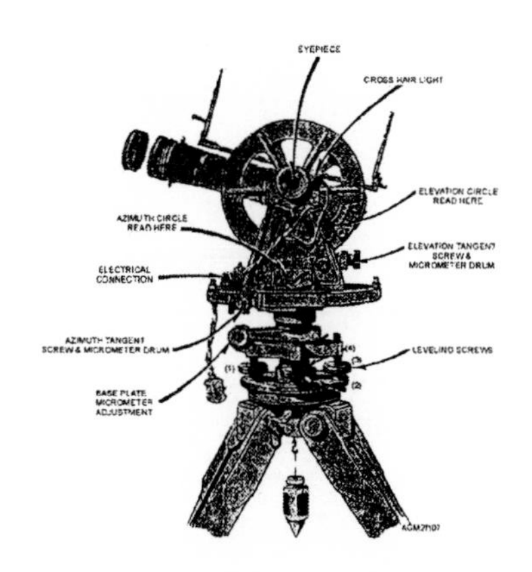

I would never have gone to Newcastle and never have met and married my wife. I would be married to a completely different woman altogether.

So what does all that have to do with anything? Well, history is full of such stories. Of What Ifs and If Onlys and Maybes. Starting with the very early beginnings of The Wars of The Roses, this book has at its heart several key acts in English history that changed things for ever. And perhaps, more importantly, there are valuable lessons to be learned.

Because the key acts are all caused by people. And their decisions not only often made them more unhappy and less successful but many, many others too. Learn those lessons yourself and live your life by The Seven Golden Rules and you will be happier and more fulfilled.

The study of history has become less popular in schools over the past few years; the proportion of students taking history GCSE has steadily declined. When it is studied, it seems to me that subjects and periods are examined in isolation, without being related to the march of events and their meaning ~ either then or now. It strikes me that history is sometimes seen in schools as an intellectual indulgence, without practical application.

And yet studying what has happened in the past helps us not to make the same mistakes in the future.

Ironically there is a great interest amongst adults in history and what we can learn from it. The 500th anniversary of Henry VIII's accession was almost treated as breaking news, with a flood of TV programmes, features and columns. Indeed, our daily news is saturated with history. The MPs' expenses scandal that happened at the same time as the accession anniversary can be appreciated only through the encrusted pattern of parliamentary privilege and a culture of moat-maintenance at public expense going back centuries. We, the great unwashed, seem to instinctively understand the importance of linking history with modern life.

And this book is effectively about the power of precedent in human affairs.

It starts with The Wars of The Roses.

To many people, The Wars of The Roses was simply a century-long feud between two rival counties. Few are aware of the causes, fewer still the outcome. One or two of the battles may ring a bell and occasionally a place name may sound familiar. Like Pontefract or Eccles, or indeed anything associated with a snack or pastry. I'm told the battle of Hob Nob was a particularly bloody affair, but the details have largely been lost with the passage of time. No matter, I'll not make them up when we get to those bits but, rather, rely on the facts as accepted by prominent historians. What I'm really interested in – and what the focus of this book will be – are the lessons we could and should learn from a particularly hairy period of history from the latter part of the 14th century to the end of the reign of the first Elizabeth over 300 years later.

The first key act I will examine that changes English history is in 1377 when Edward III dies but as his son Edward had already died, his heir is his grandson, Richard. He's only 10 so it's decided that his uncle, the Duke of Lancaster, will run the country. It's the real start of The Wars of The Roses. There are a number of lessons that we could and should learn from The Wars and The Second Golden Rule.

Arguably the biggest decision that changes things forever is in 1533 when the second son of the man who effectively ended The Wars of The Roses, Henry VIII ~ the son of a Lancastrian and a Yorkshire woman ~ decides he will marry Anne Boleyn having decided to get a divorce from Katherine of Aragon. And he changes not only the face of English history but sets in motion a chain of events that will see a quite remarkable number of people beheaded, hung drawn and quartered, burned at the stake and imprisoned and also will see his daughter, Elizabeth, die without issue and unite the Scottish and English thrones for the first time.

Was Henry VIII a vain, self-pitying, arrogant overweight bully with few scruples and even fewer morals, who was neither a marital nor a martial success? Was he simply a lousy politician and a worse diplomat who made a prat of himself abroad? Or was he our best known King for good reason?

Henry VIII

Well, Henry VIII seems to me to have been the sort of bloke who, if faced with a choice between having a lukewarm, milky drink and sticking his genitals in a hornets' nest, would inevitably head straight towards the sound of the buzzing whilst unbuckling his belt.

We English do seem to find something very appealing in the sense of daring and total commitment in the style of battle that is personified by such diverse figures as Horatio Nelson, Ian 'Beefy' Botham, 'Hurricane' Higgins and 'Captain Marvel' Bryan Robson. We took 'Freddie' Flintoff to our hearts not because he was the best wicket taker or run getter but, rather, because we could imagine him leaping between a ship's rigging, sword drawn, masts burning overhead, blood and gore spattered all around him. Like Freddie, Henry is the sort of King – the sort of 'character' you don't see very often nowadays.

Fact is, he was the pivot around which English history revolves and there are things we should learn from Henry and The Third Golden Rule for a happy and successful life.

The third section of the book looks at the reign of Henry's son, Edward and the fourth section that of Henry's eldest daughter - destined to have the sobriquet 'Bloody Mary'.

And finally the fifth section of the book concerns the reign of his third child – well the third to reign anyway - by which time the inventor of the bicycle, the potato and tobacco, Sir Walter Raleigh, as well as the bard himself, William Shakespeare, are all on the scene. Writing, peddling, and chain smoking their way through the next few decades whilst still wondering what to do with that damn spud.

So, as I say, the purpose of this book is not simply to recount the tale of The Wars of The Roses, the reign of Henry VIII and the reigns of his three children for their own sake. The story of The Wars and the times of arguably the two best known monarchs we have ever had provides us with much more than just a fascinating insight into man's inhumanity to man throughout the Middle Ages. It also tells us about every facet of mankind and provides us with uncanny parallels with 21st century life. This period is the beginning of religious life as we know it and Henry's divorce is the end of the beginning.

I use this period of English history as a conduit to outline the lessons for life, business and everything. Every chapter in this book has at least one valuable lesson in either life or business.

And there are Seven Golden Rules.

Of course, it would be easy to say that with the benefit of hindsight we could all easily learn the lessons. So I have endeavoured to avoid the 'smart after the event approach'. A very significant percentage of the failures and mistakes we have made make repeating patterns and there are usually warning signs that, in retrospect, were obvious. I shall make more than just the odd passing reference to 'The Titanic'. It has become symbolic of things that go wrong. It is a classic example of warning signs that were all too clear well before it set sail in 1912. And the very fact that people were not willing to point out those kinds of warning signs is also looked at in depth.

People throughout history have appeared not to have learned The First Golden Rule and one that permeates not only this period of history but those before and since.

The First Golden Rule:

When you lose, don't lose the lesson.

I shall explore the issue of just why men fight. It appears to be a basic part of the human psyche to battle. Be it in war, sport or business. After all, why do we play sports at all? Is it just to win? People who can run well love to run, people who can throw a ball like to do exactly that. As a golfer - and a poor one at that - I continue to play like all the other golfers because no matter how bad you are when you really hit one right, when it really flies that is such a thrill that you go back for more in the forlorn hope of consistently hitting it just like that.

So much of this book is about war. Was it just about the winning or was it like sport - a joy in itself? And when the underdogs win in sport it's usually because the 'better' team – the 'professionals' were complacent and joyless. Another theme we shall return to.

So often the defeated are guilty of hubris and don't actually learn the lesson. Too often we lose in love and in life but don't look at how and why we lost. The happy and successful people are those who analyse themselves harshly and learn the lesson before they move on.

And there is something else too. Something that is fundamental to our feelings about happiness and success.

It is that thing we call Hope. You can lose it, have it dashed, or never be without it. Some say it springs eternal, others that it never dies. But what exactly is it? Modern dictionaries define hope as *'a feeling of desire for something and a confidence in the possibility of its fulfillment'*. The key word is 'possibility'. That's why every Saturday night millions of people sit with bated breath and fingers crossed hoping that they'll get lucky. And then there are those that do the lottery.

Hope can be a rejection of cynicism and defeatism. But every business, just like every individual, needs it. In their darkest days incarcerated in a Beirut bunker, Keenan, McCarthy and Waite never lost hope that one day they would be set free. Similarly Chelsea fans knew that some time in the distant future they would once again win the league championship. It took them fifty years, of course, but at least they weren't chained to a radiator in the meantime.

Hope has proven to be the key ingredient to create resilience in captives and survivors of traumas such as natural disasters. Studies show that people who score high on hope cope better with disease, illness and even pain. When relationships are at an all time low, it's a fact that people get ill more often. Moreover, the presence of *contempt* in a marriage has such a negative affect on the immune system that it can influence how many *colds* a couple get.

A fact not to be sneezed at.

It's clear then that hope influences many aspects of our daily life and can shape our perception of reality. But, of course, as a reader of this book, what you are really interested in is how *you* can be happier and more successful by learning the lessons from the past. And I will reveal exactly that over the 25 chapters. But it all starts with daring to hope.

All the decisions made by these historical figures were made because they hoped that things would be better by making those decisions. But they appear to have, in the most part, not to have learned The Seven Golden Rules.

The Seven Golden Rules that we all need to learn to live a happy and successful life keep coming up again and again.

That's my story and I'm sticking to it.

Now here's theirs.

PART ONE
THE WARS OF THE ROSES

Chapter 1 ~ The French boy's Uncle and the Teddy Bear

1377 — 1413

The dynastic quarrel between the Yorkists and Lancastrians for the throne of England was only one aspect of the dispute that became known as The Wars of The Roses. The first real battle was actually on May 22nd 1455 in St. Albans in Hertfordshire.

Don't ask; it gets worse.

Prior to this, there had been several minor skirmishes on the Pennine border that led to a great deal of ill feeling between the two shires. It is, however, the struggle for control of the monarchy that is the most documented account of The Wars of The Roses and so it is this that we shall mainly concern ourselves with.

Although they became known as The Wars of the Roses, it wasn't until a few fights in that the tabloid press realised the two combatants shared a common symbol on their respective coat of arms. A white rose for the Yorkists and a red one for the House of Lancaster. Interestingly, the House of Fraser later adopted a white deer as its emblem but as far as we know has never been in anything more vicious than a price war.

The first proper battle in St Albans was rather neatly just after the end of the 100 years war with France. That war had begun in 1337 when Edward III invaded Normandy and actually lasted 116 years but to be fair there was a lot of injury time to play. I've no doubt Edward was telling anyone who would listen in the 14th century that the war was 'drawing to a close' and would be over by 1400...

But we really need to start our story of The Wars of The Roses - and the lessons we should all learn - in 1377 to understand what happened and why it all came to a head in St. Albans.

The population of England in the mid 1400s was just over three million. It had been as high as six million but the Black Death had taken its toll. To put it in perspective, today there are over five million people living in Yorkshire alone.

I know what you're thinking; that's a lot of lonely people.

And, believe it or not, Calais was part of England then. Edward III had believed himself to be the rightful King of France and had crossed the Channel and captured the city in 1347. The Treaty of Bretigny in 1360 formally acknowledged the city to England.

Well done Teddy.

Although it wasn't until 1455 that the two armies actually engaged in fisticuffs, it is generally acknowledged that the Wars of The Roses feud began on a nice sunny day in June 1377 when Edward III died on the front lawn of his home at Sheen Palace.

So 1377 is where we actually start.

Some say he died of a stroke brought on by severe constipation, some say through gonorrhea by his mistress, Alice Perrers. During his reign, Edward had assumed the title of King of France which had kick started the 100 years war. His French born wife, Queen Philippa had died a few years before his death and Edward, despite having fathered 13 legitimate children that we know of and countless others on the side, felt the need to take a mistress. Alice Perrers was not perhaps a good choice, but this book is full of bad choices of Kings' mistresses.

To make matters worse, his son and heir, also Edward, had died just over a year before from an illness contracted in Spain. So it was Edward III's ten year old grandson Richard - a Yorkist like his dad - who was crowned King.

The new King, Richard II, had been born in Bordeaux in January 1367 which technically made him French and no doubt very good at wine tasting. Due to his age and penchant for the red stuff, he was deemed unfit to rule his Kingdom or be in charge of any heavy machinery. Fortunately none had been invented at this time so it wasn't a big problem to enforce. Due to his incapacity, his uncle, John of Gaunt, the Duke of Lancaster, effectively ran the country. Incidentally he gained his name 'John of Gaunt' because he was born in Ghent in Belgium then called *Gaunt* in English.

The Lancastrian John of Gaunt has effectively wrestled control from the Yorkist King so it's first blood to the Lancastrians and at an early stage we see the impact of disunity.

Factions and disunity bring about downfall. Always. Even former deputy Labour leader John Prescott was able to spot it. "Disunity kills political parties" he said in one of his more profound and lucid moments. When people were worried about their jobs and quality of life and all they heard from Labour were questions about the leadership, the Conservatives were just waiting in the wings.

And so it always is in relationships in business.

Having been proclaimed unsinkable, 'The Titanic' set sail in 1912 without enough life boats on board. (We shall return later to the subject of why and how a ship designed to accommodate over 3,500 people was only required to provide lifeboat accommodation for less than 1,000.) It also suffered from a shortage of seamen, although its Parisian café employed several hundred waiters. Not surprisingly, factions and disunity were already much in evidence from the moment it left the dockside. Second Officer David Blair had been looking forward to the inaugural trip but was taken off 'The Titanic' at the 11th hour. Bosses at The White Star Line had decided that Henry Wilde, the Chief Officer of 'The Titanic's sister ship 'The Olympic' should be transferred to 'The Titanic'.

As a consequence, the existing Chief Officer became First Officer and Charles Lightoller – the First Officer - replaced Blair as

Second Officer. Mr. Blair was deemed too senior to take up the position of Third Officer and was tasked to another ship. No-one will know whether it was a simple mistake or a fit of pique but, giving him the benefit of the doubt, Blair was to suffer perhaps the most catastrophic lapse of memory in history, costing more than 1,500 lives. As the ship set off, he forgot to leave behind a vital key. Without it, his shipmates were unable to open a locker in the crow's nest containing a pair of binoculars for the designated lookout.

The Lookout was Fred Fleet. He survived the disaster and later told an official inquiry that with binoculars he would have seen the iceberg sooner. And that in itself would have been enough to save the ship from disaster. And because of the disunity caused by Henry Wilde elbowing his way on board, no-one was willing to lend the lookout their 'glasses' (as binoculars were know in those days).

On the night of the 14th of April 1912, it was the existence of factions and the creation of disunity from those factions that brought about the downfall of the biggest ship ever built.

So given that the First Golden Rule is not to lose the lesson when you lose; here is a key lesson for all groups, families, organisations and businesses:

Avoid factions and disunity. They bring about downfall.

And as for The Wars of The Roses? Well, it's one-nil to Lancashire and we're up and running.

And the lesson when a ten year old is in charge of the country?

Never send a boy to do a man's job.

England was still in a state of flux in the early 1380's. Nobody, including my editor, is quite sure what this phrase actually means but we're pretty certain no-one will pull us up on it. However, in 1383 Richard II celebrated reaching the ripe old age of fifteen by marrying Anne of Bohemia. There'd been a lot of wrangling with the great houses of Europe before he settled on Anne. Indeed, it had all turned a bit nasty. The 'Great Schism in the Papacy' had resulted in the creation of two Popes, later made into a popular TV show known as Pope Rivals.

I am not making this up. Well, maybe just that last bit.

One of the Popes, Urban VI, had sanctioned the marriage between Richard and Anne in an attempt to create an alliance on his behalf and they would all gang up against the French. The French, in turn, had their own preferred Pope, Clement, and they wanted Richard to marry a nice Italian girl; the daughter of Bernabò Visconti of Milan. On her arrival on these shores from Hungary, the ship carrying the 16 year old Anne was smashed to pieces as soon as she had disembarked. Nevertheless, Anne and King Richard II were married in Westminster Abbey in January 1382 despite neither being legally old enough.

In 1387 King Richard II flexed his muscles by taking over some of the ruling of England. Nothing too heavy; a few fishing regulations, one or two weights and measures controls, that sort of thing.

One of his interesting first appointments was Robert de Vere, 9th Earl of Oxford. Rumour had it that they enjoyed an unhealthy affection for one another and were, in fact, gay lovers.

I am not making this up.

Not even that last bit.

Anne and Richard were married for 12 years, but had no children. Anne's death from the plague in 1394 was a bit of a blow to Richard II, who had got quite used to her by all accounts.

So what with that and the rumours about him and Robert de Vere, a cunning plan was hatched for Richard to marry Isabella of France then aged just seven. As plans go, it wasn't one of the best.

It wasn't until the child bride got off the ferry at Dover clutching a teddy bear that Richard realised his error.

But, at the end of October 1396, King Richard married Isabella of France.

Yes, a seven year old French girl.

Perhaps there is another lesson we can learn from history. A marriage between a seven year old bride and a 29 year old groom is likely to have problems. So it's no surprise this one didn't quite work out and Isabella married her own cousin and died in child birth at 19.

However, it was upon the death of the Duke of Lancaster, John of Gaunt, in 1399 that things really started to hot up. He'd all but ruled England for the past 22 years and his son, Henry, was expecting to take over the family firm. However, Richard, the boy King, was now not only grown up and shaving but had already been twice married and, even more importantly, he was still alive. Naturally, he had other ideas. Not great ideas, true, but different nonetheless.

So when Henry returned from exile to claim his 'inheritance' he got something of a shock. Richard had cancelled the legal documents allowing him to inherit his father's land and instead required him to ask for them personally. Richard's reply is not actually documented but it's thought to have been supplemented with a series of lewd hand gestures later adopted by home football fans whenever an ex-player returns.

This latter point proved to be but a temporary inconvenience to a determined Lancastrian fresh from an extended jolly on the Cote D'Azur. Richard II was finally rounded up – he'd run in all directions to avoid capture – and was incarcerated in Pontefract Castle, allowed out only to attend the occasional race meeting.

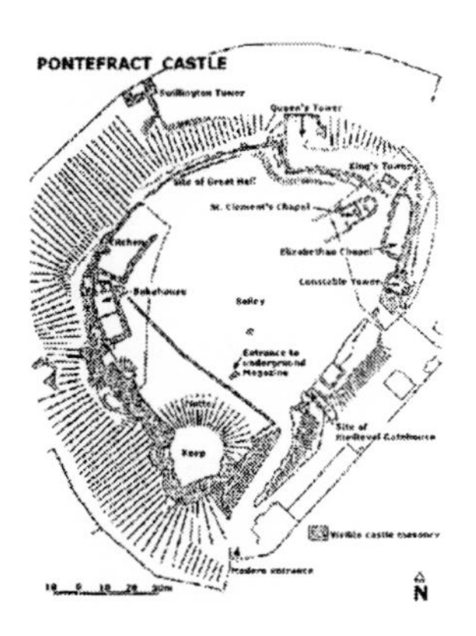

So Henry's first real problem was quite what to do with the deposed Richard. There was a bodged assassination plot in January 1400, so he simply ordered his death; most probably by starvation. There's evidence for this in the circulation of letters in France demonstrating prior knowledge of the death and sure enough, Richard died in February 1400, and his body was put on public display in St Paul's Cathedral to show everyone he was very, very dead; aged 33. Richard's crown was taken by his own cousin Henry Bolingbroke of Lancaster.

And so to the next lesson which proves to be one of many threads in this book:

You can always deny you said it. You cannot retract what you write.

Written evidence of the prior knowledge of Richard's death is a bit of a giveaway.

If you ever send an e-mail making derogatory remarks about someone it's best to assume that they will, at some point, get to read what you wrote.

And as Arthur Andersen found in 2002, when they were found guilty of shredding documents relating to Enron, getting rid of what you have written can actually help send you under.

Letters or no letters, Henry IV has the throne reupholstered and it's two-nil to the house of Lancaster.

Henry IV is obviously also the Duke of Lancaster and the Lancashire retinue was a large and hardy body willing to fight for their Duke at the drop of a hat. Unfortunately, it seems that they were very clumsy with their headgear in those days and so fights were breaking out all the time.They were the hard core of his following and a big factor in allowing him to hold on to this throne.

Henry was also pretty extravagant when it came to gifts and pensions. The patent rolls - the record of a monarch's reign - for the first year of his reign are twice as bulky as those of the next largest, the first year of Edward IV. Great in the short term to gain favour and perhaps to repay moral debts incurred in getting to be King but Parliament eventually saw him as financially incompetent.

Henry IV was to be King for just 14 years. He had already married Mary and together they had seven children. Upon his death in 1413 he was succeeded by Henry V.

And he inherited not only the throne but also his father's enemies.

Chapter 2 ~ 'Unsteadfast of wit'

1413 1377

Henry V was quite an accomplished soldier. At the age of fourteen he fought the Welsh forces of Owen at Glendower; at sixteen he commanded his father's forces at the battle of Shrewsbury; and shortly after his accession he put down a major uprising and an assassination plot by nobles still loyal to Richard II. Henry V was 27 when he proposed to marry Catherine of Valois. That's right, another French lass, demanding the old Plantagenet lands of Normandy and Anjou as his dowry. The French didn't think much of that so Henry declared war.

It really was that easy in those days.

Having defeated the French at the Battle of Agincourt in October 1415 on a split decision, by 1419 he had captured Normandy, Picardy and much of the Capetian stronghold of the Ile-de-France to add to Calais.

The French King, Charles VI, had not only accepted Henry V as his son-in-law, but passed over his own son to name Henry as heir to the French crown. Had Henry lived a mere two months longer, he would have been King of both England and France. But Henry had prematurely aged due to living the hard life of a soldier. He became seriously ill and died after returning from yet another French campaign; Catherine had borne his only son in 1421, the future King Henry VI, while he was away and Henry died having never seen his child.

Was it all worth it? He spent so much time at work he died of exhaustion and didn't get to have time with his young son. Never held his hand on that walk on the first day at Infants School. Never saw him appear in a nativity play, taught him how to swim, to ride a bike or score his first try.

As so many men find when they spend too much time at work and not enough time on the really important issues such as simply spending time with your children, the regret comes later. Or as Joni Mitchell once famously said, 'You don't know what you got 'til it's gone.'

Your children only get one childhood.

So if you are a parent, set yourself the goal of attending *all* your children's athletics contests, plays, performances and 'meet-the-teacher' evenings. Teach them to ride a bicycle, to throw a ball, to develop a signature, to cook, to bake, to fly a kite; to teach them that you will always be there for them.

Henry the Fifth was succeeded by his son Henry the Sixth in 1422. As you have probably guessed, Henry was a popular Lancastrian name of the time. Often shortened to Harry (as in the cricketer, Pilling) it was later overtaken in popularity only by such famous Lancastrian names as Clive, Farouk and Wasim.

Obviously, Henry VI was only a few months old when he became King so his father's brothers ran the shop for him. Sound familiar?

When he finally came of age he proudly maintained the family tradition of marrying a looker from across the Channel. In this case, the niece of the French King, Margaret of Anjou. Margaret's signature is shown below which clearly shows her links to the medical profession. Only a doctor could write like that.

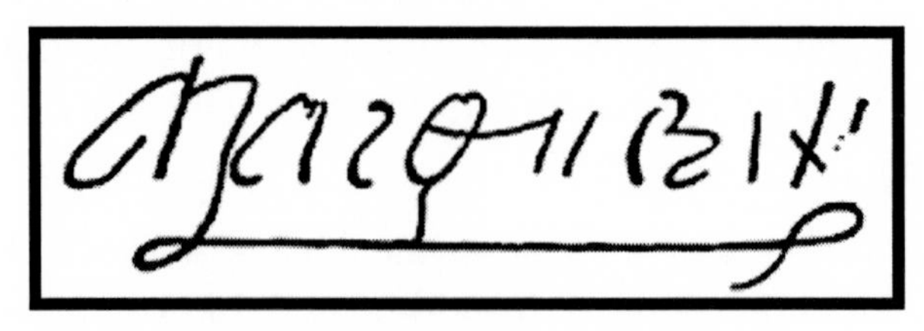

The Signature of Margaret of Anjou

By all accounts, Henry VI was a fairly gentle kind of a guy. According to his entry in Forbes he 'enjoyed needlework and dry flower pressing'. He quite possibly won prizes in pastry rolling competitions. Early in his reign he was described as 'unsteadfast of wit' which is the more diplomatic term for someone who is a catatonic schizophrenic.

Interesting this. He has all the money and position that so many people work for and yet he spends his time doing things that cost next to nothing.

If people only chase the money they will only be disappointed. When you don't work in the conventional sense of a 9 to 5 office job and cut yourself off a little, you find that your wants and needs are reduced. This is because you no longer need material compensation from the miseries you suffered as a work-slave, coupled with the fact that you no longer feel a need to impress people with your ostentatious wealth. All the people I know who only chased the money were left wondering what to do next and looking for their purpose in life. Often that meant just going out and earning even more money. Happiness comes from absorption in doing something with a real purpose.

If you only chase the money you will only be disappointed when you get to your goal.

The reign of Henry VI has a rather unwanted claim in that it is arguably the most calamitous in the whole of English history. At the start of his reign he was King of all of England and France because of all the soldiering and war mongering of his dad. By 1453 all that was left other than his homeland was Calais out of all the conquests of Edward III and Henry V.

Calais. A little bit of France left for us. It must have been strange to have been French in those days and not have to cross the channel to be in England.

Was Henry VI a loser? Was he a peaceful and pious man not suited for the harsh nature of the time he lived in? Or did he just not think positively?

Much has been written about the power of positive thinking in helping to attain goals. Believe in your own abilities and have faith in the outcome and you're well on the way to achieving your objective. But at what point is confidence bolstered by mere superstition? Or to put it another way; does wearing lucky pants really increase your chances of success, or just the likelihood of a nasty infection?

Sportsmen and women are amongst the most superstitious of all. Tiger Woods only wears a red shirt on the Sunday of a tournament. No trousers, just a red shirt. And there are footballers who won't put their shirt on until the pitch is in sight; male tennis players who refuse to shave if they're on a winning run. And cyclists who consider it extremely bad luck if they're required to give a sample.

In business, it's no different. After once winning a big fmcg account against all the odds, I always wore the same lucky tie in subsequent major pitches to fmcg clients. Although, at my colleagues request, I did put a stop to running around the room with my shirt pulled over my head. That was undignified and I've never done it since.

Is this behaviour irrational, superstitious nonsense or does it actually work by giving us more confidence and self belief? A study by German psychologist Lysann Damisch tested this very theory that simple superstitions, like crossing your fingers or using a lucky charm, improved performance on both motor and mental tasks.

In the first experiment, Damisch asked a number of golfers to have a go at holing a one metre putt. Easy peasy, you might say. But, of course, many missed. However, when he repeated the experiment on another hole, again from one metre, the number of successful putts increased by 33%. Why? Because this time he handed each golfer his 'lucky ball'. And with that, more of them simply believed they would hole the putt.

Damisch repeated the experiment twice more in studies that tested both memory and puzzle-solving abilities. Again – with fingers crossed – the results were markedly improved when the participant was given a 'lucky charm' as part of the experiment. The researchers concluded that these superstitions improved performance because they gave people the confidence to aim higher and keep trying.

So it seems that believing in superstition helps to relieve nervous tension and allows us the illusion of control in what is sometimes a scary, random world. So have a good look through your underwear drawer; fish out that favourite old tie and believe.

Maybe if Henry had had a lucky charm history would give us a different version of him.

Henry VI appears to have lacked guile. The really great Kings are those who were thought of by their enemies and contemporaries as great soldiers. They were seen to be upright, brave and forceful men. And they were seen as honest and fair. The King personified law and order; truth, justice, and character. The King's reputation was everything.

And so it is today with good leaders in business. It's not enough just to be the boss and have the title. To be a good leader you need followers. The more the better. And people follow people who are honest and fair; you have to be *seen* to be honest and fair.

You have to be *seen* to have integrity.

Henry VI had married Queen Margaret when she was 16 but it was eight years later that she gave birth to a son, Edward, in 1453. It was rumoured that the child was not the feeble-minded King's but that of the Duke of Somerset who had often been seen loitering with intent in the vicinity of her chambers. In one of his more lucid moments when Henry was shown his son he declared that Edward must have been fathered by the 'Holy Ghost'. Something that was difficult to prove in the days before DNA. In fact, it's still a bit of a bugger now.

Meanwhile, across the English Channel a slip of a girl known as Joan of Arc was making a bit of a name for herself. Joan was said to hear voices and see visions, and she told anyone who would listen that the Virgin Mary had appeared to her urging her to rescue France and to lead King Charles VII to his coronation in the champagne region of Rheims. People were understandably suspicious, particularly since Joan was known to like a drink.

Joan of Arc

Some said that her voices and visions were the result of a bad attack of sun-stroke which she suffered aged 13 or possibly through eating too much red meat. Certainly she was later to rue her catchphrase 'Make mine a steak and I want it well done'. Aware of the rumours, Joan decided that the only way to get people to take her seriously was to cut off her hair and dress as a bloke.

So, in 1429, with sword in hand and a strategically placed sock in her pants, she appeared at the Court at Chinon to see King Charles VII. Needless to say he was a bit suspicious but nevertheless had her examined by the Clergy who specialised in sexing young things. Bizarrely, they decided that she was harmless enough and suggested she was hired as a cook. However, due to a misunderstanding when signing the contract she was actually appointed 'Chef de Guerre' which means Chief of War. Any other nation would have swiftly corrected this folly but the stubborn French immediately relieved her of all her cooking utensils and instead equipped her with a banner depicting Jesus Christ supported by two angels. She couldn't actually kill anyone in battle with this but she could give them a nasty chill by repeatedly wafting it at them.

Joan of Arc had lied. As people throughout history have done. Her deception of King Charles VII is up there with Bill Clinton's 'I never had sexual relations with that woman.'

Satisfied with his appointment, the King of France sent her off to Orleans, which was then under siege by the English, with the instruction 'Kick ass' only in French. And she did; immortalising herself in the process.

Whether or not Joan was mad is hard to say but by 1453 Henry VI was certainly showing signs of insanity.

Richard, Duke of York, saw this as an opportunity to advance his claims on the throne of England and, at the same time, settle a score with the Lancastrians. Or at the very least, pull it back to 2-1. And so, on May 22nd 1455 the first battle of the Wars of The Roses took place at St Albans. That's right; we've got there at last.

The Yorkists easily defeated the King's army, killed a few Lancastrian nobles, raped, pillaged and were generally at least five points ahead in the Mori polls. The Yorkists haven't got the throne just yet but it's now two-one and they're on the scoreboard.

But wait, there's more. Still officially King, Henry VI was injured and taken prisoner. During captivity he suffered further bouts of insanity characterised mainly by mimicking the mating call of the kookaburra whilst back-combing his eyebrows. Even his most staunch supporters considered this to be grooming gone mad and so Richard, Duke of York, was made Protector of England.

It's now two-all and the White Rose fans are singing and dancing in the streets. Except there were no streets in 1455; just sort of dust tracks through villages, but you get the idea. However, their happiness was short lived. Because less than a year later, specialists from The Royal Institute of Public Health in Portland Place, London, examined the King and his habits and declared him both perfectly sane and incredibly clean. He immediately re-took the throne of England and Lancashire once again nudged ahead 3-2.

The next lesson is clear. If at first you don't succeed, check your personal hygiene. That's all that could be holding you back.

I'm serious.

Martha McClintock was just twenty years old in 1968 and in her first year at Wellesley College, Massachusetts when she did what turned out to be a ground breaking study. She simply recorded the dates of the menstrual cycles of the 135 women in her dormitory. And, as the academic year wore on, the dates became closer and closer together. In 1971 McClintock published the statistical evidence to suggest that women who live together tend to cycle together.

Scientists at the time were at a loss to explain the cause of what she called 'menstrual synchrony'. Evidence that the cause was human pheromones would come in the 1980's from Winnifred Cutler's work with George Preti and colleagues, and later in the 1998 work of McClintock and Stern at the University of Chicago.

Plants, insects, animals - and us - communicate with one another using pheromones. And it's believed that humans emit pheromones through their armpits. Pheromones are chemicals that are secreted in our sweat (and other bodily fluids). Rather like bulls, we are being led around by our noses. And there's no guarantee someone will particularly like *your* pheromones. So focus very carefully on personal hygiene. You can make the presentation of your life, but unless you deliver it from behind an impenetrable wall of Lynx's best whiff, it won't make the slightest bit of difference. Deodorant. It's the only way we can survive.

There are only two types of people in the world. The people who think everything matters and the people who don't. If you don't care about personal hygiene; about having clean shoes and clean finger nails, what else don't you care about?

If you don't take the trouble to make the best of yourself you are saying to the world that you don't care. If you don't care about your appearance and your manners in a relationship you are effectively saying 'it doesn't mean that much to me to mean that much to you.'

And what people want in relationships is the feeling that the other person truly cares about them.

And how did they conclude that King Henry VI was mad in the first place? Well, there were no real tests in those days so it must have been his behaviour; his body language. And there are two important things to know about body language. The first one is obvious; you give away what you are really thinking and the second one isn't so obvious. Your body language affects your ability to learn.

Whenever I speak at conferences, the delegates tend to fall into three categories. Those in a trance, those in a deep sleep, and those who are fully comatose. Only kidding. No, really, I am. The truth is, there are those who sit up nice and straight, obviously eager to maximise their learning. Always bright and alert and open to learning. After those come the ones who are slightly sceptical about learning anything useful but are nonetheless willing to give you the benefit of the doubt. Often they lean backwards in their chair, surveying the room in the manner of a guard dog, just waiting for the occasional tasty tit-bit to be tossed their way. And then there are the others; rather like a cross between a houndog and a St Bernard. They slouch in a slovenly manner and give the impression of not being interested in anything. Their body language tells you they really don't want to be there.

I remember from my school days that it wasn't cool to be seen sitting up straight and paying attention. In fact, if you wore two matching socks you were considered posh. But apart from indicating your attitude to the situation and your willingness to take part, does sitting up straight and not slouching actually influence how much you learn? Does the way you sit at a sales meeting or a marketing conference actually make a difference to what you take away from the event?

A study in 2009 by Pablo Briñol of Madrid University has examined how people's self-confidence and self-evaluation is affected by the pose they strike. He divided a class of students into two groups: half were told to slouch whilst the other half were asked to sit up straight. They were given some cover story about the experiment being concerned with curvature of the spine to throw them off the scent. These two groups were then split again, and half were asked to write down three positive personal traits about themselves, whilst the other half had to write down three negative personal traits.

The results showed that people who had been sitting up straight were much more likely to believe the positive things they'd written about themselves, whereas those who were slouching were much less sure. In short, their posture actually affected whether they really believed the positive or negative things they wrote about themselves. And here is the next lesson:

What you decide to do with your body position actually feeds back to your brain and ultimately affects your thinking.

So the next time you're at a conference or sales meeting, sit up straight, shoulders back, and no slouching. Because you won't just be giving the right impression, you'll learn a lot more too.

Back to the fifteenth century.

It's 1459 and the Yorkists and Lancastrains are spoiling for another fight to decide who rules England.

Chapter 3 ~ 'When they were up they were up'

1413 — 1461

A few years passed until the next big battle whilst both armies scoured the countryside for a suitable venue. Nowadays the siting of the Portaloos is crucial in such events but in 1459 it was just a case of sorting out whose side the local landowners were on. Turned down flat by Glastonbury, eventually Ludlow in Shropshire was decided upon. No surprise here though, as the chief challenger to the Lancastrian right to the throne was based in Ludlow Castle and could nip home to see his wife and kids in the evenings.

Buoyed by a home fixture of sorts, the Lancastrians punched above their weight and the Yorkists, who just a few years earlier had been invincible, were now beaten black and blue as well as several shades in-between.

4-2 to the House of Lancaster and some people think it's all over.

But wait. Some people are still on the battlefield. Perhaps the Duke of York had spent several days on some sort of residential course in leadership and motivation at a spa hotel just outside Swanage. Either way he bounced back with a vengeance by marching his men up and down a hill continuously. This caused eye-witnesses to note that when they were up they were up and when they were down they were indeed down. Local hacks eagerly scribbled these quotes but were unsure of their value. Apparently, there was some debate over how to describe their position when they were neither up nor down. Eventually, the optimists won the day with the phrase 'halfway up' whilst the pessimists who favoured 'halfway down' skulked off to cover a peace protest in Solihull.

Anyway, the important thing is that the Yorkists not only won the battle but also captured King Henry VI for a second time. Along with the imagination of the population through popular song. By now he was not only hopping mad but also completely crazy. Four-three and its Liverpool v. Newcastle in the 90's all over again.

But just as the travelling hordes were getting back their breath and checking train timetables to make the triumphant journey home, more dramatic events unfolded. Despite the King being incarcerated, his wife, Queen Margaret of Anjou, was still on the loose. Worse still, she's even more frightening than the King.

Seething mad and quite literally spitting feathers, she headed straight for Yorkshire to raise an army of Lancastrians. Well, she is in a bit of a state to be fair. You can be in the right state and you can be in a right state and, at the time, she favoured the latter.

Next lesson in life; if you are getting ready for a fight be in the right state and not in a right state.

In 2010 there was a surprise winner at golf's biggest championship, The Open. The unknown Louis Oosthuizen's victory at St Andrews was a surprise to many because, by his own admission, he wandered off mentally and struggled to get back into the moment. So his psychologist, Karl Morris, suggested he put a red dot on his glove so that he would remember, as he addressed the ball, to get into focus and just think about the next shot. In golf you must be able to concentrate fully, but you cannot expect to do it for a solid five hours. You need to be able to switch it on and off. The red dot was Louis' trigger point to get himself back in focus. It put him in the right state instead of him being in a right state.

He won by seven shots.

To be fair to the King's wife, Queen Margaret of Anjou, she had actually set out for Manchester but a series of contra-flows on the main drag through the Midlands had completely disoriented her. No matter, in December she marched her men back south and set up camp at Pontefract. As she said at the time, to her cohort, The Viscount Pannal, "That's enough walking for one day. What's for tea?"

Her enemy, The Duke of York, had a little further to travel. He marched all the way up to Sandal, a small village outside Wakefield that gave its name to a type of footwear popular at the time but which has since gone spectacularly out of fashion.

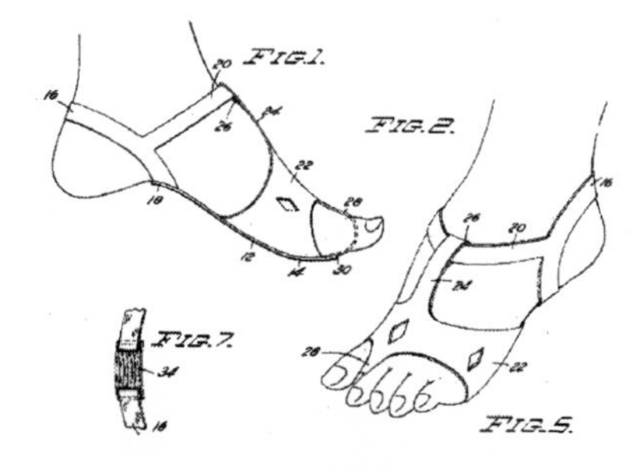

And so, on December 29th 1460, the Duke's 4,000 men took on the Queen's 20,000 strong army of Lancastrians at the Battle of Wakefield. Richard's men were 'environed on every side, like fish in a net' according to an eye witness who had obviously been drinking. The appeal for a mis-match was overruled. Both Richard, Duke of York, and his 18 year old son, Edmund, Earl of Rutland, died in the battle and Queen Margaret had their severed heads - and that of the Earl of Salisbury - placed on a pale on Micklegate Bar in York. That did nothing for the tourist trade of course. It's now 5-3 and the Lancastrians' two point advantage is restored.

Lesson for us all. Finish off your main competitor when you get the chance, or they will almost certainly come back to bite you in the bum. Or somewhere equally as painful.

We see it all the time in sport. One team has most of the play and most of the chances to take an advantage and fails to do so. And the other team see that their opponents recognise their best chances are perhaps behind them and begin to believe it's *their* turn.

Flushed with success – though some said it was the menopause – the Queen marched her triumphant army south to take on all comers. The size of her troops had been swollen not only by turncoat Yorkists, but also by bands of marauding Welsh and Scottish thugs, plus various waifs and serfs out for the weekend.

Needless to say, the trip was plagued with incidents of looting and pillaging and en route, the second battle of St Albans took place in February, 1461. These days residents would get together to discuss the merits of a Neighbourhood Watch Scheme.

Again the Queen's men defeated the Yorkists whose morale was somewhat undermined by the sight of their chief enemy riding into battle with a charger in one hand and a travel hairdryer in the other. It was now 6-3 to the Lancastrians and cries of 'easy, easy' and 'there's only one King Henry' rang around the battlefield.

It is said that all is fair in love and war. However, dismayed by the particularly barbarous behaviour of the Lancastrian forces, the Lord Mayor of London flatly refused to admit them to the City, effectively imposing the first ban on a travelling army of away fans.

It's at this point that The Wars of The Roses gets a trifle confusing. In the red corner we have the Lancastrians (based in Yorkshire) aided by an assortment of Welsh and Scottish mercenaries. Whilst in the white corner we have the Yorkists made up mainly of southerners who are based in Shropshire. This was, in effect, the beginning of the north / south divide. Also, slightly more worrying, there is a remarkable keenness to marry young French girls. The younger the better.

It's time for another fight.

Desperate to avenge the previous season's defeat on home soil, the Yorkists, now led by Edward, the son of Queen Margaret and Henry VI, fought like tigers in the battle of Towton. They would have done even better had they not been moving about on all fours but when you're 6-3 down you'll try anything. This is also thought to be the first time the Yorkists had really used the White Rose so prominently as their emblem. Edward saw it as a symbol of his father's right to some lands and a castle in the North. Rumour has it, it cost a six figure sum and was designed by a local brand development agency so he was damn well going to use it.

It happens.

So, on Palm Sunday in March 1461, just as the rest of the country were tucking into their Easter eggs and checking out the Bank Holiday sport, the rivers around Towton ran red with blood, mainly of Lancastrian origin. The Yorkists were outnumbered as they had 15,000 men and the Lancastrians 20,000. The casualties amounted to about a quarter of those involved. And for what?

The crown?

Why *do* men fight?

Since time began, philosophers and evolutionary psychologists have pondered this question. Because, since time began, men have been fighting. Perhaps aggressive behaviour is simply part of the male make-up. Or maybe it's a reduced level of serotonin in the brain that has led to duels, skirmishes, and wars. Conceding a goal in the last minute also doesn't help.

All around the world, people have attempted to find an organic, genetic basis for aggressive behavior. Several hormones and neurotransmitters, such as testosterone and seretonin, have been implicated in the quest to find why people are aggressive. Studies suggest that, in normal levels, serotonin exerts a calming, inhibitory effect on neuronal firing. Whereas when levels are low, aggressive and impulse behaviours increase. But we are far from understanding how or why serotonin explains aggression. Perhaps, in the future, with more sophisticated knowledge of the mechanism of the brain and nervous system, we will truly understand the organisation of neurons. But until then, instead of seeing aggressive behaviour as having a biological explanation, I think it simply comes back to how you were raised; the values you were given as a child.

Growing up, you can be *taught* not to want to fight. To paraphrase Dorothy Louise Law Nolte, *if a child lives with criticism, he learns to condemn and if a child lives with hostility, he learns to fight. But if a child lives with tolerance, he learns to be patient.* I think we can all appreciate man's desire to fight to defend his harem, but that doesn't explain waging war.

Why does man not simply walk away from an unnecessary challenge? It seems to me it is basic ego coupled with a lack of parenting to show there can be a passive way. I recall Jade Goody commenting on criticism of her vile and loud-mouthed behaviour during her well-publicised confrontation with Shilpa Shetty on the TV programme 'Big Brother'; "I don't know any other way of reacting" she said. By comparison, Shilpa had learned as a child how to handle conflict. Whereas Jade knew only one way:

Shout louder.

What we see in The Wars of The Roses are fairly simple fights for territory; still the most common cause of modern day conflict today.

Nowadays it's called Road Rage and Trolley Rage.

Back then, the chiefly class was developing and with it the habit of fighting under leaders; first selected for ability and suitability, then selected for life, and finally born to the job. Imagine the shiver sent down the spine of a young, peace-loving heir to the throne on the realisation that one day they may have to lead the troops into battle. You'd pretty soon be devising a strategy that saw you leading from the rear. Or possibly even an armchair back in the palace.

Of course, poor conditions often lead to the courage of the cornered rat; a deep seated resentment is what presumably drove Hitler on; but why to such lengths?

Poverty, hunger, sex, avarice, ambition, injustice and personal pride are just some of the words that could best sum it up. 'Man' wants to assert and dominate. But perhaps the basic desire to be 'right' and 'to win' comes top of the list. Maybe as long as the secretion of serotonin goes up and down then men will be aggressive?

In Tennyson's poem; 'The Charge of the Light Brigade' about the events at the Battle of Balaclava in1854 he wrote:

‘Forward, the Light Brigade! Was there a man dismayed? Not though the soldier knew someone had blundered. Theirs not to make reply, theirs not to reason why, theirs but to do and die.’

The Charge of the Light Brigade

They went into the jaws of death; they rode into the mouth of hell knowing they would most likely die. And then Tennyson used it for propaganda.

The leader had made a big misjudgment; a huge mistake. Akin to blooding a rookie goalkeeper in a vital championship qualifier on a rain soaked pitch at Wembley. (I’m sorry, that was the best I could do). Some of the soldiers must have known this was a mistake. So why did they go ahead? They knew he’d messed up. But theirs ‘was not to reason why, theirs was but to do and die.’

Perhaps it was all about courage? Perhaps it was about social conditioning and a lack of self worth at the time? At what point do you question the leader? At what point do you decide they don’t know best? Courage is difficult. It’s about knowing when *not* to do as you’re told. It’s about going back into a burning building against all advice. It’s about diving into a monstrous sea when there is little hope of saving anyone. It’s about entering

'Britain's Got Talent' when deep down you know that few people these days are entertained by the sight of a grown man putting ferrets down his pants. Even if your backing track is a funky arrangement of 'Here We Go Gathering Nuts In May'.

To be a good leader you need both courage and honour.

But courage is also about understanding the common goal and being willing to risk your own life because you believe the cause is right.

It's all about the common man. Did Hitler ever really think about the effect of his warmongering on the common man?

In the preface to this book I asked you to cast your mind back to 1971 when I was standing outside a hall in Ashton-under-Lyne Grammar School waiting to sit my Physics 'A' level paper. I was born and raised in this Lancashire mill town. As were my father, Harry Hesketh, my grandfather, also Harry Hesketh and his father too, Sam Hesketh.

My grandfather, Harry Hesketh and his brother Albert fought in World War I. My grandfather wrote letters home from Egypt and two of them were published in the 'Ashton-under-Lyne Reporter' on August 7th 1915. At that time my grandfather only had two children, George and Alice. My own father was yet to be born.

This is the article that appeared in the paper:

> Two brothers named Private Harry Hesketh and Private Albert Hesketh, sons of Mr. and Mrs. Hesketh of 79, Church Street, Ashton, are with the Ashton Territorials fighting in the Dardanelles, and news has been received that Harry has been wounded. Harry is 28 years of age, and is married and has two children. He was a spinner at Reyner's Mill, and lived in Portland Street. He had been in the Territorials for four years and had completed his time, but re-enlisted when the war broke out.
>
> During the fighting against the Turks he was struck with shrapnel in the forehead when coming out of the

trenches, and has been in hospital. Private Albert Hesketh is 24 years of age, and lived with his parents. He was a piecer at the Minerva Mill, and was well known as a footballer, and has played for Ashton and Dukinfield clubs. He joined the Ashton Territorials after war was declared. He enlisted in September, was in khaki the next day, and was on board ship the following day en-route for Egypt. Private Harry Hesketh has sent home some very interesting letters of which two are given below:-

From H.P.H. Hospital, Alexandria.

'I never expected seeing this place, which is outside the city on the coast. It is a lovely little place, similar to Cleveleys, Blackpool. It is a field hospital about 20 yards off the beach, and we have nothing to do only lie down and sleep. Even lying down we can look out across the sea, and watch the ships going up and down. I met with an accident last Wednesday morning, and before I knew where I was I found myself on a boat bound for Alexandria. So you see how soon a chap is looked after. The wounded are picked up and taken to the clearing hospital, and from there are sent here to get better, and they know how to look after you. We have plenty of food and clean clothing and the staff are very attentive.

I wouldn't mind stopping here a week or two, but I expect I shall be with the Battalion again shortly. I have sent our Albert a letter telling him where I was. I only hope and trust that he is all right, as I feel very anxious about him, as I know what it is like out there. You never know one minute from another whether you will see the next day or not. The doctor has taken the bandage off my head this morning, but I am to be examined for the nervous system, as my head pains me so much, but I expect it will wear off. I shan't be sorry to get home again, though we have done very well up to now.

A fellow gets fed up when he has been away from his home a long time, and I want to be seeing the children, as I seem to be missing the best part of them. I daresay Alice won't know me when I do get back, and I think our George will be doubtful; ten months is a long time without seeing them, but we shall soon get to know each other.'

From Base Camp Mustapha, Alexandria, Egypt, Private Harry Hesketh writes:

'I am doing very nicely, but I am not feeling as well as I did before being knocked out. Ah, well, accidents will happen, and I might have been blown to pieces, and then there would have been a mess wouldn't there? Thank God it is no worse, and while there's life there's hope, and I am hoping to come back safe and sound and live at peace when we have settled with this lot. When we have got without the Turks, which won't be long, they ought to give us a chance over in France. I can assure you the East Lancashire Division can do a bit; you ask the Turks. We shall have the Dardanelles open shortly.

We know it's no easy job, but we are determined, and when the Lancashires say they'll do it, you bet somebody is going to get hurt. The 29th Division are fine fellows, and along with the Australians and New Zealanders have made the Turks run above once, and will do so again. They don't care for the bayonet.

Captain Hamer chased a large number of them himself with nothing but the bayonet. He met a brave death, and he was a gentleman, so are a great number of the officers. We are, indeed, proud of the fact that we are engaged in the greatest military history of the world, and prove that the old country is still as good today as it was in the days of Marlborough and Wellington. Of course we are not getting off scot free, but our losses are nothing compared with the Turks. The day I came away was the end of a two day's fight when the Turks lost 7,000 killed and wounded. They were simply mown down, just like cutting a meadow. It was awful, but it's war, and the more we kill the sooner it will be over.'

....

My grandfather returned home safely at the end of the war and my father was born in 1925.

'What Ifs, If Onlys and Maybes…

If you are a parent reading this let me share this thought with you; your children's bad behaviour is your own fault. Men don't fight if they are brought up in a loving family; nice boys from nice families don't sing the blues. Well, they can't write them very well.

The famous experiments conducted by psychologist Harry Harlow in the 1950's when he separated infant monkeys from their mothers a few hours after birth are still as relevant and as powerful today as they were then. He arranged for the young animals to be 'raised' by two kinds of surrogate monkey mother machines, both equipped to dispense milk. One mother was made out of bare wire mesh whilst the other was a wire mother covered with soft terry cloth.

Harlow observed that monkeys who had a choice of mothers spent far more time clinging to the terry cloth surrogates, even when their physical nourishment came from bottles mounted on the bare wire mothers. 'Mother love' is emotional rather than physiological. Harlow showed how love and continuity of care was a far more determining factor in healthy psychological development than anything else.

Harry Harlow's Monkeys

When the monkeys in the experiments were frightened by strange, loud objects, such as teddy bears beating drums, monkeys raised by terry cloth surrogates made bodily contact with their mothers, rubbed against them, and eventually calmed down. However, the monkeys raised by wire mesh surrogates did not retreat to their mothers when scared. Instead, they threw themselves on the floor, clutched themselves, rocked back and forth and screamed in terror.

For the rest of their lives.

In subsequent experiments, Harlow concluded that 'better late than never' was not a slogan applicable to raising monkeys. When Harlow placed his subjects in total isolation for the first eights months of life, denying them contact with other infants or with any type of surrogate mother, they were permanently damaged.

You reap what you sow; an issue we will return to at the end of this feud and at the end of the first section of this book.

Harlow's work and harrowing results leave us with lessons we all need to learn half a century later.

Chapter 4 ~ 'Short, violent and hairy'

1461 — 1485

Whatever the levels of serotonin, a comprehensive win it is for the Yorkists in 1461. It's 6-4 and is this a comeback? Edward was cagey when offering a soundbite to a local reporter "It's a promising start to the crucial Easter fixtures but we're not getting carried away and there's a long way to go yet".

Nevertheless, the victorious Edward IV, as he is now known, swept into York carrying the heads of his enemies held high. These replaced the heads of the Yorkists on the Micklegate Bar and souvenir sellers ditched their out-dated stock and printed new messages of goodwill on to T-shirts and Kiss-Me-Quick hats. 'Come on you Tykes' was a popular one.

And the next lesson to be learned? Sell what people want to buy. Fish where the fishes are. Go with the flow. If life throws you lemons, make lemonade. If it throws you oranges, make orangeade. And it if throws you an assortment of fruits and liqueurs, try a cocktail.

The Yorkists' tails are up and within a couple of months of the battle of Towton, Edward IV is crowned King in June 1461.

And as for Henry VI? Well, eventually the Yorkists caught up with him.

Deposed, depressed, and in deep doo-doo, after his capture he was incarcerated in the Tower of London. On the upside, he noted that the towels were much softer than those in Pontefract Castle which he put down to the quality of the water.

As Eric Idle was fond of saying, always look on the bright side of life.

In the years after Towton, peace and some prosperity returned to the country as King Edward IV consolidated his reign, formed a stable government, either sacked or conciliated the Lancastrian supporters, sent the French naval forces packing, and married a beautiful Lancastrian widow, Elizabeth Wydville in 1464. Beautiful, yes, but a bit unsteady with a pen in my view.

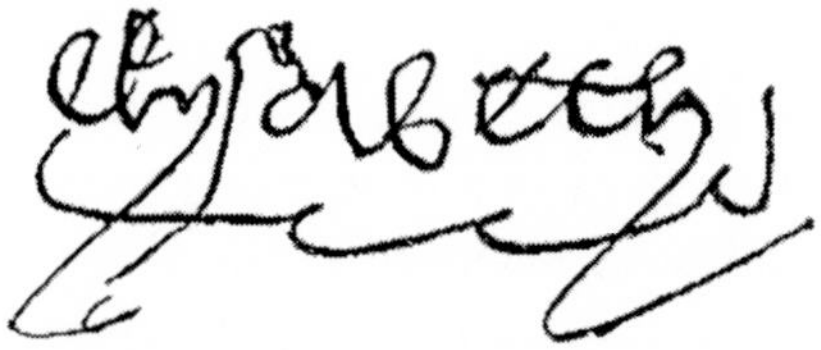

The Signature of Elizabeth Wydville

Never mind the hand writing though, his only real regret was that he hadn't checked the French boats for young girls before sending them away. Nonplussed, he set himself the task of fathering heirs to the throne and reserved Tuesday and Thursday evenings for such activity since the entertainment was always lousy. Maybe even Sundays if he was feeling up to it.

And Elizabeth provided Edward with an heir, Edward, and a spare, Richard (later to be the Princes in the Tower) and five daughters to marry off.

To be fair, the reign of King Edward IV has something to say for itself. By all accounts he was a handsome man with great personal charm, self confidence and intelligent to boot. But he was also rather impulsive. Indeed it could be argued his marriage to Elizabeth Wydville was ill advised. She was penniless and as Polydore Vergil (yes, that's his real name) commented, he 'was led by blind affection and not by rule of reason.'

But by 1470 his people were disillusioned with him. They had hoped for prosperity and peace – as the masses always do when a new Prime Minister or President is elected – and became frustrated when that didn't transpire. As the masses always do.....

So that year, King Edward IV was forced to flee when Warwick's brother, John Neville, changed to the Lancastrian side and on

October 3rd 1470, Henry VI was briefly restored to the throne of England.

How? Why?

Well, the various successes Edward had had prior to 1470 had brought the scores on the doors even closer and now the Lancastrians' lead in the series was generally agreed to be a slender 6-5. But proving that you're never more vulnerable than when you've just scored, the Yorkists became complacent and in May 1470 they agreed to release Henry VI from prison on the grounds of his good behaviour. Wacky, true, but good for him nonetheless.

The Yorkists had effectively shot themselves in the foot. Well not literally, obviously. An entire army limping into battle would have been a sorry sight and a recipe for disaster. But, metaphorically, they'd weakened their position and handed the baton to the Lancastrians. Not that there was a baton as such. That would have been really confusing.

Eight thousand men, one baton, no officials and no television replays. Anyway, a series of punch-ups in quick succession saw the Lancastrians extend their lead to 7-5 and briefly take back the throne in 1470.

They should never have allowed their enemy freedom. They lost control; they became complacent and thought he wouldn't fight back. But that's exactly what he did.

Henry VI had handled his adversity well. Whilst in prison he had controlled his own attitude. And arguably the key to controlling our attitude is how you handle adversity.

Because adversity in your life is inevitable. Leaders understand that when things are not good, it's still not time to panic because you can't win them all. If you want to be a leader be aware that people are watching you all the time to see how you handle both adversity and adversaries. Do you communicate well when things are going wrong or do you just make people feel guilty?

You can't have 'corporate belief systems' for your business and then behave in another way. Self-esteem is also key to having a good attitude. Most people have more control about how their employees, colleagues, children and partner feel about themselves than they think.

The most important thing anyone can think about you is ‘I feel good about myself when I’m near you.’

People who feel good about themselves are more likely to produce great results. Your employees will treat your customers exactly the way you treat them. When I see shoddy service in a café or bar and ask to see the manager I am never surprised to find that he or she shuffles towards me with an insouciant smile, dirty shoes, dirty fingers and unkempt hair.

It’s the next lesson.

If your team members don’t think you have credibility it shows in their work.

Henry had behaved well and shown good leadership so he still had his supporters.

But the Yorkists triumphed in a surprise counter-attack less than a year later to regain power. 7-6 and there’s still all to play for.

Time for some serious foul play.

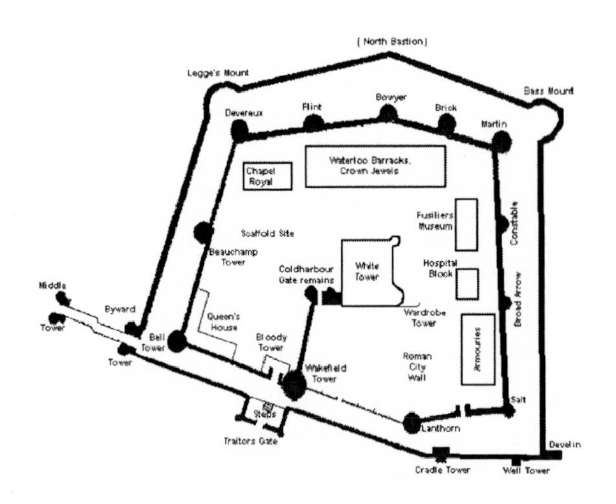

The Tower of London

On April 11th 1471 Edward entered the City of London in triumph. And on May 21st 1471 Henry VI mysteriously met his death in the Tower of London. According to his gaolers, he had just bathed and was drying himself off with his favourite fluffy towel when, as my mum would say, 'he came over all funny' and slumped to the floor.
Dead.
They also added that at no time had they strangled him or kicked the corpse around his cell like a football just in case anyone thought they had so there. On his official death certificate the Yorkists declared he died of 'pure melancholy and displeasure'. A world first.
At least the Yorkists had finished him off this time.
439 years later, the controversy over the exact circumstances of his death still raged. So much so that to clear up the mystery, King George VI ordered his body to be exhumed and examined by pathologists in 1910.

That's right, 1910.

People don't forget. People want the truth. Even if it hurts.

You may be able to sweep something under the carpet for what seems like an eternity but eventually the skeleton will pop out of the cupboard. Or in this case, the coffin.

People need closure before they can move on. They need to know the facts of what happened before they can come to terms with things. That's why we need public enquiries. And if people think the wool is being pulled over their eyes they react.

When, in 2009 MPs' expenses claims were found to have included clearing a moat, maintaining swimming pools, a 'duck island', fitting mock Tudor beams to the front of a house, buying trouser presses, bath plugs, dog food, lawnmowers and, in one case, a packet of Hob Nob biscuits, what galled us, the hoi polloi, was that the MPs had all signed a declaration with every claim that they had incurred these costs (and I quote) 'wholly, exclusively and necessarily' to enable them to perform their duties as a Member of Parliament'. But where were the checks that this was the case?

And when in 2009 The Prime Minister apologised on behalf of all political parties for some of the 'mistakes' made he saw no irony in the fact that no 'mistakes' had been made where MP's could and should have claimed for *more* than they did.......

Fact is, if you are always honest you don't have to remember anything. Life becomes a lot easier.

So what did happen to Henry VI in 1471? Well, the skeleton was found to have been dismembered before being placed in the box and not all the bones were present. Three much-worn teeth were found and the only piece of jaw present had lost its teeth before death. Most revealingly, his brown hair was found matted with blood on the skull, confirming that Henry VI had died as a result of a violent blow, possibly administered by Edward's younger brother, Richard, Duke of Gloucester.

18 year old Richard is the only person named as being in the Tower on the night of May 21st 1471.

Bit of a give away.

However, Royalists dispute this, stating that since Richard was a chronic asthmatic he could never blow that hard. That's the problem with Royalists, always missing the point.

We want to know the truth. We want honesty. Particularly when things have gone wrong. We want to hold people to account.

The beauty of always being honest is that you don't have to recall what you said to someone. Whereas whenever you lie, you *always* have to remember in case you're asked again. There are the deceitful whoppers often designed to save a bit of money, and the little white lies usually told to save someone's feelings. For example, '*No, of course, your bum doesn't look big in that*' is more likely to precede a successful evening than if your answer includes a reference to say, a baboon or a sumo wrestler.

The truth is, lies are very difficult to detect. Even the classically studied tell-tale signs are no real indicator. Today, people rarely fidget or look away when they're lying. They don't scratch the back of their neck, act nervously, or change the pitch of their voice. If they touch their nose it's probably itching. If they touch yours, you're standing too close.

So how do you tell? Well, years of researching real police interviews allowed Dutchman, Aldert Vrij, Professor of Applied Social Psychology at The University of Portsmouth, to provide some guidance about what non-verbal signals represent. Firstly, it's important to consider a person's natural behaviour. A friendly, gregarious outgoing character who turns up on your doorstep asking to borrow an axe is more likely to get assistance than someone who's a dead ringer for Hannibal Lecter. Similarly, introverts or socially nervous people sometimes give the false impression that they're lying. As a teenager I would often fidget nervously when chatting up a girl even though I was deadly serious about the proposition. Even the bit about the custard.

Vrij's researchers concluded that the way to spot a lie is to study someone's behaviour when telling the truth, and then to compare this with their behaviour when suspected of lying. You see, lying places high cognitive demands on an individual and the more awkward questions asked, the more pressure they feel, and the more physical signs they display. This is basically how a lie detector works, highlighting the difference in things like facial movements, heart rate and sweat glands.

Of course, if you have a meeting with your boss and you need to know his *real* plans for next year, it's probably not the done thing to wire him up first. So here's a tip. Rely on your intuition. If you're a sales person it will doubtlessly be finely honed any way. If you're in a meeting and something doesn't quite *feel* right it's probably means that something *isn't* quite right. Either that, or your underwear is on back to front.

In a nutshell, implicit or broadly unconscious processes can be more effective at detecting a lie than conscious directed thought. It's a big nutshell, granted. So if you want to be sure of the truth, ask someone to recount the story over and over again. And don't forget to look out for the TNTs – Tiny Noticeable Things – that are different, as well as any discrepancies in the answer. As they say on the telly, the truth is out there.

Back to 1471.

It's 7-7 and, as Sir Alex Ferguson likes to describe it, squeaky bum time.

Yorkist Edward IV is back on the throne. He was a popular murderer (it wasn't an oxymoron in those days) and right up until his death in 1483 was known in royal circles as King Edward, the original Spud-U-Like. He had pretty much ordered the execution of every important Lancastrian but one - the teenager, Henry Tudor. Henry's mother gave her son a bit of good advice to leave the country for a short while and leave he did.

For France.

For over a decade, licking his wounds and planning a Lancastrian come back. The young Henry was, of course, to make quite a come back and father Henry VIII. But we'll read about that later.

If you create enemies you create plots against you.

A lesson Anne Boleyn will learn too. But that's for the second part of the book.

King Edward IV was a notorious womaniser, Jane Shore being one of many mistresses, and Edward's life of debauchery and self indulgence ended in 1483. He died wealthy, respected and in his own bed after he'd caught a bit of a chill whilst out fishing on the Thames. Dying in your own bed was no mean feat for a 15th century ruler. His son and heir, the 12-year old Edward Junior, took over his father's role - minus the debauchery bit, obviously. Previously the Prince of Wales, he was proclaimed King Edward V. However, as is often the case with boy Kings, his uncle Richard, Duke of Gloucester, had other ideas. Cunningly, he told anyone who'd listen that he'd sent the young royal and his little brother out for an ice cream with plenty of cash along with the instruction not to forget the flake and raspberry sauce. Then, during the youngsters' prolonged absence caused chiefly, he said, by the non-synergy of ice cream and confectionery vendors at that time, proclaimed himself King Richard III.

His reign mirrored himself exactly.

Short, violent and extremely hairy.

Richard III

But why did he feel the need to take the throne? Richard genuinely grieved for his brother, Edward, and he sent a nice copper-plated handwritten letter of condolence to Queen Elizabeth, promising to do all that lay within his power to ensure the smooth succession of her son, Edward, Prince of Wales, now King Edward V.

But then he began thinking. He pondered what the future held in store. He was now 31 years of age with a distinguished career as a soldier already behind him. As the new King's uncle, he could expect to be prominent in the counsels which governed the affairs of the land, and the future looked bright indeed.

Of course, he was immensely wealthy but he knew that at any moment his status could be taken away on the whim of his nephew. He could be brought low, his estates confiscated and then forced into the ultimate sacrifice - made to marry a French girl still at junior school. This last thought actually cheered him up a little but it soon passed. Paranoia, avarice and fear of loss ensured he kept the kids in the tower.

Inevitably, this led to more violent clashes but Richard III wasn't called Richard The Lion Heart for nothing. In fact, he wasn't called Richard The Lion Heart at all - that was Richard I.

Just testing.

Nevertheless, he was an effective adversary to the Lancastrians and he saw them off again in 1484 to finally give the Yorkists a richly-deserved lead, 8-7.

The next lesson is here for us all to see. Richard is pretending to be something he's not. As bald men with cheap toupees seem to forget; acting as though you have something and actually having it are not the same thing and anyone who looks closely can tell the difference

Richard began to really believe he was omnipotent; more than just flesh and blood. Not for the first time in this book arrogance and contempt has crept in. In Roman times, generals were allegedly reminded of the fickleness of their glory by a slave carefully positioned in earshot on the triumphal parade route.

'Memento mori' the hapless servant would whisper to the wreathed victor as his chariot rattled along Rome's jubilant streets: 'Remember you are mortal.'

The difference between a boss and a leader is that a boss gets people to do what *he* wants them to do whilst a leader gets people to *want to do* what he wants them to do. More than ever, over 500 years on, communication is the critical test for leaders.

When things go horribly wrong as, for example, when the Icelandic volcano erupted and grounded planes all over in Europe in 2010 the biggest complaint from the great unwashed – literally – was not that their planes were not leaving but that there was not enough communication from the authorities.

But the authorities don't tell you what's going on. They do it their way.

Never say 'we've always done it that way' as an excuse for not changing.

We live in times that demand constant change. Doing the same thing over and over and expecting different results is a ridiculous notion.

Lots of us make New Year's resolutions but few of us see them through to the bitter end. So what's the trick? How do you change the habit of a lifetime? Is there a technique you can use that helps you lose weight that doesn't involve wiring up your jaw? You may enjoy high fashion but do you really want a designer gastric belt for Christmas? I didn't think so.

The good news is a study by Dr Philippa Lally – Doo to her friends – revealed some interesting facts about how to successfully form new, long lasting habits. Together with her colleagues at University College London she recruited people who wanted to get into the habit of doing something healthy like eating a piece of fruit each day or taking a 15 minute run. Participants were then asked daily how *automatic* their chosen activity felt. Questions included things like whether the behaviour was 'hard *not* to do' and could be done 'without thinking' and 'What's that cream bun doing in your back pocket?'

Not surprisingly, the normal plateau curve occurred. That's to say, after a period of time either the habit was formed and became automatic, or it became too much of an effort and they returned to reading a copy of 'The Racing Post' in the local snug. Typically, the plateau in 'automaticity' was reached after 66 days. Which meant that the new activity had become as much of a habit as it was ever going to be. However, although the *average* was 66 days, there was a marked variation in how long habits took to form. Anywhere from 18 days up to the thick end of nine months is possible. I think as a teenager it took me about three days to form the habit of drinking beer but I can't remember very much about it now.

As you'd imagine, drinking a daily glass of water became automatic very quickly but doing 50 sit-ups before breakfast required more dedication. So what does this research tell us?

Firstly, never try to do fifty sit-ups whilst drinking a glass of water. It's not clever and it goes everywhere. But perhaps more importantly, it revealed that when we want to develop a relatively simple habit like eating fruit or taking exercise, it could still take us over two months of *daily* repetitions before the behaviour actually becomes a habit. And, while skipping single days isn't detrimental in the long-term, it's those early repetitions that give us the greatest boost in automaticity.

Arguably the pain of uncertainty is worse than the certainty of pain. But we need to have uncertainty and challenge to grow and develop. Back in 1485 though, Richard III had created uncertainty with regard to the whereabouts of his nephews, disunity in the court and factions in the family.

Out of interest, in 1674 two small skeletons were discovered in the White Tower under the stairs leading to the chapel. They were subsequently reburied in Westminster Abbey as ordered by King Charles II. The skeletons were believed to be the remains of the bodies of the two tragic Little Princes, Edward V and his younger brother Richard, Duke of York. In 1933 a forensic examination conducted by Tannery and Wright was unable to confirm whether the bones discovered in the White Tower were those of the Princes in the Tower. The mystery goes on to this day.

Time for the last fight in The Wars of The Roses.

With the French, as usual, in the thick of it.

Chapter 5 ~ The Battle of Bosworth and Turkeys at Christmas

1461 1501

And so it was that in August 1485 the final battle of The Wars of The Roses took place in Market Bosworth between Richard III and Henry Tudor. If there'd been television they'd have made it a 5 o'clock slot and have billed the battle as 'Richard & Tudor Live.'

Henry Tudor had been born in January 1457 and descended on his father's side from an 'unauthorised' liaison between Henry V's widowed Queen, Katherine of Valois and Owen Tudor, a cabinet maker from Kendal in Cumbria.

Henry's mother was one of John of Gaunt's illegitimate children, Margaret Beaufort. Margaret was twelve years old when she married Henry's father, Edmund Tudor, and was pregnant by the time she was 13. They had been living together as man and wife - or boy and girl strictly speaking – and when Edmund died in November 1456 she went to live with her brother-in-law, Henry VI, at Pembroke Castle. Before she'd hit 14 she had been married, widowed and given birth to a future King. Maybe that's what toughened her up for what was to come.

Time for a recap.

It's 1485. Henry, a 28 year old Lancastrian who had been based in France for over a decade, decided to confront the Yorkists, based in London, by invading England via Milford Haven in South Wales armed with fewer men than travel to Hull to watch their team, Stoke City, play in a football match. They then travel up country to the fight venue somewhere in Shrewsbury. Naturally, Google Earth was not available to them at the time and orienteering was still in its infancy, which helps to explain why he took the long route.

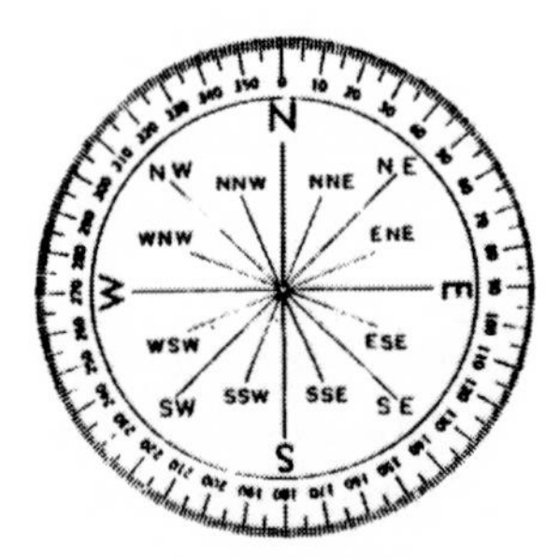

To compound the problem, the 2,000 French mercenaries he brought with him spoke little English and were reluctant to ask directions. Henry made a mental note to bring their wives as well next time.

Meanwhile, the Shrewsburyites were rather reluctant to see their town burned down by this new challenger to the throne. So they made Henry Tudor wait at the town gates for a night and a day as well as promise to replace all their wrecked furniture afterwards. This was, in effect, the second ban on a travelling army of away fans but now also came with some community service thrown in.

Frankly, Richard III was caught napping. With the August Bank Holiday looming, most of his army had already committed themselves to a weekend at the coast with the family. To make matters worse, the men Richard did have at his disposal were horribly out of position. He had sent Viscount Lovel to Southampton to guard the south coast, and ordered the Duke of Norfolk and his men to the Essex coastline to defend the eastern border. Finally, he positioned Sir Robert Brackenbury, the Constable of the Tower, just a few miles down the road just in case Henry Tudor arrived there.

Thinking he had all the bases covered, he relaxed and took himself off to Bosworth for the punch up with what he imagined would be a bedraggled assortment of perhaps a few dozen disenchanted Lancastrian supporters, probably from Gwent or somewhere like that. So it came as a bit of a shock when he drew back his curtains on that fine summer's day to be confronted by Henry and two thousand French lunatics. Stunned by the news that they had arrived via Milford Haven and got straight through customs without a raised eyebrow, he barely had time to unleash his sword when he and his men were cut down in a flurry of mortal blows.

Incidentally, this also caused pub landlords up and down the land to spend the night hastily painting over their White Boar signs - Richard III's emblem that had been patriotically displayed everywhere until 1485 - with whatever blue paint they had in the house - leaving Britain with its surfeit of Blue Boar pubs to this day.

So, 108 years after the first minor quarrel, the score stood at a respectable eight a piece and Henry Tudor was finally crowned Henry VII. Apart from the odd minor rebellion, The Wars of The Roses were all but over.

And the lesson to be learned from this final Battle of Bosworth?

Well from a Lancastrian point of view, perseverance and a good plan are a powerful combination. But maybe get a SatNav next time. And the Yorkists should have never allowed themselves to get complacent. Plan for the unexpected and you won't be caught napping.

A theme we shall return to again and again.

Having won the throne after Bosworth in 1485, Henry VII married Elizabeth, the daughter of his ex-enemy Edward IV, in January 1486. He did this partly to show there were no hard feelings, partly because that's what three clever women had decided was best for them, and partly because she was tall, fair haired, and had an amazing bone structure. Elizabeth was also gentle natured and could speak perfect English, albeit with a Yorkshire accent.

This act united the two houses that had been at war for many years. An altogether different act consummated the marriage and took not nearly so long. To symbolise the union, Henry took as his emblem a cucumber - but was later persuaded to abandon this for the Tudor Rose, which combined the white rose of York with a red rose of Lancashire. Though not necessarily in that order.

Nine months after the marriage in 1486, the new Queen had a son. Nice one, Henry. They called him Arthur and surely he'll become King and we'll all live happily every after? Well, as I'm sure you know, it didn't quite work out that way. The birth of Arthur was followed by a daughter, Margaret, destined to be Queen of Scots. Now if Henry VII had gone through with his plans for a vasectomy – two bricks and a meat cleaver in those days - the whole structure of England would have been very different. But in 1489 - yes, you've guessed it - they had a second son and called him Henry.

But more of him later.

Interestingly, the Crown still owns land as a result of all The Wars of The Roses activity over 500 years ago. Our current Queen, as Duke of Lancaster, is a major Yorkshire landowner. In over thirty years of The Wars of The Roses there were only 13 weeks of actual fighting and more people died of plague than from battle wounds. But the memories of Towton have lived on for many years.

There is something of a dearth of historical accounts of Henry VII's reign from 1485. It seems to fall between the two stools of being after The Wars of The Roses and the dramatic disappearance of the Princes In The Tower and before the main event of Henry VIII.

Even Shakespeare left him alone.

So before we look at the events of Henry VIII's reign it might be worthwhile seeing if we can learn something from the big man's dad. As we've said, Henry was born in January 1457 in Pembroke Castle in South Wales and the first fourteen years of his life were spent in Wales.

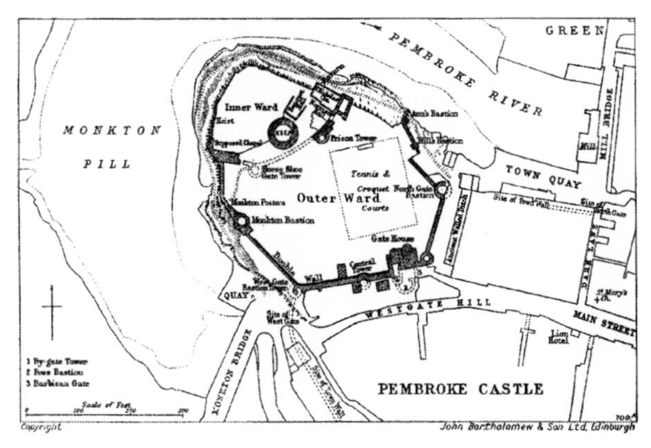

Pembroke Castle

He had been born after his father's death and his mother had remarried twice before Henry was 16. The next fourteen years of his life were spent in France. Basically when he came to the throne he'd spent very little time in England, knew hardly anyone in the country, had never managed land of his own, spoke French better than he did English and had no personal knowledge of government.

Fact is he's the man who decided that a young Spanish girl would marry his son and heir. And perhaps that's the biggest legacy he left.

But there is something else about Henry VII. William Wilberforce made a passing reference to him in his anti slavery speech.

People look after themselves. Certainly Henry VII did.

And people look to have people around them who can also see the benefit - to themselves - in behaviour that should not be encouraged; behaviour that sometimes, on reflection, beggars belief.

History is full of powerful people who did some very bad things because no one was brave enough to stop them.

The next lesson comes directly from William Wilberforce's speech on the horrors of the slave trade in the House of Commons on May 12th 1789. He said 'All that is necessary for the triumph of evil is that good men do nothing.' (Or words to that effect. It's thought he was quoting Edmund Burke). His view was that it was simply avarice that was the key motive for every monarch to go to war. If the King of Barbessin wanted brandy all he had to do was send his troops, in the night-time, to burn and desolate a village with its captives then being used as commodities that could be bartered with British traders.

Whilst good men stood by.

Wilberforce said 'What if I should be able to show this House that in a civilised part of Europe, in the time of our Henry VII, there were people who actually sold their own children? What if I should tell them that England itself was that country? What if I should point out to them that the very place where this inhumane traffic was carried on was the city of Bristol?'

In the reign of Henry VII Ireland was used to drive a considerable trade in slaves with England. When a great plague infested the Emerald Isle the Irish were struck with a panic that the plague was a punishment sent from heaven for the sin of the slave trade, and therefore abolished it. They only stopped it when they truly believed there was a message from on high.

Wilberforce asked if any man could contradict 'the dictates of his conscience, the principles of justice, the laws of religion, and of God.' Even when they could no longer plead ignorance bad men would continue to feather their nest until 'a few good men' became a cabal and grew.

And the abolition of slavery began with a few good men with a conscience believing that a wrong should - and could - be put right.

And the lesson we should learn is all around us.

Don't expect turkeys to vote for Christmas.

Wembley football stadium's official capacity is 90,000, but with over 17,000 seats reserved for Club Wembley members, whose investment paid for the stadium to be built, its effective capacity is no more than 72,000.

On the biggest day and biggest football match in the English football calendar, the FA Cup Final, only 50,000 tickets go to the fans, with a further 22,000 or so going to various football clubs, charities, sponsors, the Football Foundation, the Premier League, Football League, Football Conference, PFA, International Associations, Fifa, Uefa and County Football Associations.

Pretty much everyone agrees that it would be fairer for the supporters of the two finalists to have more tickets. But the largest single beneficiaries of the tickets are the Counties and the 115 members of the FA Council, sometimes known as 'football's parliament'.

The councillors themselves receive up to eight tickets each, four of them complimentary. The entire system is overseen by the

Council itself, whose members include the chairs of all 51 County Associations.

And they decide on the allocation.

The FA also point out that it is almost impossible to balance the competing demands for tickets, and that the FA Cup final is no different to the Champions League or Carling Cup finals, where around a third of the tickets are shared beyond the competing clubs.

But that doesn't make it right.

Turkeys don't vote for Christmas. It takes one of the councillors to speak and not be wracked with self interest for things to change. It takes someone to do 'the right thing'.

The rest of Henry VII's reign was fairly uneventful. There seems to be little or no change to Parliament during his reign. No significant changes in procedure, composition or electoral arrangements.

Needless to say he had gone down the rather traditional and well worn route of declaring war on France - in 1491 - but even that ended in a damp squib whereby he didn't actually invade until the autumn of 1492 and eventually agreed to withdraw for a cheap bribe.

But he did spend most of the latter part of the 15th century worrying about usurpers.

So before we get to Henry VII's sons it's worth making reference to a little side plot that threatened his rule. Welcome to the stage, Lambert Simnel who was a child pretender to the throne of England, and Perkin Warbeck, a fellow imposter who was a Belgian backed by the Scots.

Time for chapter 6. I have not got enough imagination to make up what happened next.

Chapter 6 ~ The Warbeck and Simnel Side Plots

Perkin Warbeck and Lambert Simnel were not just unlikely names but also both unlikely imposters who both - and separately - rather bizarrely threatened the rule of King Henry VII.

The 'rebellion' led by Warbeck was a rather long, drawn out affair and lasted between 1491 and 1499 and it's this one we shall look at first. Perkin Warbeck's father, Jehan de Werbecque, was a poor Frenchman and in 1491 Warbeck himself was working for a Breton silk merchant called Pierre Jean Meno. Warbeck arrived in Cork in the autumn of 1491 on one of Meno's merchant ships selling silk.

For whatever reason, the people of Cork thought that the French speaking Warbeck was the Earl of Warwick. By all accounts Warbeck denied that he was the Earl but, rather liking the idea that the young girls of southern Ireland found him attractive as part of the landed gentry, and fortified by a couple of pints of Guinness, he claimed that he was Richard, Duke of York – the younger of the two princes in the Tower who had mysteriously disappeared leaving their Uncle Richard III in power.

As he said to his Dad at the time, "In for a penny, in for a pound."

The Princes in the Tower

With neither prince having been proved to be alive or dead and he being the right sort of age he somehow continued to get away with the scam and the following year Charles VIII welcomed Warbeck to Paris with, by now, about 100 supporters of the House of York gathered behind him. From Paris he moved to Flanders where Margaret of Burgundy took him in as her nephew and from there Warbeck gained yet another supporter – none other than the Holy Roman Emperor Maximilian. He too recognised Warbeck as Richard IV of England.

And so in July 1495, Warbeck attempted to land at Deal in Kent planning to march to London and claim his throne.

I am absolutely not making this up. When James Thurber wrote 'The Secret Life of Walter Mitty' in 1941 he was probably inspired by Perkin.

Anyway, there was no-one to meet him on the beaches of Kent so he sailed for Ireland and unsuccessfully laid siege to Waterford – a town loyal to Henry – but was unsuccessful. From Ireland, Warbeck sailed for Scotland to try his luck there. And this time James IV gave Warbeck refuge and a pension of £1,200 a year. James probably just saw Warbeck as an opportunity to disrupt England and get up Henry's nose rather than believe that he was *actually* the Duke of York. But either way, Perkin had developed and honed his selling skills. Given his original job was bringing silk over in one of Pierre Jean Meno's ships, it was probably he who inspired that expression about making a silk purse out of a sow's ear.

Using his pension to finance the whole thing, Warbeck attempted an invasion of England.

He was a trier, Perkin.

It was an absolute disaster as no one south of the border was willing to support him and so, via Ireland, Devon and Beaulieu

Abbey in Hampshire, he was eventually persuaded to give himself up. As a foreigner Warbeck could not be tried for treason so would not have had to face the butchery of being hung, drawn and quartered; but surely he would be sent to the block?

No; believe it or not, Henry allowed Warbeck to remain at court. Henry wanted to keep an eye on him.

We have no idea why.

When Warbeck rather foolishly tried to run away he was caught, put in the stocks, humiliated and sent to the Tower. Henry's patience had finally run out and in November 1499, Warbeck was hanged.

You can't fool all the people all the time.

And believe it or not he wasn't the only one claiming the throne during Henry's reign.

The other imposter, Lambert Simnel – if that was his real name - was born around 1477. He was of fairly humble origin but at the age of ten was taken as a pupil by an Oxford-trained priest named Roger Simon who had set himself up as a Kingmaker. In his time he'd taken many boys up the back alley to ascertain their credentials but nothing was ever proven. He chose Lambert after detecting an uncanny resemblance between him and both of the supposedly murdered sons of Edward IV. So he duly set about teaching the boy some courtly manners and all the necessary etiquettes to hang out with royalty. Which fork to use, how to cuff a footman; that kind of stuff.

He got the young boy to behave as though he was royal. He encouraged him to behave in a way that people would think he really *was* of Royal descent.

Nowadays it's called body language and it's well-known that our body language influences how other people perceive us. Striding purposefully into a room to deliver an important presentation gives you an air of confidence that the butterflies in your stomach might possibly belie.

Fortunately, nobody can see the butterflies, just the confident stride. But what is the evidence that you can use body language to your advantage? If you closely mimic the mannerisms and gestures of someone that you want to get to like you, such as a new client or colleague, will it work?

Displaying a degree of empathy with a potential client can obviously help to bolster a relationship. But is it as simple as copying a hand gesture, a particular way of standing or sitting, or a distinctive nod of the head?

Well, there is evidence to suggest that subtle mimicking of another person's body language can increase their liking of you. For many years, Bush and Blair were thick as thieves. Or, should I say, enjoyed a 'special relationship'. They both developed a style of public speaking that was almost identical. It would start with dramatic pauses and simple hand gestures, continue with subtle arm movements and then often conclude with the invasion of a small country. Coincidence? I think not.

But if you're still a little sceptical, here's the proof. Psychologists John Chartrand and Tanya Bargh of New York University carried out a series of experiments to determine whether mimicking another person's habits really does influence how much they like you. Testing what they called 'The Chameleon Effect', they divided up their sample of guinea pigs into two groups. Each group spent twenty minutes or so chatting to a member of the researcher's team whom they had never met before. One group of researchers were instructed to subtly mimic the person's body language such as folding their arms, scratching their nose, tapping the arm rest, waggling their foot – in fact any little nuance that they could mimic without being rumbled.

Meanwhile, the researchers in the control group sat quite still throughout their conversation and didn't attempt to mimic any body language at all.

Afterwards, the participants were asked to provide a mark out of ten to indicate how much they liked the person they had been talking to and how well they had got on with each other. The results supported the theory that mimicking a person's body language does, indeed, increase their liking of you; with the group whose actions were imitated consistently giving higher scores than those whose body language wasn't mimicked in any way.

Naturally, you should never copy these traits at exactly the same time as the other person is doing them because that would give the game away.

It'll look like you've been on a course or read a book. They would probably start to shuffle uneasily in their chair. And when you do likewise, they may even begin to sweat a little. And if you can replicate that, you'll soon find yourself being frog marched off the premises, whilst screaming to the security guards 'Keep in step, boys'.

That would be taking it too far.

So try 'The Chameleon Effect' yourself the next time you meet someone new you want to impress and get to like you. Just be careful not to over do it. Because if they've also read this part of the book you may find yourself acting out a bizarre Laurel and Hardy routine.

So with all the lessons learned, Roger Simon rebranded Lambert as Richard, Duke of York, son of King Edward IV, the younger of the vanished Princes in the Tower.

However, his plans were to take a dramatic twist on learning of the death of the Earl of Warwick during his imprisonment in the

Tower of London. Apparently, he'd slipped on a bar of soap whilst showering, pulled the plastic curtain off its rails, got tangled up inside it, and asphyxiated. The guard's thought it was a bizarre sex game and left him to it.

It happens.

Anyway, this was excellent news for Roger Simon who, along with his cohorts Smith and Higgins, realised that the Earl had a boy about the same age as Lambert with a bit of a claim to the throne as the son of the Duke of Clarence, King Edward IV's brother.

Passing Lambert off as that son, Simon's plan worked like a dream and the young pretender was solemnly crowned King on May 24th 1487.

Not surprisingly, when Henry found out he was steaming.

Mad, that is, not drunk.

Well, possibly a little drunk, but definitely vexed. He summoned his peers and bishops and together they devised a series of measures for the punishment not only of Simon and Lambert but all his secret enemies. When one bishop asked the not unreasonable question, "Who are these secret enemies?" Henry, leant forward, tapped his nose, and said out of the corner of his mouth, "I don't know; it's a secret. Now pass me that chicken leg."

To add to the confusion, Henry's first act was to proclaim a free pardon to all his former opponents. He then offered a £1,000 reward to anyone who could produce the body of the sham Plantagenet. In today's money, that's the equivalent of about seven billion pounds and though excited at the idea of being rich, people worried that their mattress wasn't going to be big enough. You couldn't trust the banks, even back then.

Meanwhile, Lambert, buoyed by the crown, fortified by drink and supported by a dozen Irish cronies, took a boat from Ireland and landed at Foudrey in Lancashire. None of them knew why, it just seemed like a good idea at the time.

Henry was shaking with rage and trepidation, though some say it was the DTs. He got together his own forces and headed towards Coventry which seemed like a convenient place for a fight. In the event, the by now hostile armies met at Stoke.

Don't ask.

Anyway, after a brief but bloody one day contest it was all over. Henry's men were victorious and the young pretender and his mentor were taken prisoner. Although Roger Simon was a monk he had passed himself off as the boy King's butler and there was further confusion when the pair were paraded in front of Henry. Introduced as 'Lambert and Butler' the King replied, quick as a flash, "Tipped or full strength?" It was to be another five hundred years before anybody got the joke.

When questioned, Lambert Simnel spilled more than the beans. He protested his innocence and blamed Roger Simon for leading him astray. "I thought I was going to a fancy dress, honest." was his pathetic excuse. When he revealed his real parentage, Henry didn't know whether to laugh or cry. After a brief pause, he decided to laugh. Then, much to Lambert's relief, Henry pardoned him on condition that he worked as a scullion in the royal kitchen. The boy did well and was eventually promoted to the rather cushy position of falconer. He died peacefully in his sleep in 1534.

Roger Simon faired less well but did manage to claim some sort of ecclesiastic loop hole and escape the axe. However, he was kept 'in custody' for the rest of his life. There was little in his cell to occupy his brilliant mind and keep him busy but once a day, by way of a little light entertainment, a guard would enter the room and tell him the Lambert and Butler joke. And every day, as the guard turned and left, Simon would mutter under this breath, 'I still don't get it.'

Chapter 7 ~ 'Yikes, it's Katie' and The Second Golden Rule

1501 1509

Marrying young French girls was considered rather passé in the early part of the 16th century so Henry VII decided that his eldest son, the future King Arthur should take his pick from the European girls sunning themselves over the border in Spain. As Henry himself said, "They're right little crackers but a lot less gobby". I know it's not very PC; I'm just reporting the facts. It's not a view necessarily shared by the author or his publisher.

Of course, the future King couldn't marry just any young Spanish girl; it had to be a royal princess. This considerably narrowed his selection but finally he chose the King of Spain's daughter, Katherine of Aragon.

Or rather, his dad chose for him.

Pacing nervously up and down the quayside at Portsmouth awaiting his new bride's arrival, the young Arthur looked forward to embracing Katherine's lithe, olive-skinned body and running his fingers through her typically Spanish long, dark locks. He probably had in mind the kind of look portrayed by Maria Doyle Kennedy in the subsequent BBC drama 'The Tudors' and his expectations were running high.

So, as you might imagine, there was a good deal of cursing and looking to the Heavens in disbelief, as the pale-skinned, grey-eyed, strawberry blonde Katie cleared immigration and stepped out into the English sunlight for the very first time. 'Yikes!' was the first word she heard from Arthur, yet to his credit, he never explained this term to her. Unfortunately, this meant she spent the rest of her life greeting everyone she met by taking a sharp step backwards and exclaiming 'Yikes'.

They were married ten days later on November 14th 1501 at St. Paul's Cathedral. He was 15 and she was 16. Only 16. But he loved her so. She was too young to fall in love and I can't quite remember the rest of the lyric.

The next lesson is clear. Don't always believe what you are told. There are no guarantees in life. And in particular, when it comes to mail order brides, you pays yer money, you takes yer choice, and there are seldom any refunds.

Due to the inclement December weather and the general mayhem surrounding the Christmas shopping period, Katie and Art - as the tabloids would no doubt these days dub them - postponed their honeymoon until they were old enough to have sex the following Spring. They chose Ludlow Castle in Wales and booked in for a long weekend.

Now we've all experienced wet weekends in Wales, but the nightmare for our young lovers proved far worse. Day one, he sneezed, day two, she sneezed. Day three he wheezed and coughed, day four she wheezed and coughed. Day five they couldn't go home because they were both too ill.

And it's worth asking a question right now that becomes absolutely critical many years later. Sir Antony Willoughby - a body servant of Arthur's - was subsequently asked to tell what the teenage Arthur had said to him whilst sneezing and coughing on the morning after the night before at Ludlow Castle. He apparently bragged to Sir Anthony, "Last night I was in Spain!" Was this just teenage bravado or a true statement of accomplishment?

And did anybody remember this properly anyway?

Our recollection of events is more fallible than we realise. The idea that we remember where we were when we heard of a great historical event, for example, is a common one. The top three being the death of the Princess of Wales, 9/11 and the assassination of John F. Kennedy. But this idea that we have a 'flashbulb memory' is just plain wrong. People can't remember accurately what they were doing when they heard about the assassination of JFK.

They just *think* they can.

There was a study conducted in America on the day after 9/11 whereby people were asked what they were doing when they first heard about the twin towers. And then, one, six or 32 weeks later the same subjects were asked to recall the event again.

And the longer the gap before they were asked again, the less consistent their memory and the more false details - vivid but wrong - were added. They were totally confident that their memory of 9/11 was right. But they weren't recalling 9/11 more accurately, they were just more confident about their inaccurate memory.

President George W. Bush was reading to school children when he was informed that a second plane had hit the twin towers and that America was under attack. Yet he has twice publicly recalled that before entering the classroom he had watched on television as the first plane hit the tower. And although that's not possible it's led to conspiracy theories. Fact is he can no longer remember where he was. He just thinks he can. We all do it. That's why you shouldn't always believe what you are told.

But back in 1971 I ***<u>was</u>*** outside the main hall at Ashton Grammar School waiting for the Physics exam......

Anyway, Katherine and Arthur were married for a good few months. Two horny teenagers in a damp and cold castle; was the marriage not consummated or was it under the covers and whoopsy daisy?

Either way, day six, he sneezed again. Day seven he wheezed and coughed again. You get the idea.

Day one hundred and seven, he croaked. I don't know about you, but I'd want my money back.

And that's how Henry VIII (born on June 28th 1491) became first in line to the throne.

Let's summarise Spanish Katie's position at this point. She's sixteen years old and has been living in a foreign land for less than a year. She's met a fifteen year old prince and married him within a fortnight. From day one, she believes 'Yikes' is the customary greeting in England. And when she finally gets to grips with the cold weather, the language and the greasy breakfasts, she finds herself widowed. How could things possibly get worse? Well, how about if your father-in-law decides that you should now marry your dead husband's eleven year old brother? That's got to come pretty high up.

Eleven!

I am not making this up.

This required the Pope (Julius II if you are interested; that becomes important later on too) to grant a dispensation based on the fact that her marriage to Arthur was never actually consummated due to his obsession with fly fishing and what with all the brass monkey weather in Wales and all. Suppressing a wry smile which some even described as a snigger, the Pope duly obliged, wishing her better luck next time and encouraging her to hide her new husband's rods.

Sensibly, the hapless couple - sorry, the happy couple - waited a while before tying the knot. They wanted to make sure that the ceremony was a really joyful occasion and so they naturally waited until Henry VII died.

But there was another reason they waited for Henry VII's death. Also included in the Papal dispensation for his younger son to marry his brother's widow was a proviso that allowed Henry VII himself to marry his widowed daughter-in-law if he wanted to.

Cheeky bugger.

Henry VII is about to draw his last breath.

Time for The Second Golden Rule before we move to Part Two.

It's natural. It's in the Bible (Galatians 6:7-10) and is the immutable law of Karma. Indeed, it's at the very heart of all religions and faiths.

You reap what you sow.

Throughout The Wars of The Roses we see time and time again how the behaviour of each King and so many of his cohorts has come back to bite them.

They kept losing and also lost the lessons they could and should have learned. So much unnecessary bloodshed. So little consideration for others.

So here is The Second Golden Rule for a happier and more successful life:

The Second Golden Rule:

Treat others as you would like them to treat you

If you plant corn, you don't get potatoes.

If you do, take it up with whoever supplied the seeds.

For every action there is a re-action; a result. If you gossip, you're likely to lose friends. If you lie, you'll become known as untrustworthy and lacking integrity. If you make others happy through service, charity and kind acts, you sow happiness like a seed, and it will give you the fruit of happiness. If you make others unhappy through harsh words, insult, ill-treatment or cruelty you sow unhappiness like a seed, and you too will eventually suffer misery and unhappiness. That's why the purpose of life is to develop loving relationships and make a meaningful, positive contribution.

Treat others as you would like them to treat you is The Golden Rule at the heart of the world's greatest religions and philosophies. It is the foundation upon which decency and morality are based.

The Golden Rule is also the foundation upon which success is based. Those who follow it will be happier, wealthier, have better relationships, achieve more in their careers and lead more rewarding lives than those who don't.

Most parents are aware that a teacher's expectations of a child become self-fulfilling prophecies. If a teacher believes them to be slow, the child will believe that too and indeed learn slowly. The lucky child who strikes a teacher as bright will pick up on their expectation and rise to fulfill it. This finding has been confirmed so many times, and in such varied settings, that it's no longer even debated.

It turns out that self-fulfilling prophecies are just as prevalent in offices as they are in elementary school classrooms. If a manager is convinced that the people in their charge are first-rate, they'll reliably outperform a group whose manager believes the opposite - even if the innate talent of the two groups is similar.

Focus special attention on an employee's first year because that's when expectations are set. Make sure new employees get matched with outstanding supervisors and are 'buddied' with excellent people. And don't forget to set high expectations for yourself.

In George Bernard Shaw's 'Pygmalion' Eliza Doolittle explains: "You see, really and truly, apart from the things anyone can pick up - the dressing and the proper way of speaking, and so on - the difference between a lady and a flower girl is not how she behaves but how she's treated. I shall always be a flower girl to

Professor Higgins because he always treats me as a flower girl and always will. But I know I can be a lady to you because you always treat me as a lady and always will."

Some managers naturally treat their subordinates in a way that leads to superior performance. Encouraging and cajoling, praising where praise is due, and setting them tasks that help them to develop their skills and talent. But most managers are like Professor Higgins. It may be unintentional, but often they treat subordinates as substandard, setting them lower targets than they are capable of achieving which leads naturally to lower performance.

In short, what a manager expects of an employee and the way they treat them largely determines the employee's performance and career progress. Expect great things and you'll get great things. Expect very little and you'll get just that. Of course, that doesn't explain all the successful people whose school report said they would never amount to much. They are the exceptions to the rule and usually turn out to be exceptionally talented in ways not possible to detect in their youth.

The idea that we can become conditioned to react in a certain way isn't a new one. Over a hundred years ago Russian psychologist, Ivan Pavlov, demonstrated this with his famous experiment that he called 'The Ivan Pavlov Canine Conditioning Experiment'. Unfortunately, the publisher of his paper thought this a little too long and cumbersome and persuaded him to change the title to the much shorter and catchier 'Pavlov's Dog' adding to a slightly put out Pavlov, "You'll thank me for it in the long run".

Ivan Pavlov

In his experiment, Pavlov placed food on one side of a room and some hungry dogs on the other. When the dogs got a whiff of the food they began to salivate and Pavlov rang a bell. He repeated this enough times to create an anchor between the bell ringing and the dog's salivating. Finally, he placed no food in the room and just rang the bell. And despite not a crumb of food being present, the dogs would salivate. He'd successfully conditioned them into behaving a certain way. Then they attacked him.

Only kidding.

It is the same with humans. A touch, a voice or even a look can induce a certain state in us. The sound of a firework can bring back terrifying memories for war veterans. An incident in a swimming pool can make some people afraid of water for life. And on a lighter note, whenever an England goalkeeper rushes out to collect a high ball, the nation's football fan's hold their collective breath. We can't help it - it's just that we know what might happen.

So can you use this information to your advantage in business? Well, if you bring to mind a time when you achieved an exceptional performance, you can use it as an anchor to create another exceptional performance. Here's the proof of the Pavlova. I mean, pudding.

Back in the early 60's, when we in Britain were learning to swing, driving Minis around town, and dabbling in hallucinogenics, the Russians were doing experiments on their top athletes with a view to world domination. As far as running, jumping and throwing went, at least.

To prove that simply *visualising* a great performance could lead to one, they divided their athletes into two groups. One was sent off to a special camp where they were trained exceptionally hard for a month. Let's call them the short straw athletes. I say that because the other group were ordered not to train at all. Instead, all they had to do was sit at home and 'visualise' a great performance. A month later, the two groups went head to head in competition and the athletes who had done nothing more than 'visualise' a great performance won hands down. Russia's domination of track and field in the 60's and 70's was thought to be partly the result of using this technique.

Not to be outdone, the Americans decided to test this theory for themselves. Dr. Blaslotto at the University of Chicago set up an experiment with basketball players. He divided them into three groups and recorded their success at shooting baskets when given a number of free shots. Each group were then given different instructions and told to come back in 30 days' time. One group was told not to practice free shots at all; one group was told to practice free shots every day; and the third group was told to practice free shots only in their mind by *visualising* a successful shot.

A month later the groups were tested again and the results compared to their initial performance. Perhaps not surprisingly, the first group who had not practiced at all showed no improvement whatsoever. However, the second group, who had been asked to practice, showed an improvement of over 20% in their successful shots. Again, not surprising, since practice makes perfect, right? So what about the third group who had just been sitting at home, eating pretzels, drinking cola and watching daytime television? Well, remarkably, they too recorded an improved performance level of over 20%. I know what you're thinking; that sounds like my kind of training regime too.

The ability to do great things, to literally change the world, always comes from within. The essential element is invisible to the eye. So it's not enough to just treat others as you wish to be treated or behave as you wish others to behave towards you. You have to behave as you wish to be *perceived.*

The best way to predict the future is to invent it yourself. Don't just wait to see what turns up, decide what you want and then make it happen if you want to be truly happy.

Try this exercise. Write down where you think you will be ten years from now. Detail things like where you will live, the kind of house you live in, the kind of car you will drive, how your family has developed, how much money you will have and, most importantly, how and why you are satisfied doing what you have decided to do. There's a good chance that you will come very close to achieving what you write down. Because the best way to predict the future is to invent it.

According to a 2007 survey by the University of Chicago amongst workers in America, the clergy are the happiest and most satisfied in their jobs. A whopping 87% reported being 'very satisfied'. And they wouldn't lie. Firefighters came second with an 80% satisfaction rate. In fact, all of the top ten most satisfying jobs were professions that involved caring for, teaching or protecting others. Jobs that polled satisfaction rates of 60% or more included education administrators, painters and sculptors, teachers, authors, psychologists, special education teachers, and operating engineers.

Another study released by the Institute for Research on Unlimited Love and conducted by such top universities as Harvard and Chicago, has also found that the happiest people are those who either give to or help others on a regular basis. They all treat others as they would like to be treated themselves and they reap what they sow.

Least happy in the survey were petrol pump attendants. And not just because they're forever out on the forecourts changing the prices. People don't treat them well. They don't feel important. They don't feel what they are doing is especially worthwhile. And their two basic psychological needs are left unfulfilled.

Even though we may spend a lot of time looking up to them, roofers didn't fair too well either. Having a roof fixed can be an expensive business but it's not something that is admired when it's finished. We have a basic psychological need to be loved and a basic psychological need to be important; to feel that what we are doing is worthwhile. If you want to get the best out of someone you need to let them know you truly care about them and appreciate the efforts they go to.

Particularly your children.

Treat others as you wish to be treated yourself and you will be happier and more successful.

That's a lesson the Kings of England could and should have learned. A lesson J. Bruce Ismay should have learned. In the event, he made it off 'The Titanic' whilst so many perished. If he had treated others as he wished to be treated himself he wouldn't have changed the design of the ship and reduced the number of lifeboats to a pitiful number. He wouldn't have put the Chief Officer through the embarrassment of being demoted to First Officer; of Charles Lightoller being demoted to Second Officer and David Blair having to leave the ship.

With the key to the locker in the crow's nest tucked in his pocket.

The Balinese have a view on life and balance they call Tri Hita Karana Sanskrit, meaning 'three causes of welfare and security, through harmonious relationships with God, with fellow human beings and with the environment.'

Tri Hita Karana provides a comprehensive set of universal values and practices designed for the Bali people to live by. They achieve prosperity, peace and happiness through the harmonious interaction of people with their surrounding world. That is, their relation with fellow humans, with the environment and spiritual companions, respectively called pawongan, palemahan and parahyangan.

Each of those worlds contains a specific body of knowledge, beliefs and practices that must be adhered to if one is to achieve harmony and balance between and within these worlds with the Balinese values of mutual aid, equity and solidarity in community life.

Tri Hita Karana teaches the doctrine of deed and retribution called karma pala. Basically, this means that whatever is sown, reaps a corollary harvest.

You reap what you sow.

In their different ways, most ancient religions such as Hinduism, Buddhism, Shintoism, Confucianism and Taoism teach the same respect for nature. They all describe a world where human beings, together with animals, plants and non-living things, participate equally in one organic and universal system.

The Second Golden Rule

Treat others as you would like them to treat you

Always

Because you reap what you sow

Eventually

PART TWO
THE REIGN OF HENRY VIII

Chapter 8 ~ The 4 minute mile and 'The Great Matter'

1509 — 1527

Henry VII died on April 21st 1509. He presumably had had second thoughts about marrying his son's young widow and never did re-marry.

On that same day, Henry VIII was crowned King and Thomas More wrote in a poem that was presented to Henry at his coronation: 'This day is the end of our slavery, the fount of our liberty; the end of sadness and the beginning of joy.'

Sounds like Margaret Thatcher in May 1979. Strictly speaking she quoted from St Francis of Assisi, 'Where there is discord, may we bring harmony' etc but the misplaced expectation is all there. And again like the sort of thing Tony Blair said in May 1997. David Cameron said 'I want to try and build a more responsible society. Those who can should and those who can't we will always help' in May 2010.

Misplaced expectation.

And who held the important title of 'Squire Of The Body' and walked along in the King's funeral procession, clad in his newly issued black livery?

None other than Thomas Boleyn. Already scheming to achieve higher status through his own political efforts or by using his children. His youngest daughter, Anne, was 8 at the time.

When she was 12 years old in 1513, Anne Boleyn left England to be a maid of honour in Brussels. Not quite France but near enough. And the purpose of her leaving these shores was to 'be finished'.

It's called a Gap Year now.

She was to live abroad for nine years. Quite a bit of finishing needed obviously. Thomas Boleyn's decision to send his daughter to Belgium and work for Margaret of Austria was presumably prompted by the opportunities created by working abroad; learning a language or two and a bit of music and dance. It would do wonders for her prospects on her return.

It is easy to underestimate the importance of entertainment in those days. The work ethic is all well and good but once leisure is plentiful, managing it becomes a serious business. Ask anyone who's a member of a golf club that is owned by the members. Or on the committee of the local Working Men's Club. We all have a need to be important and if we don't get that through work we turn our attention to seeking a position in a voluntary capacity. Beware the motives of people who do.

Everyone has a need to be important; to feel that what they are doing is worthwhile. So tell people what they are good at. If you employ people, treat everyone you employ as a volunteer. It's a lesson we should all learn.

We will obviously hear more of the Boleyns later in the book.

Back to 1509 and Henry VIII's coronation.

With The Wars of The Roses a distant memory and Katherine now used to English breakfasts, the 17 year old Henry VIII became King in the Spring of 1509. And, with his father having not taken up his 'option' he is able to marry the 23 year old Spanish girl on June 11th 1509 - known to her Ladies in Waiting as Katherine of Arrogant.

Yikes.

Surprisingly, the marriage between Henry VIII and Katherine seems to have started as a happy one. In the first few years of marriage he commissioned the 'Mary Rose' - the flagship of the Navy - and focused on warring with France. By now that's a basic expectation for a King of England.

He busied himself being King and being busy means you spend less time doing things that don't need doing. When we come to The Fourth Golden Rule we will look at the downside of doing things that are neither important nor urgent. It's widely thought that it was Chaucer in the 12th century who called idle hands the devil's tools and maybe that's a lesson that Henry should have learned. As any good parent knows if you keep your kids busy doing worthwhile things they don't have time to get up to mischief.

In September 2008 twenty five people were killed when a Metrolink commuter train crashed head-on into a Union Pacific freight train in Los Angeles, California. It is thought that the Metrolink train ran through a red signal while the conductor was busy text messaging.

He was texting for goodness' sake.

Wrongful death lawsuits are expected to cause $500 million in losses for Metrolink.

It's called work for a reason. Whatever you are doing you should do your absolute best. You should concentrate. Particularly if people's lives are on the line. The subject of The Second Golden Rule.

Anyway, Henry and Katherine had their ups and downs like all couples do, but generally things went pretty much according to plan for the first 10 years or so. Until, that was, Henry had his mid-life crisis which in those days kicked in before you got to your thirties. The rejection of Katherine appears to have begun shortly after the seven year itch, a movie made famous over 400 years later by Marilyn Monroe standing over a grid with a white dress on. They had had a son, born on New Year's Day 1511 named Henry and Christened on January 5th but he died less than eight weeks old. It was to prove to be a turning point in British history. Of course, they did have a daughter, Mary, in 1516. But male ego gets in the way and he wants a son.

Three years after Mary was born, Henry VIII's affair with his teenage mistress, Elizabeth Blount, had led to the birth of his illegitimate son, Henry Fitzroy. Young Henry was born at the Priory of St Lawrence at Blackmore, Essex, in June 1519. And Henry was ecstatic. He was not only full of paternal pride as Henry Fitzroy had more than a passing resemblance to himself; he was also looking at evidence that not only was he capable of producing a fine, healthy heir, but that his Spanish Queen could not.

Basically it wasn't his fault. There was something wrong with her or the marriage.

And perhaps this was the real turning point. The point at which Henry VIII believed he could father a healthy boy but not by Katherine. A lesson that a certain sub four minute miler could and should have learned back in 1954.

Roger Bannister

When you ask people to name the first man to run a mile in less than four minutes even people born well after 1954 can tell you it was Roger Bannister. On May 6th 1954 at the Iffley Road track in Oxford the 25 year old British medical student became the first man to run a mile in less than four minutes. 3 mins 59.4 seconds to be precise. And, of course, beat someone else's world record.

But ask people to name the man who was the world record holder up to that point or, indeed, to name the next man to run the mile in under four minutes - and beat Bannister's time - most people struggle.

On the 12th December 1953, in Melbourne, Australian John Landy had set a new Australian Mile Record of 4-02.0, equaling Roger Bannister's Empire Record, set earlier in the year. After the race, he predicted he would never run a four-minute mile. "If I do so before I retire from serious competition, it will be only luck" said Landy. Since July 1945 the world record for the mile had been held by Sweden's Gunder Hagg, who was affectionately known as 'Gunder the Wonder'. He had set the new world mile mark of four minutes, 1.4 seconds.

Gunder's record had stood for a full nine years and yet just 46 days after Bannister achieved the feat, on June 21st 1954 in Turku, Finland, Landy achieved a time of 3:57.9 (ratified as 3:58.0). Landy had improved by more than three seconds in one race and taken the world record off Bannister. The second man to do so.

Landy held the world record for over three years until, on 19th July 1957, Yorkshireman Derek Ibbotson posted a time of 3:57.2.

Landy had not believed it was possible. It was only when desire and real belief came together that there was then a conviction.

Bannister simply believed he could do it and put a comprehensive plan together to achieve it. The previous World Record Holder had held the record for nine years; the holder *after* Bannister held the record for three years. Bannister was World Record Holder for less than two months.

But he's the one who got Knighted. He's the one we remember.

The lesson that John Landy should have learned from Henry VIII is that you don't always need hard evidence that something can be done before you plan to do it. It just seems that way.

Henry VIII had been unhappy with Katherine - his bride of some ten years - and needless to say she's unhappy with him as Henry made his illegitimate son Earl of Nottingham, Duke of Richmond and Somerset. He went on to also give his son several other important posts including Lord High Admiral of England, when Richmond was only six years old. He later became a Knight of the Garter.

The Queen firmly put her foot down when Henry wanted to appoint Richmond King of Ireland. Henry appointed his son Lord Lieutenant of Ireland instead.

After the birth of his son, Henry had a number of affairs whilst his marriage was on a one way ticket to nowhere. And he turned his attentions to Anne Boleyn after discarding her sister, Mary Carey, having previously added the girls' mother to his list of sexual conquests.

What was Mary Boleyn thinking when she got married to Bill Carey on February 4th 1520? Mary Carey. It's a bit like Oprah Winfrey marring Deepak Chopra and becoming Oprah Chopra. Or Sven Erickson's old flame meting up with and getting hitched to rugby legend Lawrence Dallaglio and becoming Nancy Dell 'Olio-Dallaglio.

The chronology and pattern of royal grants to William and Mary Carey suggest that Mary's affair with the King started shortly after she married. And there were very significant grants to William Carey in 1524 and 1526 when Mary had children. He seems to have been rewarded particularly well for his compliant role as nominal father to the King's bastards. By all accounts Henry VIII would not have countenanced sharing the sexual favours of any of his mistresses, even if they did have a husband; he required chastity from his sexual partners.

But she had served a purpose and her younger sister Anne was the next young woman now in focus.

Henry VIII had fallen well and truly in love.

Anne Boleyn

One of the impressive pieces of evidence we have about how Henry VIII felt about Anne is the 17 letters he wrote around 1528. Ten of them in French and seven in English which is impressive in itself.

And we repeat a lesson from when Henry IV put it in writing that he was going to have Richard II bumped off. Never write down the words, 'I love you.' You can always deny you said it. You cannot retract what you write.

Henry's conviction that he could have a divorce from Katherine in order to marry Anne Boleyn, comes from his view that in the Bible (Leviticus 20: 21) it clearly states 'If a man shall take his brother's wife, it is an unclean thing....he shall be without children'. Much is made of this but the piece was obviously in the Bible when he married Katherine all those years ago and they got a dispensation from the Pope as they argued her marriage to Henry's brother wasn't consummated.

As my mother used to say, 'you can't have your cake and eat it too'.

Lesson? If the lawyers get involved, check the small print. If Henry's right then Pope Clement VII has to accept there has been a Papal mistake, they've exceeded their own powers and he'll have to eat his words. And we don't like doing that.

The key thing here is that Henry really and truly believed in his side and the Pope thinks like my Mum; you can't have your cake and eat it. Once that happens there are going to be tears.

As in businesses, factions are part of the scenery. It is easy to dismiss factions as back-biting, bitching and seeking self advantage but it is to miss the point. And often, the prize. Factions are the form politics and businesses take when its focus is the will of one man. In this case, Henry. Look at the stories of Hitler, the Byzantium, Roman and British empires and Stalinist Moscow. More latterly Idi Amin, Saddam Hussain and Robert Mugabee. I could go on. If direct opposition to the omnipotent one is impossible rebels become conspirators.

Anne Boleyn had gone the direct route and gained the King's favour. And that means losers and that, in turn, means conspirators. And if there are factions, people are not focused on the common goal.

So here's the next lesson.

If you run a business or manage a team, keep people focused on the common goal.

Companies are at their most successful when people are focussed on the common goal. Factions make people face inwards and eventually everyone can lose. The expression 'live by the sword, die by the sword' should in Anne's case be reworded 'Gain power by seeking favour with one man and beware the ramifications when you fall out of favour.' Anne Boleyn's subsequent fall was a consequence of her allies eventually recalculating in the most calculating way when she produced no son and Henry's head was turned by Jane Seymour.

For now though, in 1525, there's a Battle Royal developing between Anne Boleyn, her naturally conspiratorial father and the King's loyal servant and confidant for many years, Cardinal Wolsey. Meanwhile the Spanish King, Charles I is winning a war with Francis I of France.

Cardinal Wolsey

Cardinal Wolsey, in turn, is entering a battle between himself and the Pope as he has been charged by Henry with the responsibility of getting the King a divorce from Katherine. Or at least an annulment. The Papacy was a job that Wolsey had coveted for years. And Katherine is unhappy that Wolsey is constantly between her and her husband. Frankly, she's hopping mad and spitting feathers with the Cardinal.

And Anne's unhappy with the Cardinal too. And Anne's dad. And the Pope. And, pretty soon, Henry himself. You couldn't make this up could you? The Cardinal is between a rock and a number of hard places. For once his reach seems to have exceeded his grasp.

To complicate things further, Henry VIII has two sisters who are not raving fans of Wolsey either.

Henry's sister, Margaret Tudor, was two years older than the King and had married King James IV of Scotland twenty years before. But James had died in a battle against the English ten years into their marriage (Margaret will eventually become grandmother of Mary, Queen of Scots which becomes relevant in part five of the book if you're still with me). Less than a year after her husband died, in 1514, Margaret married Archibald Douglas. Despite being Earl of Angus, he was an England supporter so she was removed from the regency and exiled to England. But, as is often the case when people see greener grass on the other side of the fence, Margaret rather quickly changed allegiances and supported the pro-French regent, John Stewart, the duke of Albany. She won an annulment from Douglas, and then married Henry Stewart.

Basically she's got an agenda for her son, James.

Henry's other sister, Mary Tudor, had been born some five years after Henry. She had been betrothed to Katherine of Aragon's nephew, Charles (by now the Holy Roman Emperor) but, surprise, surprise, there'd been a fall out and some misunderstandings between Spain, the Holy Roman Empire and France and so Henry cancelled the betrothal.

There was some good news and some bad news for Mary. She probably had no desire to marry a French boy four years younger than her but the bad news was that Henry's choice for a replacement was 34 years older than Mary - King Louis XII of France, described as 'feeble and pocky'.

By all accounts Mary was a bit of a looker and in love with Henry's friend, Charles Brandon, the Duke of Suffolk. So, weeping, sulking and with a long face, the 18 year old went off to France in 1514 and married the 52 year old King of France, with the Boleyn sisters Anne and Mary behind her wiping her tears for her. Whatever Mary did with him and for him, she did a grand job and Louis XII died on New Year's Day 1515, after just three months of marriage.

Good news or bad news? Well, she's lost the husband she didn't want to marry but her future is now uncertain.

Everybody gets bad news and it makes us all feel sad and depressed. But then, after a while, a funny thing happens. We don't feel quite so bad. Did you read about the guy who mistakenly threw away a £100,000 winning scratch card? Naturally, he was gutted at the time. But now he's probably having a right good laugh about it.

Or maybe not.

However, for most of us - and certainly for Mary - bad news often turns out to be nothing like as devastating as we first feared. Why is that? Well, a study by Daniel Gilbert at Harvard University has come up with a theory. To test it, he set up a series of classic social psychology studies that most people would be familiar with: going for a job interview and getting rejected. Of course, as with all these experiments, things weren't quite what they seemed. Firstly, all the interviewees were led to believe there was an actual job on offer. Then they were asked to complete a questionnaire which included a section about how they would feel if they didn't get it. To quantify their disappointment they were asked to predict the change in their mood on a scale of 1 to 10 where 10 was happy at getting the job. All agreed that their mood would worsen by two points to eight if they were rejected. One woman, who'd arrived in a bit of a mood anyway, said it could drop to four, rise to eight, drop to four again, and then she'd probably thump someone.

Naturally, nobody was offered the job. What Gilbert was interested in was their reaction to the bad news, and in particular, how this differed from their prediction. But there was another little twist in the tail. Half the group was interviewed by just one person, and half by a panel of three. This made it easier for those rejected by one person to rationalise the decision as just one person's preferences. But for those who were rejected by three people it was naturally more difficult to dismiss, since this was seemingly a considered judgment by a panel.

The results showed that, immediately after the rejection, those interviewed by just one person could rationalise the decision and their good mood only fell by 0.4 of a point, whereas the ones rejected by the panel of three saw their mood drop further, to 1.25, but still not as low as they had predicted. On being told that it was all an experiment and there was never any job on offer the woman who'd threatened to thump someone overturned the desk, set fire to the curtains and stormed out.

So why is it that we don't feel quite so bad as we thought we would? Well, we all have an inbuilt psychological immune system that recalibrates our perception of the world and our feelings. So whenever life kicks us in the unmentionables, the psychological immune system gets to work rationalising what's happened and, over time, stopping it hurting as much as we feared. Of course, that's still no excuse to start a conga at your granny's funeral, but at least now you know why it wasn't so bad after all.

Not only did Mary soon get over the bad news of losing her husband, she married Charles Brandon before her brother could marry her off to a Spanish prince. Henry was not best pleased but Mary and Charles named their first child, born in 1515, Henry.

Good move, Charlie.

Mary was a good friend of her sister-in-law Katherine of Aragon, and was a supporter of hers in 'The Great Matter' of the divorce and rejected Anne Boleyn. So Wolsey had Charles and Mary to contend with too.

It's like working for a family business but not being part of the family as far as Wolsey's concerned.

At least Cardinal Wolsey's made himself rich, famous and important whilst he's been doing the King's bidding. Rumour is he's been embezzling and funding his colleges at Oxford University where he took his degree at the age of fifteen. He probably has as many illegitimate children as Henry VIII himself; he's got himself the positions of Archbishop and Lord Chancellor and has his own abbey in St. Albans.

However, to make things more complicated for Wolsey, in May 1527, the Hapsburg troops have ransacked Rome and imprisoned Pope Clement VII. He'd chosen the wrong horse to back and sided with France in the League of Cognac.

This is not, as you might suspect, a competition involving brandy drinking.

It's time to recap who's who and what's what in the summer of 1527.

The King of Spain is Charles I. He is also Holy Roman Emperor, Charles V. He is Belgian born but of Spanish descent. His maternal grandparents are the parents of Katherine of Aragon who, in 1527, is still Henry VIII's wife.

The King of England is Henry VIII. He has shifted his support from Spain to France yet wants to divorce his Spanish, Catholic wife of 18 years in order to marry Anne Boleyn.

Cardinal Wolsey - the King of England's loyal number two - is trying to restore peace in Europe and also endeavouring to get Pope Clement VII to agree to Henry divorcing Katherine of Aragon whilst the Pope is entirely under the thumb of his captor, Charles V, who is Katherine's nephew.

In the three year period from 1527 to Wolsey's eventual demise in 1530 the political shenanigans puts what happens in most companies in the present day well in the shade.

The French have a lovely expression; Plus ça change, plus c'est la même chose, which loosely translates as 'The more things change, the more they remain the same'. Of course, they have ones even lovelier than that but just not as appropriate to this part of the book. But all things do change.

And that's a useful lesson for us.

However good or bad a situation is, it will change. And so will our perception of it.

Wolsey had been all powerful during the early part of Henry's reign. He had been his right hand man and facilitator; his political manoeuvres were legendary. He had seen mistresses come and go. Indeed, he had fixed for various attractive young women to be brought to the King's bed chambers and organised for the various illegitimate offspring of Henry to be born quietly and their mothers cared for.

But he's made enemies as he plotted and schemed to his own advantage.

Wolsey had assumed that Anne would become nothing more than the King's mistress and if the King were to marry again it would be to a French queen.

Wolsey hasn't treated Anne as he would wish to be treated himself and he's about to pay the price.

Chapter 9 ~ The Pot Bull, Aunty Dot and Lady Wallop

1527 — 1536

So why did the Pope refuse to give Henry his divorce? Why was Wolsey unsuccessful?

Well, it's not just that the Pope's in the pocket of the wife of Henry's nephew. The two sides have reached a stand off. Edward Fox, Doctor of Divinity, and Stephen Gardiner, Doctor of both Civil and Canon Law, had unsuccessfully gone to Rome on the instructions of both Henry and Wolsey to convince the Pope to grant Cardinal Wolsey the power to rule on the King's case. And the Pope knew what that ruling would be.

In April 1528, Pope Clement agreed to send to England the Italian Cardinal Lorenzo Campeggio, to 'try' the case with Cardinal Wolsey, but did not agree to give either Cardinal the power to pronounce sentence. Cardinal Campeggio arrived in England at the end of September 1528 and the 'proceedings', such as they were, began the following month. Cardinal Campeggio had come with the rather unhelpful suggestion that Henry reconcile with the Queen - which went down like the proverbial lead balloon.

Complicating the situation somewhat, Anne Boleyn and her ever helpful father suggested to King Henry that Cardinal Wolsey was not really doing his absolute best to obtain the annulment. And there's a pot bull involved too.

The Italian Cardinal had brought with him the ornamental bull that authorised him to adjudicate on the case. So the King kept nagging Cardinal Wolsey to get the bull from Cardinal Campeggio, without success.

In early 1529 the Pope became conveniently ill so the court didn't convene until May of that year. During the interval, Cardinal Wolsey had been doing what he could to get the bull from Cardinal Campeggio. In June, the Italian cardinal told Cardinal Wolsey that the Pope had prohibited the use of the bull, adding confusingly "And no bull."

In July, Pope Clement (who was being leaned on by Emperor Charles V if you remember), rescinded the commission to Cardinals Campeggio and Wolsey and the court was formally closed.

We don't know what happened to the bull. It may have ended up in a china shop.

Anne blamed Wolsey for the failure of the process and whilst Wolsey is focusing on getting that damned bull, Thomas Boleyn and his brother-in-law, Lord Norfolk, are plotting against him. He has made plenty of enemies on his way up the political ladder and when people see him falling from grace and popularity they jump on the bandwagon. He has fewer and fewer friends. So that doesn't help.

The same is true today in business. If you make enemies on your way up the greasy pole, they will wait to get you when you are on your way down and accelerate your decline.

Despite the finely worded efforts of Wolsey and his lawyers and all their scheming, the fact is his enemies were plotting against him. A deliberate leak of information on Wolsey's dealings with Rome, the Emperor and Francis I was made to Anne - or her father - and the distance between the rock and the hard places was getting smaller. When Cardinal Wolsey failed to obtain the divorce from Rome, he was replaced with Sir Thomas More.

In October 1529, Wolsey was deprived of the Chancellorship and required to return the great seal. His number is up and he knows it. He's been nice to everyone he wants something from. And here's the next lesson.

People who are nice to you usually do so because they want something.

Trying to avoid the inevitable, the Cardinal gave the King most of his properties and begged him for mercy. In February 1530 King Henry formally pardoned Cardinal Wolsey and confirmed him as Archbishop of York. Anne was not at all happy. Wolsey left London for York two months later to lick his wounds. He couldn't reach all of them and had to get a servant to do the tricky ones. However, whilst in Yorkshire he was charged with treason on November 4th 1530. Wolsey pleaded guilty to absolutely anything and everything that the King could think of charging him with and threw himself at his mercy. He died aged 59, at St. Mary's Abbey, Leicester three weeks later on his journey south. Well, if you were charged with treason you'd take your time getting down from Yorkshire to London wouldn't you?

But it's Henry versus Pope Clement VII that is still the big fight. If Henry hadn't gone at it like a bull in a china shop the story might have ended differently. Maybe that was the message about the bull?

Henry strongly believes that the Pope at the time of his marriage to Katherine, Julius II, had exceeded his powers in going against the statement in the Bible.

But there again who wrote that?

Who is to say that if a man marries his brother's wife he shall be without children? Is there any evidence to support this? Well, obviously not but it's in print in the Bible so it must be true.

For his part, the Pope doesn't want to be seen to be backing off. His cohorts are saying that Henry has no right to force the Pope not only to see things his way but also to accept his own interpretation of Canon law. And what we really have here is an old fashioned ego-driven power struggle. It's a case of 'mine's bigger than yours'.

In many respects the First World War was also an ego driven power struggle of 'mine's bigger than yours' between two cousins. With Charles V on the Pope's side it's become a 'mine's bigger than yours contest'.

Plus ça change, plus c'est la même chose.

Maybe if they had got together over a cup of tea it might have all turned out very differently.

Unfortunately, the importing of tea into Britain didn't begin until the 1660s with the marriage of King Charles II to the Portuguese Princess Catherine of Braganza (will they ever find a nice English girl like Kate Middleton?). Catherine is thought to have brought tea with her. Certainly Samuel Pepys has him describing drinking 'a china drink of which I had never drunk before'.

Instead of posturing through their cohorts, countless lives over the next 500 years might have been saved. Indeed even the complexion, names and fan base of Britain's biggest football teams might have been very different.

Maybe I would have married Susan Garlick.

Back to the plot.

It would be easy to explain Henry's behaviour by saying that he is in love. Passionately in love. He's approaching 40 in 1531 and

Anne's in her 20s. His wife isn't interesting any more. He wants a son. And he's willing to do anything. And, because he's King, he does.

He elevates Anne's father to the rather odd but much coveted title of 'Earl of Ormonde' and that makes Anne's brother Viscount Rochford. And shortly after that, with Anne regularly by his side at banquets, Thomas Boleyn replaces the Bishop of Durham as Lord Privy Seal, the fifth ranking officer of state.

The drive to marry Anne has become not only a power struggle between him and the Pope but a campaign to vindicate his Kingship.

He should have learned the lesson that Crosby, Stills, Nash and Young would sing of many years later; 'If you can't be with the one you love honey, love the one you're with' - as many 40 odd year old men who have found women in their 20's very attractive but when the thrill of the chase and the excitement of a night in the Premier Inn has gone they have to crawl back with their tail between their legs and face chagrin.

Anne is beginning to enjoy herself and abuse the position she's found herself in at court. She's what my mum used to call 'a right little Madam'. And she's set herself up for a fall. Lesson? If you've got it, don't flaunt it. Don't rub people's noses in it. The law of causality will come to find you out; for every action there is an equal and opposite reaction.

She didn't live her life by The Second Golden Rule.

As the whole issue of the possible divorce dragged on, Henry VIII's mind appears more and more to be focusing on whether a Pope can tell a King what he can and cannot do. If both are appointed by God (a moot point in itself) then who is to give in when they disagree? Frustration all round.

And the argument is focused on whether Katherine had consummated her marriage with Arthur (thereby making Mary a bastard). But the dispensation given by the Pope to Katherine and Henry at the time was one to cover against all possible eventualities and therefore also against the possibility that Katherine had indeed consummated her first marriage. Henry VIII, of course, denied the Pope's right to grant such a dispensation in the first place - the central issue of the whole affair and not so much the Queen's virginity.

People look for evidence to support an opinion they have already got.

And they can usually find it.

But very often it's just not right. When Louann Brizendine, founder and director of the University of California, San Francisco's Women's Mood and Hormone Clinic, published 'The Female Brain' she claimed that women speak an average of 20,000 words per day, nearly three times more than the 7,000 spoken by men.

A fact still quoted by people who assume that it's right. But James Pennebaker, chairman of the psychology department at the University of Texas had been collecting data on the topic for a decade before Brizendine got her 15 minutes of fame. And he was able to prove that the sexes are about equal when it comes to a war of words. But then he hasn't met my mother-in-law.

Instead, he had people wearing a device he called EAR (Electronically Activated Recorder). It's a digital recorder that subjects can store in their purses or pockets in a sheath similar to a case for glasses. The EAR samples 30 seconds of ambient noise (including conversations) every 12.5 minutes.

Researchers used this device to collect data on the talking patterns of 400 people in Texas, Arizona and Mexico. And the average number of words spoken by men and women were similar at about 16,000 words a day. He did find that women tend to chat more about other people whereas men chat about cars and beer. But as far as the myth of women being more chatty than men it is, quite simply, not true.

Many people who have been very near to death and then revived, report the sensation of walking towards a bright light and see it as a religious vision and confirmation of an afterlife.

Books have been written on the subject and people who want to believe in the after life see it as confirmation that there is something out there for us all when we draw our last breath.

I may decide to paint mine, because I'm lousy at drawing.

Of course, there may well be something beyond death. But the brainwaves of dying patients always show a surge of electrical activity in the moments before their lives end. According to Lakhmir Chawla, an intensive care doctor at George Washington University medical centre, the near-death experiences are caused by a surge of electrical energy released as the brain runs out of oxygen.

As blood flow slows down and oxygen levels fall, the brain cells fire one last electrical impulse. It starts in one part of the brain and spreads in a cascade. It is *this* that gives people the impression of being bathed in bright light and a sense of peace as they start to walk into a light-filled tunnel and the vision of Jesus or Muhammad or Krishna. Sam Parnia at Southampton University's school of medicine has interviewed hundreds of people who have had cardiac arrests and been brought back to life. Most of them don't have the bright light experience. So if it is a sign of the after life why do only a minority experience it?

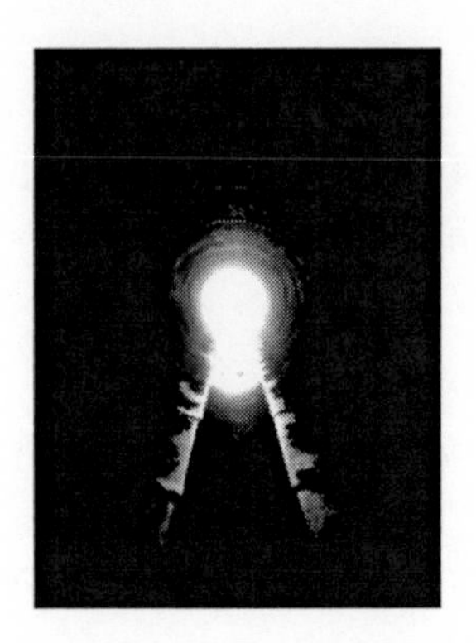

But people who want to believe that when you die you will see a shaft of light and 'the other side' don't want to know about the work of people like Chawla and Parnia.

Incidentally, those people who have had a near-death experience become happier, more altruistic, less afraid of death and less materialistic according to a Dutch study published in 2001 in The Lancet. So before we return to 1531 here's the next lesson; don't assume what someone is saying is true. Say 'What evidence do you have to support that?'

Henry VIII is doing exactly what most people do - he's searching for evidence to support his view; he's looking for books that say a King is omnipotent. And he finds those books, starts reading them and gets from them what he wants. Like a drunk clinging onto a lamp post, he's using the findings for support rather than illumination.

Eventually Henry used Parliamentary legislation to end the dependence of the English clergy on Rome. In a Parliamentary act granting pardon to the clergy found guilty of the violation of the Stature of Praemunire, Henry VIII was recognised as 'protector and only supreme head of the church and clergy in England' in 1531. In addition, Parliament passed a law prohibiting appeals to the Pope in matters of marriage.

Henry took Anne off to Dover in October 1532 together with an entourage of twenty plus ladies including her Aunty Dot and Lady Wallop. They all boarded the ship 'The Swallow' and ten years after she'd left it, she found herself back in Calais. "It's not pretty but at least we can get some cheap booze" she was overheard to say. However, Calais, at this time, is still part of England, so there was a bit of explaining to do going through Customs & Excise on her return.

It seems likely that this is the point at which Henry at last sleeps with Anne. There was definitely a lot of movement in their cabin but that could have been the rough sea crossing. For ten days Anne acted the role of Queen and for his part, Henry is living like, well, a King. They had a wedding ceremony of sorts in January 1533 and, bingo, she's pregnant.

William Warham, the Archbishop of Canterbury had died in August 1532. Henry needed the holder of that office to annul his marriage (rather than be seen to be doing it himself) so rather conveniently appointed Thomas Cranmer; his own man. By March 1533 Cranmer was consecrated and instituted at Canterbury, with the assistance of confirmatory Papal bulls. (Not the pot kind; this is more of a formal proclamation issued by the Pope and sealed with a leaden 'bulla'.) And Cranmer proceeded to do what was expected of him. As Archbishop of Canterbury he declared the King's marriage to Katherine of Aragon void from the beginning, and pronounced the marriage to Anne Boleyn valid. On June 1st 1533 she was crowned Queen. Needless to say Pope Clement VII excommunicated Henry.

It's called a rigged deck nowadays.

It's also called burning your bridges.

And the repercussions would last for hundreds of years.

So, all's well apart from the fact that there are three people in the marriage. Henry, Anne and Katherine. And as Diana, Princess of Wales, was to also find out over four hundred years later, when there are three people in a marriage it's not easy...

Following the breach with Rome, Henry VIII, Thomases Cranmer and Cromwell undertook a reorganisation of the church and state.

Thomas Cromwell

Cromwell was an interesting guy. For some fourteen years he was a solicitor for Wolsey but saved himself from the car crash that was Wolsey's demise by changing horses so fast you couldn't see his feet move. In November 1534 the Act of Supremacy acknowledged that the King 'justly and rightly is and ought to be the Supreme Head of the Church in England'. Henry formally assumed the new title in early 1535.

It was to prove to be a particularly bloody summer. During June and July, John Fisher, who was Bishop of Rochester and Sir Thomas More, the King's former Chancellor, were convicted of high treason against the King and sentenced to be drawn, hanged, disemboweled, their bowels burnt before them and then, just in case they were still wriggling, beheaded and quartered. And, to make double sure, the various body parts to be strewn 'in such places as the King should assign'. The treason was denying that the King was Supreme Head of the Church in England.

It created what is now known as a 'PR issue' for Henry. In the next five years Parliament passed a series of laws aimed at dissolution of the monasteries and reformation of the Church of England in the direction of Protestantism. But for what? Anne had produced her daughter in September 1533.

If the baby girl, christened Elizabeth and destined to be Queen, had been a boy the face of English history would have been different.

On such things does history turn.

In 1534 the Act of Supremacy had set them up for a happy life and in 1535 the Archbishop of Canterbury agreed that Henry and Katherine are divorced.

26 years after they were married.

But by 1536 Anne Boleyn has been executed on charges of adultery. Yes, that's right. Henry spends the thick end of six years or more fighting with Rome as to whether or not he can get divorced, but by May 1536 Anne - and Katherine - are both dead and buried.

What went wrong? To spend so much effort to get your own way and then cast aside the very thing you fought so hard for?

In the summer of 1535, whilst the beheadings were going on – or rather, coming off - Henry spent most of it on a progress to the Severn and then across to Hampshire in September. The sport was good - in particular the 'hawking'. Anne accompanied him throughout the trip and by the time they returned to Windsor in October she was pregnant again.

They had called at Wolf Hall in Wiltshire on the way home and had stayed as guests of Sir John Seymour and Margery

Wentworth. The eldest of their eight children, Jane Seymour, was lady-in-waiting to Anne Boleyn, having previously been in the service of Mary Tudor, Henry's sister, and also Katherine of Aragon. And she's about to play a part.

At the end of 1535 with Henry having fallen out with Rome, the French refusing to co-operate and acknowledge Anne as Queen, no son and heir and a lot of unhappy English Catholics, it's no longer the Cardinal who is between a rock and a number of hard places. It's Henry and it's his reach that seems to have exceeded his grasp.

On January 7th 1536 Katherine of Aragon died at Kimbolton Castle after a short illness. As far as Anne Boleyn and her family are concerned all it needs now is for Mary to go the same way as her mother and all their worries are over. She and Henry have a 16 month old daughter and she is pregnant with what will hopefully be a healthy son and heir. They celebrate the news of Katherine's death the following Sunday by wearing bright yellow from tip to toe. They must have looked like a couple of bananas.

Pride cometh…

Anne miscarried a boy on January 29th and there were 'signs of deformity and abnormality' according to a report by the Spanish Imperial Ambassador to England, Chapuys. There is little or no real evidence to support this so, as I promised in the introduction, I'm not going to make it up. What you don't need to make up is that, just like everyone else at court, Chapuys has his favourites, his agenda and, of course, his self interest and self preservation in mind. He was one of Katherine's and Princess Mary's closest allies and despised Anne. And Anne, being Anne Boleyn, returned the feeling.

Chapuys had confidently predicted Anne's fall for several years. He can see the King's shift from Anne to Jane and it suits the

King for there to be a deformity. Henry began to believe that Anne would never give him the healthy son he craved.

We don't really know to what extent Anne fell out of favour because she couldn't produce a son or because Henry fell in love with Jane but the expression 'whirlwind romance' is probably apt.

Anne has made plenty of enemies. Even her father is about to distance himself from her. And she is now beginning to learn the knock on effect of ignoring The Second Golden Rule:

You reap what you sow.

By April 1536 Cromwell discreetly suggests to Jane's brother, Edward, that he and his wife move to Cromwell's rooms which are connected through a secret passage to the King's apartments which will allow Henry private - and secret - access to Jane whenever she happens to be visiting her brother.

Which she then did on a regular basis.

Cromwell knows which side his bread is buttered on.

But here's the next lesson. If you are in a secret relationship, you probably shouldn't be in it.

When it comes to going after what you love in life, you shouldn't take no for an answer too easily. But sometimes it's best for everyone that you do.

It's 1536. Jane Seymour has gained the King's affections and just three years after she married the King, Anne Boleyn's days are numbered.

Chapter 10 ~ The Musician, the Brother and the Bottom Wiper

April 1536 — July 1536

Born in 1508 and therefore 28 to Henry's 45 in 1536, Jane Seymour could only just about read and write her own name. Not what you would call a Scholar. She worked for Queen Katherine and when Anne Boleyn became Queen she served Boleyn. The first report of Henry VIII's interest in Jane Seymour was in February 1536. She was pale and blonde, the opposite of Anne Boleyn's dark hair and olive skin.

And so the factions begin all over again. As in businesses once factions begin, the main protagonists want people to take sides. And people close *do* take sides and seek favour so that if they've backed the right horse they will be ultimately be rewarded.

Anne has seen Henry get rid of one wife and unless she produces a male heir she knows he can do it again. "Am I not a man as other men are?" Henry allegedly says. His ego is getting in the way again and he can't face the fact that he might be the one to blame for the lack of a son. Henry is looking for a reason to rid himself of Anne and, if you look hard enough for it and have enough acolytes, you can soon put together a case.

And that's what Cromwell does. Anne's brother's wife is willing to testify that her husband and Anne have been inappropriately intimate and once the people at court realise that the King has decided that Anne is to go they start shifting horses too. Anne is on her way out with no way back. She's arrested on the grounds of adultery with her brother and others. And, of course, the King needs the most senior people in the church to find a way to annul his marriage.

Just as Jeffrey Skilling needed Arthur Andersen to give credence and credibility to Enron's scandalous activities. As the service provider (Arthur Andersen) you take the King's Shilling if you do as he bids. Bonuses all round. And if you resist and go with your conscience you are left in the waste lands. Over the years it happens.

Again and again.

Arguably the surest sign that a major corporation is headed for trouble is when management experts and professors of business at universities start touting that corporation as a model for every other company to follow.

As they did with Enron.

When Enron spectacularly collapsed in December 2001 it was then the biggest bankruptcy in corporate history. It ripped open the catastrophic fault line of unchecked economic avarice, incompetence, selfishness, lies and greed that ultimately led to Bear Stearns, Lehman Brothers, HBOS, Icelandic banks and various other meltdowns. It had taken just 16 years to grow to assets of $70 billion and 24 days to go bankrupt. A company praised by many pundits as a new business model that met and exceeded its targets and was used in universities as a model for others to emulate was, with the benefit of hindsight, a house of cards built over a pool of petrol with a lighted match nearby.

And it's not just avarice that causes a fall.

It was 1973 when Paul Simon sang 'Mama don't take my Kodachrome away'. Thirty six years later Kodak finally did it. The Eastman Kodak Company took Kodachrome off the market after a run of 74 years. It was, of course, yet another victim of the digital revolution. It might have captured some of the most famous wildlife imagery; indeed, Abraham Zapruder's 8mm reel of President John Kennedy's 1963 assassination was shot on Kodachrome. To be fair, it's difficult to think of anything else that was invented in 1935 that is still being used today. But it went the same way as Betamax, Video tape, vinyl records, Royal Doulton and Woolworths.

Of the biggest one hundred companies in the world when the Titanic set sail in 1912 less than 20% are still in the top one hundred companies in the world today.

When the Titanic set sail there were more than 500 steel works in Britain. Now there are more people work in Indian restaurants in Britain than work in the steel industry.

It's a big lesson for anyone in business. You have to keep up with change.

Toyota was always renowned for its reliability but in 2010 recalled over two million vehicles amid reports that some models were suddenly accelerating - a pretty nasty idea if you're reversing down a tight driveway. At the same time the Japanese authorities wanted Toyota to investigate the brake system in the Prius Hybrid.

Of course Toyota's reputation hadn't fallen as far as that of Enron which was once hailed as 'America's most innovative company' almost up to the point it was exposed as a glorified Ponzi scheme. Enron made its reputation through complex financial transactions that turned out to be a disguise for massive fraud. As is often the case with companies that fail it is their own corporate philosophies which contain the seeds of their destruction. The more anybody goes for swift global expansion the more difficult quality control becomes.

In my home town of Harrogate, Bettys is held up as an icon of how a business should be run. It consistently wins awards for its products, its service and also for being a great employer. It's no coincidence that Bettys will only open up where it can deliver fresh product from its own bakery each day. Similarly Booths supermarkets in the North West has continued to do very well against the major supermarkets because it has grown steadily, prudently and not gone for the swift global expansion.

The people who run those two companies truly care about their company, their customers and their staff. The live their lives by The Seven Golden Rules.

And it shows.

Back in 1536 Queen Anne, of course, denies the charges that she has been 'inappropriately intimate' with her brother and others but the King has his way.

At the end of a long weekend contemplating the future, on Easter Tuesday, April 19th 1536, Henry has convinced himself that he needs to make a change. Anne Boleyn has to be found guilty of something - witchcraft, treason, adultery, whatever. In fact, Henry's brief seems to be to make it up if necessary.

And make it up they do.

The Boleyn family's fortune are about to change.

And change fast. It's worth following the chronology of the events of April and May 1536. The Tower of London was a busy place for a few weeks that Spring.

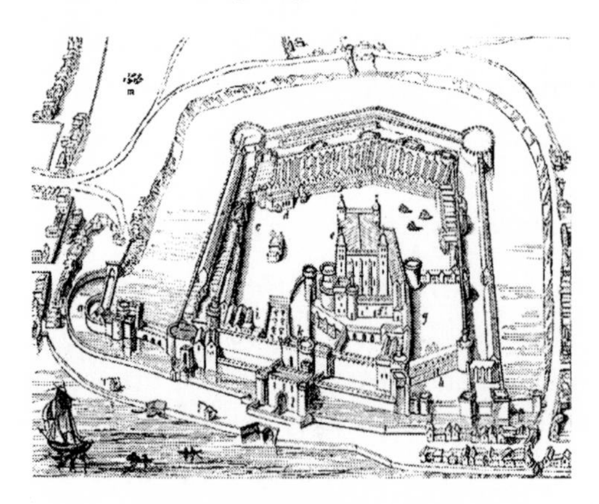

The Tower of London in 1536

23 April: George Boleyn finds he isn't to receive the Order of the Garter, whilst Nicholas Carew - hostile to the Boleyns and one of the court conservatives - does receive the honour.

27 April: Writs go out to summon Parliament - even though it had only been dismissed on the 14th.

29 April: Jane Seymour is given a purse of gold sovereigns and a royal letter whilst she is at Greenwich with Anne. And she refuses to open them. She kisses the letter and hands it back to the delivery boy unopened. We all want what we can't have. Henry is hooked.

30 April: Sir Henry Norris is the first of the 'Philandering Three' to be arrested. He was 'Groom of the Stool'. Basically he had the job of wiping the monarch's bottom after a bowel movement. He's one of those accused of adultery with Anne. He's in the doo dah in more ways than one.

On the same day, the musician Mark Smeaton is arrested and taken to Cromwell's house in Stepney. Questioned, tortured and working out he's probably plucked his last string, he soon confesses to 'violating the Queen' three times.

1 May: Anne attends the May Day tournament at Greenwich with her husband. By all accounts Henry was out of sorts, bad-tempered and left in the middle of the event. Well, if a week is a long time in politics then the fortnight from Easter Monday to May Day must have seemed like a lifetime.

Anne would never see Henry again.

2 May: With Henry having tried to get Norris to confess to charges of adultery, but the bottom wiper pleading his innocence, he is escorted to the Tower. Never mind the evidence - or lack of it - down you go. And leave the backside cloth for the next man when you leave.

On the same day Anne is arrested by her Uncle, Thomas Howard, Sir William Fitzwilliam and Paulet on the grounds of adultery with the musician, the Brother (George Boleyn) and the Bottom Wiper.

12 May: Norris and Smeaton - along with Sir Francis Weston and William Brereton were tried at Westminster Hall and found guilty.

15 May: Anne and her brother are tried in the King's Hall of the Tower of London. Guilty as charged.

Were they guilty? Well, as far as the majority of the charges of adultery and treason are concerned there are huge holes in the evidence. More than half of the specific charges are impossible as either Anne or the man concerned was elsewhere at the time; for example Anne was accused of soliciting Norris at Westminster on October 6th but she was in Greenwich recovering from childbirth. Fact is when the charges include the proviso from the prosecution that if we can't find you guilty of committing adultery and treason on the days we specify then we'll assume you did so on 'other days and places before and after' you're doomed.

So why was Anne Boleyn arrested, convicted and ultimately executed if she wasn't guilty? Either Henry VIII quite simply wanted her out of the way to marry Jane Seymour and produce a male heir - Anne's miscarriage of a deformed foetus caused Henry to believe that she would never give him a healthy male heir - or the whole thing was orchestrated by Thomas Cromwell and her other enemies.

Every day, all over Britain, people gather in groups to make decisions. Some big, some small, some important, some fairly trivial. That's the decisions, not the people. The outcome could affect anything from the way a business develops, to the route a new trunk road takes. It could create a hundred new jobs or add a hundred to the dole queue. And the really frightening thing is that most executives are happy if they get just 60% of decisions right. Which means they don't much mind if they get almost half the decisions wrong. Not surprisingly, governments and businesses waste billions every year making bad decisions. And often it's because the decision was made by a group.

In many areas of life there's such a thing as safety in numbers. For instance, when confronted by an unruly mob of away fans at a train station or perhaps encountering a pride of lions whilst out on safari. But it doesn't really work when it comes to decision making thanks to what leading psychologist Irving Janis rather imaginatively terms 'Groupthink'. It's a bit like group sex but a lot less interesting and you get to keep your clothes on. Groupthink happens when you get together a group of people with very similar backgrounds, values and interests.

Like a management board, for instance. People who either like, or at least have a healthy respect for, one another. Because of this, a consensus of opinion usually emerges when deliberating a decision and any evidence to the contrary is automatically rejected. Sometimes even ridiculed. A slap on the thigh, followed by hilarious, raucous laughter and a knowing look usually does the trick.

I should know - my thighs are red raw.

The bottom line is that individual members don't want to rock the boat because it might damage their personal relationships, or even their careers.

A number of experiments have shown that people are quick to adopt the majority position and, crucially, they ignore all the potential alternatives and all the conflicting evidence. So what do you do about it if you want to make better decisions? Well, it's down to someone to make the group aware of the problems with the consensus view and offer alternatives. And as my good friend Alan Dedicoat, the Voice of the Balls, likes to say, it could be you.

Someone needs to be appointed Devil's Advocate with the job of trying to spot holes in the decision-making process. According to another leading psychologist in the field, Amiram Vinokur, a key part of this role is to nurture authentic dissent and mould it into constructive criticism. Because if mistakes are not spotted and dealt with in the meeting, they can be a lot more costly and difficult to put right at a later date. Or to put it another way, if nobody is prepared to 'rock the boat' in the meeting, the boat will almost surely get rocked later.

But everyone is frightened of Henry. He is omnipotent. No one is asking him whether it's fair and right that Anne has to go. Maybe she has committed these crimes, maybe she hasn't. She deserves a fair hearing. But with an all powerful leader and no one challenging his views the 'team' are all working towards one goal and that is Anne's demise.

Anne was condemned and due to die. On May 16th Cranmer heard the first of Anne's confessions, on the 17th her marriage to Henry was annulled - because of Henry's liaison with Mary Boleyn - and Anne's alleged lovers were executed.

Anne had asked if a popular, famous French executioner (there were those people in those days) could chop off her head but the executioner from Calais was delayed until noon and then again until the next day.

It happens.

On May 19th 1536, after a hearty breakfast, the Lieutenant of the Tower came for Anne. She wore a black gown, a red petticoat, an ermine mantle and a gable hood. And why not? Her reputation and her legacy is, like everyone else's, affected by how you show up.

Top tip:

No matter how you feel, get up, dress up and show up.

People often ask me what is the most important thing about being a professional speaker and I answer in all honesty and humility that it is turning up. You owe it to the people who have faith in you. When people have booked you the thing that worries them on the day is what will happen if you don't turn up. So I endeavour to arrive earlier than I said I would.

Which is nice for them.

Apparently she looked behind her quite a bit; perhaps worried the executioner might strike whilst she wasn't looking. Well, you would wouldn't you?

She made her speech and knelt before the block. To make sure she looked in the right direction, the executioner called to a member of the audience: “Bring me the sword.” Anne turned her head, and the executioner struck; the ‘Sword of Calais’ had been hidden in the straw. Trick of the trade I suppose. That’s what you pay professionals for. To know what to do and how to do it when the pressure’s on. It’s nice being good in the kick about; it’s when you’re on the pitch playing for real that you get paid for and what separates the men from the boys.

Anne was quietly buried in the Chapel of St Peter ad Vincula inside the Tower of London. Three years and thirty seven days after she had first dined abroad as Queen in 1533.

Anne of just slightly more than a thousand days.

On May 20th 1536, the day after Anne’s execution, with Anne’s former marriage - the ‘Great Matter’ that Henry fought so hard for - having been made null and void her daughter, Elizabeth, is illegitimate. So is Mary; Henry’s daughter from his ‘marriage’ to Katherine. The very day after Anne loses her life, Henry became betrothed to Jane Seymour and by the end of May, Henry has his third wife.

On July 20th 1536, Henry received the devastating news that his only known illegitimate son, Henry Fitzroy, Duke of Richmond, had died at the age of 17.

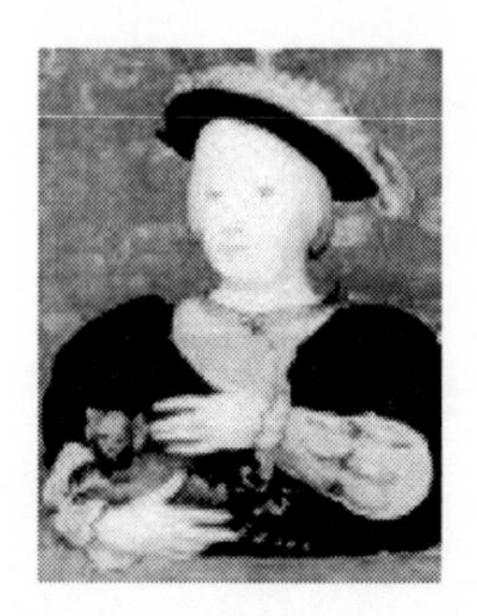

Henry Fitzroy, Duke of Richmond

So let's recap as of the start of the school holidays in July, 1536; because all this makes Kevin Keegan and his relationship with Newcastle United look positively sanguine:

Henry's just hit 45. Although he's been a very active man in the past, he's suffered a thigh wound in a jousting accident that year that's become ulcerated. He's been on the throne since 1509; the same year he married his dead brother's Spanish wife who was six years older than him. They have an illegitimate daughter but he wants a son. He splits the church, causes factions, death and in-fighting amongst many of England's families, marries his mistress's sister and they, too, have an illegitimate daughter. He's rid himself of many of his loyal servants and friends but the influential religious leader, Thomas Cranmer, has become Archbishop of Canterbury and has been let loose to get Protestantism embedded in England.

Twenty seven years after coming to the throne, Henry has divorced his wife of 26 years, murdered his second wife, lost his much loved bastard son, has a three year old illegitimate daughter, Elizabeth, brought up as Protestant as well as an illegitimate daughter Mary who's coming up to 21, is a staunch Catholic and got a mind of her own.

He also has a new wife, Jane Seymour. As Jim Croche subsequently wrote; 'Which way are you going, which side will you be on? Will you stand and watch while all the seeds of hate are sown? Will you stand with those who say, let his will be done? One hand on the Bible, one hand on the gun.' Quite prophetic, Jim. You could well have been writing about Miss Seymour in May 1536.

So The Wars of The Roses where it's Lancastrians versus Yorkists is over but within 50 years of Henry VII - the Lancastrian if you remember - marrying the Yorkist Elizabeth in 1486, Henry VIII has managed to create a Catholic versus Protestant wrangle that will last for over 500 years and counting. It's the price of a Prince.

Chapter 11 ~ Died, divorced, beheaded, survived

1536 — 1547

On the evening of Anne's execution Henry had dinner with Jane Seymour at a little restaurant on the Strand.

They did that sort of thing in those days.

He then took his barge up to Hampton Court. By six o' clock the next morning Jane had joined him there and after a good breakfast they made a formal announcement to anyone who wanted to attend the press conference that they were to be married before the end of the month.

Henry wants a new beginning. Many people do. But his 20 year old daughter still won't accept him as Head of the Church and there's the small matter of Elizabeth too. Still, Henry busied himself whilst at Hampton Court for a week to get the monogrammed linen changed, swapping the coats of arms and generally ridding the various Royal Palaces of Anne's presence.

Jane Seymour

On May 30th 1536 Henry and Jane were married at Whitehall Palace. Jane had seen what had befallen Anne by having too much to say for herself and opted for a submissive, adoring role.

What she wanted was a son and to help further her family's ambitions. Her oldest brother, Edward, became Viscount Beauchamp, 1st Duke of Somerset and given land and privileges. His position appeared unassailable. The other older brother, Thomas, was made Lord High Admiral but didn't fair quite so well and resentment crept in. He was still unmarried and he possibly saw himself as a husband to either Princess Mary or Princess Elizabeth.

Their father, Sir John Seymour, was to not only fill his boots and get himself a position at court but to embark on a love affair with Edward's wife.

That's right; his own daughter-in-law. When it was discovered, the marriage was annulled and their children declared bastards. Obviously their legal grandfather might also be their biological father. No way of knowing.

And no, I have not made that up.

Probably the entire Seymour family had been party to the plot to bring Anne to the scaffold. Fact is, after Jane became Queen, her family scaled the social ranks, as was befitting the family of a monarch.
And it would be easy to see this new cabal that the Seymour family are creating as simply about power and status. But for them - and for the others who want to join a new powerful group such as this - it is also to help fulfill a deeper psychological need we all have.

Why do we like to join social groups? Well, it's staring you in the Facebook. The popularity of social media websites serves to underline a basic need in us all. No, not just to share embarrassing pictures with the rest of the world but rather to 'belong'.

In fact, it's one of three basic human needs; the other two being to be loved and to feel important. But what's with this in-built desire to join social groups? In the animal kingdom the reason is easy to understand since it's mostly about survival. That's why wolves hunt in packs, birds fly together for safety, and ants achieve more by working in unison. Like Ant and Dec, for instance. However, for humans, belonging to a group helps us form a view of our social identity which, in turn, contributes to our sense of who we are.

It wasn't just for the money, status and reduced likelihood of being beheaded that everyone suddenly wanted to be part of the Seymour power base Henry was happy to encourage.

Fifty years ago, a famous study by Tajfel demonstrated how complete strangers stuck together even when they had only the smallest thing in common. In his experiment, a group of boys were gathered together and then told they were to be split into two teams. Despite not knowing each other at all, most favoured being in a team with those immediately around them rather than those furthest away. Better the devil you know, I guess.

It's a bit like meeting your countrymen abroad when on holiday. Walking along the prom of a UK resort, you would happily pass by without saying a word. But in a foreign country you're likely to at least exchange pleasantries when recognising that they're from these shores. Wearing Union Jack shorts helps in this respect.

What's more, a funny thing happens when we join a group. We start to behave just like everyone else and follow the 'group norm'. Even when there's nobody in the group called Norm. One of the most famous experiments showing how easily we conform to unwritten group rules was conducted by Solomon Asch of Rutgers University in New Jersey. He asked participants to sit amongst a group of strangers and judge the length of queues that were being formed in front of them. What he didn't tell them was that all the other people had been instructed to lie when asked which was the longest queue. Sure enough, 75% of participants denied all the evidence from their own senses and instead conformed to the group view.

A similar experiment run by psychology Professor Philip Zimbardo of Stanford University wasn't quite so successful. His idea was to place young men into a simulated prison environment with some assuming the role of prisoners whilst others played the part of guards complete with riot gear. Despite being a psychologist, he clearly hadn't thought through the consequences of the experiment and the likely long-term affects on the mental health of the participants. After less than a week the experiment had to be scrapped when some of the 'prisoners' were becoming too submissive and some of the guards a little too zealous when metering out discipline. Needless to say, the emotional fallout from the experiment outweighed any positive conclusions. In fact, I think some 'prisoners' are still on the roof protesting.

So if you want to join a group and become its leader, the first thing to do is conform. Then, when you feel trust has been gained, it's safe to start to show the way. And if you decide to start a group outside of work, don't forget to invite me. Because just like everyone else, I hate to be left out.

However, the Seymours had begun to accumulate enemies and grudges during their rise in royal favour. Sound familiar? John died in December 1536, but his royal daughter did not attend the funeral.

In 1537 Jane became pregnant and Henry was delighted when she gave birth on October 12th to the much wanted son and heir. He was named Edward and Christened on October 15th but Jane was weak after the birth and died just 12 days after giving birth.

Henry had already been preparing his own tomb at St. George's Chapel at Windsor Castle, which was where Jane was buried. In the end, she would be the only one of Henry's six wives to be buried with him. She ensured the King's lasting affection when she gave birth to Edward. The infant prince was the only male Tudor heir of his generation; he had two sisters and Henry VIII's sisters Mary and Margaret had several daughters. With Edward now here, Henry felt confident that the throne would not pass to a woman and the Tudor dynasty would survive.

Little did he know.

To his death Henry talked of Jane in much more affectionate terms than he ever referred to his other wives. Was it the fact that she was the one who bore him the son? Was it love? Or was it that she died prematurely?

Those who are cut off in their prime leave memories that improve with time. For many musicians, death is not a final reckoning - it's the best career move they ever made. Rock and pop stars live life in the fast lane and they are twice as likely to die early than the rest of the population. Eddie Cochrane 21, Buddy Holly 22, Jim Morrison and Kurt Cobain both 27, Marc Bolan 29, Glenn Miller and John Lennon were both 40, Elvis Presley was 42 and Freddie Mercury 45.

Within a week of Michael Jackson's untimely death at 51, five of the top ten albums in the UK were his.

In terms of her legacy, dying at 34 turned out to be a good move for Jane.

Within three years of Jane's death, Henry had turned his thoughts to a wife for political alliance. His last two wives had been chosen from the previous Queen's team of ladies in waiting. This time he married his fourth wife, Anne of Cleves, to gain a political alliance in Europe. He saw her picture, painted by Holbein, thought she was pretty and agreed to the marriage.

Anne of Cleves

He's coming up to 50 and now relies on pictures. But just as men who now go on the internet dating sites and then fix to meet the woman of their dreams find, portraits are done to show the ladies' best sides. He was sorely disappointed when they actually met and after only six months the marriage was annulled on July 9th 1540. I don't know about you but I think I'd want my money back.

To be fair he had apparently said to Cromwell on his wedding day; 'My Lord, if it were not to satisfy the world, and My Realm, I would not do that I must do this day for none earthly thing.'

His 'gut feel' was that it was the wrong thing to do. I think it is without exception that all the CEO's I know can tell several stories of how they have had a negative 'gut feeling' about a potential employee; but that they went with the CV, the view of colleagues and the impressive performance at interview and rued the day they did.

We all form a view of someone very quickly indeed and we all use the expression 'I had a gut feeling' when we have a thought or, rather, an intuition. Even when we know someone well we have an intuition that we can't quite explain that things are not as they appear to be. They lack verisimilitude.

We often have a view or opinion but are unable to rationally account for it. And, more importantly the 'gut feeling' turns out to be right.

So where do 'gut feelings' really come from and should we trust them? Do we only and exclusively use our brains to assess and decide? Well, Dr. Candace Pert (formerly Professor at Georgetown University and Chief of the National Institute of Mental Health in the USA) has discovered that the entire lining of the gastrointestinal tract, from the oesophagus to the large intestine, is lined with cells that contain neuropeptides (once believed to exist only in the brain) and receptors.

When I teach people presentation skills they all tell me that they feel their 'insides have been twisted into knots' before a big speech; they talk of 'butterflies in the tummy' so there is no doubt the stomach listens carefully to the brain. The connections between the two systems are so tight that scientists often refer to them as one entity: the brain-gut axis.

We also make 'snap' judgments on people. We don't forget the first impression that someone makes on us but we form that judgment in seconds and without actually thinking. So can thinking that takes place so quickly be at all useful? As children growing up we've always been told that we make better decisions when we take the time to carefully evaluate all the relevant information we can find

'More haste, less speed', 'Look before you leap' and so on. 'Gut feelings' and the kind of thinking that goes on in our subconscious brain when we first meet someone have two remarkable things in common. Firstly they are not deliberate, conscious decision-making processes that we usually associate with 'normal' thinking and, secondly, people consistently tell me that this kind of thinking produces consistently better results.

So should we listen to our instincts, hunches and even our dreams? Well, according to Dr. Candace Pert we could do worse. Next time you are asked to justify your gut feelings, tell them that the entire lining of the gastrointestinal tract, from the oesophagus to the large intestine, is lined with cells that contain neuropeptides and receptors. That should have them doing some 'real' thinking about you....

Back to 1540.

Heads had to roll of course and it was Cromwell, as the marriage's chief architect, who was accused of high treason and executed on 28th July 1540. There's no record of what the King said to Holbein.

Having tried the portrait route and keen to have a mother for the young prince, King Henry VIII had already turned to the tried and trusted formula of looking around at the various ladies in waiting for a new wife. And so he met his fifth wife, Catherine Howard, at the English court where she was a lady-in-waiting to Anne of Cleves.

Catherine Howard

If you recall, he met Anne Boleyn when she was a lady in waiting to Katherine of Aragon and met Jane Seymour when she was lady in waiting to Anne Boleyn. Did nobody warn Anne of Cleves or was it all part of a plan? Catherine Howard was Anne Boleyn's cousin. Enough said. People look after themselves.

Only a few days after Anne of Cleves was sent back from whence she came, Henry was married to his fifth wife, Catherine Howard. But soon she was also found guilty of adultery and executed on 13th February 1542.

It was no surprise that King Henry VIII met his last and sixth wife, Catherine Parr, at the English court. By all accounts, she didn't love him; her affections were with Sir Thomas Seymour, who she later married. But she was forced into the marriage through duty and obligation and on July 12th 1543 Henry married his sixth and final wife Catherine Parr.

Catherine Parr

That's four wives in the seven years since the beheading of Anne Boleyn; Catherine narrowly escaped punishment for her religious disputes and survived her spouse. The last four go: died, divorced, beheaded, and survived. The jousting accident in 1536 had been a major factor in the King's declining health and he died in 1547 in London at the age of 55. At his death King Henry VIII left three children from his first three wives and they all were to have a turn on the English throne: Edward VI, Mary I and Elizabeth I.

King Henry did all he could to protect his son's health; the infant prince lived in safe seclusion until his father wed Catherine Parr. Henry's last wife became a beloved mother to Edward and he adopted the zealous Protestantism which she and Edward championed. He had also grown close to his half-sister Elizabeth, with whom he shared a household for some years. His older half-sister, Mary, was an equally zealous Catholic; her religion and the vast difference in their ages prevented a close relationship.

Before we move to the next Golden Rule that comes from this period, let's put Henry VIII's life on a different time span to give us a good look at it. If Henry's 55 years had been run in a week whereby he was born very first thing on Monday morning, then he'd have come to the throne very early on Wednesday morning, been married to Katherine of Aragon for all of Wednesday, Thursday and Friday and the other five marriages, two children and other shenanigans would have happened on Saturday and Sunday.

Edward is to become King before his tenth birthday, but his Seymour uncles thought they should run the country. Sound familiar? They battled with and ultimately lost the Protectorship to the ambitious John Dudley, Duke of Northumberland.

The story of Henry VIII is echoed in the Great Depression of 1929, the financial crisis of 2009, Gerald Ratner and, of course, 'The Titanic'. And it summaries The Third Golden Rule to live a happy and successful life.

The need for the Devil's Advocate.

Chapter 12 ~ The Third Golden Rule

Whenever people gather in groups to make decisions someone needs to challenge the group's view and the leader's conclusions. As we discussed in chapter 10, if nobody is prepared to 'rock the boat' in the meeting, the boat will almost surely get rocked later. And often there are not enough life belts to go round.

As we saw in 1912.

No one was strong enough to stand up to J. Bruce Ismay when he jettisoned the original design for 'The Titanic' and reduced 48 lifeboats by a staggering 32. And if we go back to The Great Depression we see how omnipotence and the lack of a Devil's Advocate allowed financial ruin.

Back in 1929 enormous power was wielded by a quartet of central bankers: Emile Moreau of the Banque de France; Hjalmar Schacht of the Reichsbank; Benjamin Strong, the founder governor of the New York Federal Reserve; and Montagu Norman, Governor of the Bank of England. They were the guardians of the financial markets. Their actions determined the economic health of nations. They arguably had a bigger impact on the prosperity of the world than any individual government.

Detached from elected politicians and accountable to nobody but themselves, these were the guys who oversaw the world's descent into economic chaos. And, luckily for them, they did it in an age when there were no Sky News journalists to push a microphone under their nose and demand a soundbite. To be fair to the quartet, they hadn't been dealt the best of hands; there was a huge burden of debt heaped on Germany after World War I in the form of reparations, plus corresponding amounts owed to the US by Britain and France.

But even more worrying, all four made big decisions without anyone being allowed to question their conclusions and decisions. The actions taken by Montagu Norman crippled British industry. France took an unfair trading advantage for its exporters; Schacht took a reckless gamble in encouraging overseas lending to Germany; and in the USA interest rates were kept too low in the late 1920's. Benjamin Strong helped to pump up Wall Street's bubble, but that sucked in precious capital from Europe and the whole thing ended in a devastating crash. The pressures on them were enormous.

Just as they were on Henry VIII.

Strong was the Alan Greenspan of his day, perhaps even more powerful for a period than the erstwhile chairman of the Federal Reserve Board, in that Greenspan was at least obliged to explain himself to Congress from time to time.

Henry VIII had a succession of lackies in More, Wolsey, Cranmer and Cromwell to name but four. But anyone who truly answered back, anyone who offered an alternative view, was not only dismissed but occasionally also dismembered.

You see, Henry lacked a Devil's Advocate. He was omnipotent.

It might feel good at the time but omnipotence breeds arrogance and hubris. And it always ends in tears. To be truly happy and successful you need someone to be your Devil's Advocate.

It's The Third Golden Rule.

For years, Green Tree Corporation had been very successful in the consumer loans industry in the US. With a $17 billion portfolio, it was the leading lender for owners of trailer homes. And it made its Chairman and Chief Executive grotesquely rich. At one point he claimed to have the highest CEO salary in America.

From 1991 to 1998 annual sales of trailer homes in the US more than doubled. And to make buying one easily affordable, Green Tree was happy to provide mortgages with terms of up to 30 years.

However, there was a major snag with this policy; a huge problem that should have been obvious from the start but which nobody seemed to care too much about. They were all too busy making money.

A trailer home is not like a real house that appreciates in value over time. It's more like a car that depreciates in value from the moment it's bought. And to compound the problem, most only have a life span of twenty years. As they say in the US, 'do the math'. Anybody who did obviously didn't wake up and smell the coffee.

The long-term problem was swept under the carpet and replaced with a short-term rug known as affordability. This was the only thing people saw; the only thing that was sold to them. Why was it allowed to happen?

Because there was no Devil's Advocate.

And whose fault was that? The people who can't see further than the monthly payment or the guy who in 1995 trousered a base salary of $433,000. (They were big pants). He also benefited from a whopping cash bonus of $6 million and a stock bonus of $60 million.

At the start of the 21st century, the US Treasury Secretary was forced to stuff billions of taxpayers' dollars into the ailing insurance giant AIG. But no-one played Devil's Advocate and asked the 'What if?' questions. No-one thought to attach conditions to the new funding so that obscene bonus payments were impossible. The lunatics were running the asylum. AIG had got rich in the country's heyday insuring the concrete and steel of

American industry, only to destroy itself chasing phantom fortunes at the Wall Street card tables. Like a dissolute King gambling away a country's hard fought assets.

The bailout came just after AIG had posted the largest quarterly loss in American corporate history - some $61 billion. In the final three months of 2008, the company lost more than $27 million every hour. That's $465,000 a minute. My suggestion that they double the lunch hour and save over $120 million a week fell on deaf ears. The problem was that no mechanism had been put in place to search the balance sheets of companies like Enron, AIG and Lehman Brothers. Companies that held life-or-death power over ordinary people.

Who allowed this to happen? It needed a Devil's Advocate.

A strong one.

In the case of Enron it was a journalist, Bethany McLean, who was brave enough to ask CEO Jeffrey Skilling how Enron actually made its money. That was in March 2001. The Wall Street Journal began to dig but even in October 2001 Chairman Kenneth Lay said there was 'absolutely no accounting issue, no trading issue, no reserve issue.'

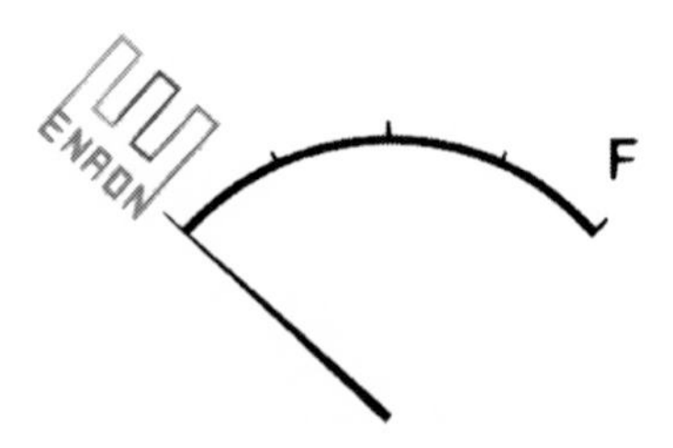

What was within the walls of their impressive building in Houston was hubris, greed and downright stupidity. And that created all the infighting.

The very shape of our country and the divisive religious beliefs is not an unfortunate accident. It's down to Henry VIII's greed and stupidity and lack of real concern for others. And the repercussions of his reign are still felt. The economic fiasco that was created by people on Wall Street and in the City of London at the start of this century was down to selfishness, greed, stupidity and the lack of a Devil's Advocate.

Just as 'The Titanic' was allowed to set sail with over 2,000 souls on board but only enough life boats for less than half.

Edward Liddy of AIG admitted mistakes were made when the company strayed from its core insurance competencies to launch a credit-default-swaps portfolio in 1987. But he makes it sound like a latter day Oliver begging for more soup; hungry and sick from being left out in someone else's financial weather. The fact is they had spent more than a decade systematically scheming to evade US and international regulators and making colossal, world-sinking $500 billion bets with money they didn't have, in a toxic and completely unregulated derivatives market.

After they wrecked the financial world, they then rather cunningly granted themselves almost unlimited emergency powers to clean up their own mess. And so the leaders of companies like AIG ended up not penniless and in jail, but being helped out by 'our partners in the government' as Liddy rather insouciantly described it. Banks who knew they were selling bad debts managed to get AAA ratings for them by not relying on their actual underlying assets but on crazy mathematical formulas cooked up by the banks to make the investments look safer than they were.

AIGFP - a London-based subsidiary of the American insurance company - ought to have been regulated by our own Financial Services Authority. But the Office of Thrift Supervision in the US (OTS) which supervises the industry that offers 'affordable' home financing for Americans, managed to convince us that it had the muscle to regulate its own giant companies. But they didn't. At least, unlike Henry's regulators, no-one at the OTS was sent to the scaffold. They concluded there was no big credit risk because they were told there was no big credit risk.

Just like people believed J. Bruce Ismay when he said 'The Titanic' was unsinkable.

AIG had no one doing the counter balance checks. When Joe Cassano, the head of AIGFP left the firm, he had led the company into the largest bail out in American financial history. However, they not only allowed him to keep $34 million in bonuses, they kept him on as a consultant on a nice little earner of $1 million a month. After all those years letting him run wild and paying insane bonuses, AIG decided to pay a further $450 million in bonuses to the employees in his old unit, AIGFP. Cassano was an autocratic bully who thought he could do anything. True, he brought many people to their knees, but at least he couldn't send people to the guillotine.

However, for those who lost money, it probably felt like it.

The Herald of Free Enterprise

Seventy five years after the sinking of 'The Titanic' Britain suffered its second biggest peace time, maritime disaster when 'The Herald of Free Enterprise' capsized on leaving Zeebrugge harbour. At first it appeared to be a terrible accident. But then we learned that the ferry had sailed with the bow doors open. Despite being against regulations, this was common practice to allow vehicle exhaust fumes to clear the deck more quickly. Also, vehicles and lorries had not yet been chained to prevent them from moving. Again, this was against regulations but it ensured the ship left port on time. The capsizing of 'The Herald of Free Enterprise' wasn't an accident but rather an accident waiting to happen. One day, in rough seas, water was bound to flood in through the open bow doors. One day, this was bound to cause vehicles to slide to one side and make the ship list dangerously. And one day, it would eventually capsize with a great loss of life.

That day was March 6th 1987.

A total of 193 passengers and crew died because nobody was willing to play Devil's Advocate. After a public inquiry, Lord Justice Sheen published a report identifying a 'disease of sloppiness and negligence' at every level of the Townsend Thoresen's hierarchy. Blame was attributed to the company's management and, in particular, four crew members of the ship.

The company and seven of its employees were subsequently charged with corporate manslaughter. However, the Old Bailey trial in 1990 collapsed when the prosecution failed to provide a case of manslaughter. By this time, most of the claims had been settled.

Alan Rogers summed up the feeling of his fellow survivors seven years after the event; "The worst thing is that to this day, no one from P&O has even written to say sorry. That would have gone a long way, wouldn't it?"

Our next lesson is echoed in the words of a famous Michael Jackson song. If you're going to make a change, you need to start with the man in the mirror. Unless, of course, you're a woman.

Either way, if you want to make the world a better place then take a look at yourself and then make a change.

Take responsibility.

When Adam Applegarth was at the helm at Northern Rock his Group Financial Director, Bob Bennett, was arguably his Devil's Advocate; his 'safe pair of hands' to Applegarth's 'energetic, youthful, growth-orientated individual' to quote Bennett. But Bennett retired in 2006 and, in common with many building societies, they ignored repeated warnings from the Financial Services Authority to clean up their books without any censure.

Following the collapse of Dunfermline Building Society, FSA chairman Lord Turner wrote to the Chancellor listing warnings made over a five year period from 2003 against the dangers of commercial property lending, the risks of buy-to-let and the dangers of mortgage book acquisitions.

Despite the FSA's concerns, Dunfermline Building Society was allowed to increase its commercial property book five-fold to £628m between 2004 and 2008 and buy mortgage books worth £467m from Lehman Brothers and GMAC. The watchdog finally intervened in October 2007 to prevent Dunfermline acquiring another £160m mortgage book from Credit Suisse.

RBS, Dunfermline, AIG, Northern Rock, Bear Stearns; the list goes on. To give you an idea of the bail out cost to the taxpayer, imagine if a fund had been set up during the reign of Henry VIII. Every week £1 million of taxpayers' money is paid into it. And then one day, almost five hundred years later, it's all handed over to the banks.

That's about the size of it.

So who's to blame?

The individuals who were guilty of greed, hubris and then disunity? Well, that's basic human nature. It's what happened to

The Beatles, Gerald Ratner and Marks and Spencer under Rick Greenbury. It is what happened to Manchester United after becoming the first English team to win the European Cup in 1968. They were relegated within six years. The same time it took Henry to have Anne Boleyn beheaded after first wooing her.

It is what happened to Liverpool F.C. after three years of being owned by two guys who despised each other; Tom Hicks and George Gillett. Liverpool failed to qualify for The Champions League for the first time since they had last won it five years before and ended up in the courts.

Liverpool F.C. used to have the key component of all successful empires: continuity. They had a sound boardroom, a judicious succession of managers steeped in the same great tradition and a dynasty of players. At the time - for those who have not studied history - it seemed inevitable that Liverpool would carry on for ever. And whilst rivals gloat, they also have to live with the real truth: that all empires decline and fall. Even those that appear unbeatable.

Fact is, everyone is trying to beat you. So you have to work that little bit harder to stay ahead. The people at the top must not be greedy or complacent. Instead they must work together and accept the need to constantly improve. Because when you recognise that change is necessary, you are more likely to make the right changes.

In 2007, Deloitte & Touche failed Dunfermline Building Society by suggesting that bad loan provisions might be too high, rather than too low. Arthur Andersen failed Enron – and us all – by not looking better and deeper and truly considering other people.

The UK and the US governments became gigantic holding companies which consisted of remarkably large and risky hedge funds, controlling stakes in struggling businesses and huge investments in a group of teetering megabanks. And these new holding companies had no mechanism for auditing themselves.

It's easy to say that the people who claim to have foreseen this unholy mess only crawled out of the woodwork after the bad news became public. But there were those, like Paul Wilmott, one of the world's leading financial mathematicians, who had been warning for years that the models used by banks to value their assets were just plain wrong. Wilmott stood up in front of paying audiences and declared that the formulas were relied on too heavily and that bankers were paid too much. Quite a few people stormed out of his conferences, slamming the door for effect on the way out. He pointed out that following the formulas was like relying on your seatbelt to drive crazily; it might save your life but it won't stop you from crashing. And the FSA can't afford to pay the best people so they aren't strong enough to be the Devil's Advocate. We need people who are clever enough not only to realise that something is wrong but also understand what it is and be strong enough to say it.

Paul Wilmott was not alone. Niall Ferguson - a Professor at Harvard no less - offered his thoughts to the great and good of the rich and self-satisfied bankers in autumn 2006 and was dismissed as an alarmist. The suggestion was even made to the organisers that instead of having an outside speaker they should offer a screening of 'Mary Poppins'.

Given that this was suggested by an American, the irony of the film's plot - a run on the bank - was sadly lost.

John Paulson was convinced that housing would implode and was desperate to find plenty of toxic mortgage products to bet against. So he went to Goldman Sachs and other banks asking them to manufacture more bad mortgages. At the time, experts on Wall Street laughed at him. Looking back, regulators argue that investors should have been warned that Paulson had a role in the creation of some of these investments. Once he had helped to pick the bad assets, Paulson then bet that its assets would go down by entering into credit default swaps with Goldman Sachs.

As one banker subsequently said, 'It's a bit like making a bet with someone on the outcome of a penalty shoot-out without knowing that the guy you are betting with is one of the goalkeepers.'

Investors lost $1 billion while Paulson's bet yielded a profit of $1 billion. Our own RBS was exposed to the deal through an insurance contract.

And how was it that Bernie Madoff was able to pull off one of the biggest Ponzi schemes in history?

Bernie Madoff

The secret life of Bernard Madoff unravelled as he stood in his Upper East Side apartment in a pale blue bathrobe and slippers, facing two FBI agents. “We’re here to find out if there’s an innocent explanation.” they told him. “There is no innocent explanation.” Madoff replied. He was responsible for over $50bn worth of global losses. In its conception, the scam is a timeless classic. Madoff later confessed to his sons, Mark and Andrew, that his money-management business was “just one big lie... a giant Ponzi scheme”. Clearly unimpressed, it was his sons who shopped him to the authorities. Madoff managed $17bn directly for clients but, through derivatives, an estimated $50bn was banking on his performance. Yet the complex trading he claimed to be carrying out in his closed-off eerie on the 17th floor of the Lipstick Building in mid-town Manhattan was a sham; the magic returns were simply cash brought in from new victims.

The list of Madoff’s victims was vast and eclectic. They ranged from charities to such well known names as Steven Spielberg. The fact that he often turned down would-be punters only boosted his cachet; people spent years trying to get onto his client list. Those he turned down no doubt felt hurt and rejected - but they were the fortunate ones that presumably he liked too much to rip off.

But just as it was with Cassano, Liddy, Ismay, Spelling, Applegarth, Maxwell, Goodwin and Henry VIII (to take just a handful of names from a very big list) there were, with hindsight, plenty of red flags. No one seemed to know what Madoff was doing. Regulators who visited in 2005 and 2007 gave him a clean bill of health - despite reports that the auditors of his massive fund consisted of three people operating out of a 13ft by 8ft office in what the Americans call ‘Nowheresville’.

When Madoff described his investment method as ‘a split-conversion strategy’, no one knew what it meant, but took it as another sign of his investment genius. He could have told them it was a split-personality-double-bluff technique and nobody would have raised an eyebrow. Except maybe Bernie, himself, who had eyebrows the size of his ego. Now he is assured of his place in history. As Warren Buffett likes to say; when the tide goes out, you see who's swimming naked.

And it would be easy to conclude that this 'crash and burn' we saw in 1929 and the early part of the 21st century as a modern phenomena, but we can go back as far as the 17th century to see how avarice and a belief that things could go on forever left people in ruins.

In the 1630's the price of tulip bulbs rose spectacularly and, one after the other, the Dutch rushed to the tulip markets like flies around a honey-pot. Everyone imagined that the new-found passion for tulips would last forever and that wealthy people from every part of the world would flock to Holland and pay whatever prices were asked for them. Farmers mortgaged whatever they could to raise cash to begin trading and tulip mania reached its peak during the winter of 1636-37, when some bulbs were changing hands ten times in a day and a particularly rare Violetten Admirael van Enkhuizen bulb, that was about to split in two, sold for more than ten times the average annual salary at the time.
But the tulip market crashed spectacularly and, as usual, the fall was even quickly than the rise.

Time for the next lesson before we look at The Third Golden Rule:

If things seem to be too good to be true, they usually are.

There was no doubt a failing in the regulatory regime in America but the get-rich quick investors – now renamed 'victims' were also guilty of stupidity, greed and carelessness.

In April 1986, the world witnessed what has been arguably the costliest accident ever. The Chernobyl disaster has been called the biggest socio-economic catastrophe in peacetime history. Over half of the area of Ukraine is in some way contaminated. Over 200,000 people had to be evacuated and resettled while over one and a half million people were directly affected by the disaster. The death toll attributed to Chernobyl, including people who died from cancer years later, is over 100,000. The total costs including clean-up, resettlement, and compensation to victims is over $200 billion. The cost of a new steel shelter for the Chernobyl nuclear plant cost $2 billion.

The accident was officially attributed to power plant operators who violated plant procedures and were ignorant of the necessary safety requirements. They were also guilty of stupidity and carelessness. As I said in Chapter 8, it's called work for a reason. Whatever you are doing you should do your best. You should concentrate. Particularly if people's lives are on the line. It's the subject of The Second Golden Rule and brings us neatly to The Third.

The Third Golden Rule:
Always have a Devil's Advocate

A good one.

And you have to listen properly.

The Devil's Advocate needs to start at the beginning; they need to imagine the chain of events from scratch and foresee the future, rather than be bound by the paths already trodden. Everyone in business has pursued a debt or two. Sometimes you've pursued it for so long that you feel bound to carry on. Often it takes someone else to point out that you need to let go. If you want a simple example think of a time when you spent hours on a

PowerPoint presentation. You no doubt spent far too long and ended up with far too many slides. But it's difficult to edit them down – which will always make it much better – simply because you had already spent so much time getting to where you are. And it seems like a waste to throw it all away.

Running your own finances is actually pretty simple. Indeed, running a company's finances is straightforward. Don't spend more money than you can afford to lose; if you're going to have debt make sure you can pay it back; always have a Plan B and always be ready to tighten your belt if the ride gets rocky. Government debt is not only bad economic policy but also morally unacceptable because it makes your children responsible to pay for what you bought.

Of course, there's a neat irony in that if, like me, you seem to spend most of your money on them in the first place.

However, generally speaking, if you are personally in debt you have no-one to blame but yourself. It's your own damn fault. You needed a Devil's Advocate - a good one.

And you have to listen. Gerald Ratner had a Devil's Advocate. She was called Lynne Franks. She strongly recommended that he didn't refer to his own product as crap. She strongly recommended that he didn't suggest an M&S prawn sandwich would last longer than a pair of his ear rings. But he didn't listen. J. Bruce Ismay was strongly advised to use 'Best Best' rivets on the bow of 'The Titanic'. But they used a grade down from the best-quality iron, known as No 3, graded simply 'Best'.

Grade 3 rivets have higher levels of slag and are more likely to splinter when put under intense pressure. 'The Titanic' was designed to stay afloat if up to four of its sealed compartments were flooded. However, pretty soon rivets were popping faster than the buttons on John Prescott's shirt after a blowout at the

Chinese. And so a fifth and fatal compartment flooded, condemning the vessel to the depths.

Ismay was advised against having only 16 lifeboats on a ship that would travel on its maiden voyage with over 2,000 souls on board.

But he didn't listen.

Simon Cowell is one of the most successful television and music executives the world has ever seen. And he recognises the need for The Devil's Advocate. In the boot camps he himself insists on each judge having a sounding board. Including himself. On all his TV shows he is not the only judge.

The first Devil's Advocate (the Advocatus Diaboli) was appointed by Pope Leo X in the early 15th century; his duty was to prepare in writing all possible arguments, even at times seemingly slight, against the raising of anyone to the honours of the altar. The Church's aim was to prevent anyone from receiving those honours who were not worthy. In a nutshell, to list everything unfavourable about the candidate. Sixtus V formally established the office in 1587 and the office was abolished in 1979 by Pope John Paul II.

Why did he abolish it?

It's just as relevant today as it's ever been.

The Third Golden Rule:

Always Have a Devils' Advocate
Someone has to check the checker
Always
Have a good Devil's Advocate
Have a good, conscientious checker
Listen properly

PART THREE

THE REIGN OF HENRY VIII'S SON, EDWARD VI

Chapter 13 ~ Teddy's Uncles and The Nine Day Queen

1547 —————————————————————— 1553

At any stage today, on the very day you are reading this book, you will be carrying out activity which is in one of four quadrants. Often known as the 'time management matrix' and attributed to Stephen Covey, you are either doing something that is urgent and important (quadrant one), important but not urgent (quadrant two), urgent but not important (quadrant three), or doing something that is neither important nor urgent. The activity in quadrant four is not important to you nor anyone else and probably has little or no implications or repercussions. For you or anyone else.

But you still spend time in quadrant four.

	Urgent	Not Urgent
Important	1	2
Not Important	3	4

We all spend too much of our time doing things that are not important, not urgent and not particularly enjoyable either. In fact, let me contradict myself. If something is not important but it *is* fun then it has a degree of importance in your life.

Because fun is underrated.

Most people don't see the real value of having fun with friends, the importance and joy of developing loving relationships and making a positive contribution. It's easy to decry the arts - and in particular comedy - as irrelevant but it is to miss the point. What is the purpose of it all if we don't have any fun?

Of course we have to do things that are important and urgent. In business, that often involves doing things that are necessary to make money, keep the company afloat, do deals etc. But often the fire fighting aspect of doing things that are important and urgent (and it's often the pyromaniacs who like fire fighting the most) is that these things are not done as well as they might have been done if they had been done when they were important but not urgent. Because most things that are important and urgent started in the quadrant of important but not urgent.

We spend too much time doing things that are not important and not urgent. We spend too much time doing things that are urgent but *seem* to be important. Often they're important to someone else.

What Edward VI seemed to spend most of his six short years on the throne doing was things that were important for other people but not for him or his subjects.

Let's recap.

The son of Henry VIII, Edward, had been born on October 12th 1537 at Greenwich Palace in London and his mother, Jane Seymour, had died twelve days later. On the death of his father in January 1547 he became Edward VI at an age when most youngsters have not finished junior school. Henry had already appointed Edward's uncle, Edward Seymour, to serve as Lord

Protector of the Realm and Governor of the King's Person whilst the young King was playing out like kids should, but the nine year old himself had always preferred his more flamboyant uncle, Thomas Seymour, the Lord High Admiral. They were both brothers of his late mother and there was no brotherly love lost between them.

Thomas decided to bet. And lost.

He plotted against his brother, Edward, and was executed within two years of Edward VI coming to the throne - on March 20th 1549.

Uncle Edward Seymour (The Duke of Somerset) was, in turn, deposed by John Dudley, 1st Earl of Warwick, and executed in January 1552. Henry VIII had appointed a well-balanced council but as the opinion of the members of Council changed, the plans of Henry VIII suffered. Uncle Edward had some strong opinions and practically ruled England from 1547 to 1549. It was he who declared war against Scotland as they refused the marriage proposal of Edward (that's him not his nephew, the young King) with Mary of Scotland. Mary was married to the French Prince, resulting in poor relations between England and Scotland.

You are forgiven if you have a sense of déjà vu here. We have a young boy as King, two uncles squabbling for power and a political schemer in the mould of Wolsey and Cromwell in John Dudley. Relations between England and Scotland aren't too clever either.

Sound familiar?

John Dudley was 35 when young Edward VI came to the throne and his father, Edmund Dudley, had been Henry VII's finance minister. Despite the fact that Edmund had been found guilty of 'constructive treason' in 1509 and executed in 1510, the Dudley family had managed to hang on in there and John Dudley had made a name for himself fighting the Scots in 1544 and the French in 1545. Dudley was a Protestant and formed a convenient partnership with Edward Seymour against the Catholic Duke of Norfolk.

In spite of a portrait of Edward as a vivacious two year old he was a frail child and a short life was anticipated for him from his early years.

That didn't prevent him benefiting from a good education but that, in turn, only taught him to conjugate some Latin verbs and read a bit of Aristotle's 'Ethics'. No match for Dudley and his pals high on self interest. Interestingly he recorded with apparently cold-blooded indifference the execution of both his uncles, and he certainly made no attempt to mitigate the harassment of his Catholic sister, Mary.

Fact is young Edward had been so impregnated with the divine right of Kings and the divine truth of Protestantism that he thought he was entitled and bound to override the succession as established by law and exclude a Catholic from the throne. His last recorded words were vehement injunctions to Thomas Cranmer to sign the will. He was brought up believing he was special and could live by special rules and get away with anything.

Bit like Tiger Woods really.

When he was crowned there were no less than three crowns placed on his nine year old head. Cranmer emphasised to the young boy at the coronation that no one had the right to hold him to account. He was answerable only to God. The implications of the absolutism established by Henry VIII were now there to be seen.

As a child he wrote that the Pope was 'a bad man; the true son of the devil'.

When someone believes they are omnipotent it always ends in tears.

Edward himself was by all accounts a decent young man. Despite not being allowed to run the country as such he was responsible for introducing a uniform Protestant service in England based on his Book of Common Prayer in 1549.

He was eleven years old.

Marriage vows, in the form 'To have and to hold from this day forward, for better for worse, for richer for poorer, in sickness and in health, to love and to cherish, till death us do part' have been recited at UK church weddings since the publication of Edward's efforts.

His father had amended the rules to marry several times; Edward never married himself but the wedding service that we are all so familiar with in Britain now was written by these two individuals.

Henry VIII didn't really have a religious policy, beyond demanding that the clergy were obedient to him rather than the Pope. He was a greedy, cynical, tyrannical, providential egomaniac who happened to lay the foundations of our modern religious and political tradition. His son merely carried on his good work and Edward VI's legacy is there for all to see and hear whenever you attend a marriage in a British church.

Looking back, he rushed The Book of Common Prayer, written mainly by Cranmer but credited to the boy King. It was important - to him at any rate - but he thought it was urgent and he should have taken more time to fully think through the implications of such a book.

The Book of Common Prayer was the book to which all English people must pray and live by. The book was Edward's attempt at finishing off Catholicism in England.

At a family Christmas party in 1550 with Edward and his two sisters together a family quarrel developed.

Well, it happens.

The 13 year old Edward upbraided his 34 year old sister Mary about her continued devotion to the Catholic religion and daring to break his laws and take Mass. But Mary was having none of it.

When she was next summoned to court a few weeks later she did so with all her cohorts carrying rosaries to hammer home the point she was Catholic. And she had a trump card. Unless Edward allowed her to practice Catholicism she would ask her Spanish cousin, The Holy Roman Emperor, Charles V, to declare war on England.

Quite a family quarrel.

Edward backed down and as it became apparent he would not live long, the issue of succession became a major issue. He needed a male, Protestant relative he liked and his sister didn't fit any of the criteria.

But Mary was, after all, the rightful heir to the throne.

And time was not on his side. Edward's potential would never be realised.

In 1549 Dudley was appointed Lord Admiral. In 1550 he became Grand Master of the Household. In 1551 he became the Duke of Northumberland and also Earl Marshall of England. That was the year Edward Seymour was executed for conspiracy. Then Dudley increased his wealth by taking a great deal of Church land.

Shocking.

Perhaps a little too ambitiously, John Dudley arranged for the marriage of his fourth son, Guildford Dudley to Henry VIII's grand daughter, Lady Jane Grey. And Dudley then persuaded the sickly, fourteen year old Edward to name Lady Jane Grey as his heir. Dudley saw it as important AND urgent.

With Dudley almost certainly standing over him and playing the religious card, Dudley got the King to hand write a document on June 21st 1553 that excluded both Mary and Elizabeth from succeeding to the throne on account of their illegitimacy and his wish that his successor should be Lady Jane Grey.

In his schoolboy handwriting the document he wrote entitled 'My device for the succession' still exists.

My deuise for the succession.

For lakke of issu of my body, To the L Fraunceses heires masles, for lakke of such issu, to the L' Janes heires masles, To the L Katerins heires masles, To the L Maries heires masles, To the heires masles of the daughters wich she shal haue hereafter. Then to the L Margets heires masles. For lakke of such issu, To theires masles of the L Janes daughters To theires masles of the L Katerins daughters and so forth til yow come to the L Margets daughters heires masles.

And with Edward's signature at the bottom, that meant that John Dudley's 17 year old son would be King.

The expansion in Dudley's influence and potential wealth had this happened is difficult to estimate - but politically he would have been all but untouchable. However, there was one major weakness in this plan - it had to work. If it failed, the consequences for anyone associated with it were obvious. If it wasn't to be Lady Jane Grey then there's quite a queue. In addition to Edward's half sisters, Mary and Elizabeth, there was also Edward's aunt, Lady Frances Brandon, who was the daughter of King Henry's younger sister Mary by Charles Brandon.

Looking back it was a very high risk strategy for the Protestant John Dudley. Having been effectively running the country whilst Edward was alive, if his plot to get Jane Grey to be Queen failed it would result in facing the worst of what the staunchly Catholic Mary would throw at him.

And before the end of the summer of 1553, throw she would.

There's a lesson that Dudley didn't learn and that all gamblers need to learn. Don't bet more than you can afford to lose. Especially on a game where you don't know all the rules.

Dudley had not bargained for the instinctive reaction of the people to support the person who they saw as being the legitimate heir to the throne; Mary. As we will see, she fled to East Anglia - the region where Dudley had ruthlessly put down a rebellion. It was an area where there was little support for the man who had done nothing to help the rural poor and where most were conservative and would have had an instinctive loyalty to the daughter of Henry VIII. Having 'lost' Mary, Dudley's supporters in London started to abandon him and he became a very isolated figure.

And there's another lesson from Dudley for anyone who wants to be a leader; we don't want someone we agree with all the time; but we do want someone we trust all the time.

It is rumoured that Dudley cruelly prolonged the illness of Edward, who was in excruciating pain, in order to prepare for the succession of Lady Jane Grey. The King eventually died an agonising death on July 6th 1553 at Greenwich Palace when only 15, possibly from a combination of tuberculosis and the measles. He, like his half-sister Mary, had congenital syphilis from his father, Henry VIII, and his condition was complicated by consumption

Henry had reaped what he had sown well after his death.

Such was the sensitivity of Dudley's scheme that he managed to keep Edward's death secret from most people for three days. In this time he put into being the plan that he had been so careful to construct. Lady Jane Grey, the Protestant 15 year old granddaughter of Henry VIII - who most likely never really wanted to be Queen - was actually proclaimed Queen of England four days after Edward's death.

Lady Jane Grey

Who by? Well, er, John Dudley.

He really was deceiving himself at this point.

Apparently, 94% of university professors believe they are better at their job than their colleagues. Most people think they are better than average. You probably do too. And by definition, that must mean that most people think they are better than most. The question is, does it matter? Is self-deception a good or bad thing in the work place?

Americans George Quattrone and Amos Tversky conducted a classic social psychology experiment to study self-deception. As is often the case in such experiments, the researchers lied to the participants about every aspect of the study. Firstly, they told them the study was about the 'psychological and medical aspects of athletics'. Then they tricked them into believing that a measure of good health could be gauged by the length of time you could submerge your arms in very cold water.

Naturally, this was nonsense. All it showed was how ready they were to deceive themselves and what they would do for fifty dollars. Typically most people could endure the cold water for about 30 seconds. To make participants believe the study was real they were given other tasks to do as well. Walking over hot coals with no shoes on wasn't one of them but it would have made an interesting foot note. Instead, they did a stint on an exercise bike.

Crucially, they were then given a short lecture about how life expectancy depended on your type of heart. Lying through their teeth, and presumably just managing to suppress a giggle, the researchers revealed that there were two types of heart: one associated with poor health and one associated with top class athletes.

Continuing with the porkies, the researchers then said it was possible to tell which type of heart you had by measuring your tolerance to cold water *after* exercise. They'd just worked up a sweat on the bikes, remember. But here's the rub. One half were told that an *increased* tolerance to cold water indicated a strong heart, whilst the other half were told that it was a *decreased* tolerance to cold water.

You can probably guess the outcome. Everybody deceived themselves into believing that they had an athlete's heart by either enduring the cold water for less or more time than previously - depending upon the lie they were told. One man was determined to deceive himself so much he submerged his whole head into the water for three minutes and then called for the hot coals 'for good measure' as he was led away to the ambulance. Or did I just make that up?

No matter. What this study suggests is that for many people self-deception is easy. So if you manage people why not tell them they are very, very, good indeed? Because the more they believe, the better they'll be.

Back to the only period in English history when we had three monarchs in less than a fortnight.

Whilst John Dudley was busy believing in his own omnipotence and making the necessary arrangements for Jane's arrival at the Tower, he asked a few soldiers if they would pop up to Mary's house in Hunsdon in Hertfordshire and make sure she wasn't going to make a fuss.

He had totally underestimated not only the will of the 37 year old daughter of Henry VIII but also the number of supporters she had. Mary had escaped and gone east.

She was, after all, the rightful heir to the throne according to Henry VIII's will.

Meanwhile on July 10th 1553 Lady Jane Grey was brought from Richmond and crowned in the Tower. She and her husband, Guildford Dudley, arrived by barge and as he was much taller than her she wore stilts under her dress so that when they walked in procession she'd look a little taller.

No, I am not making that up.

Stilts.

On her coronation.

Amazing.

One poor chap by the name of Gilbert Potter criticised the crowd for their lack of defiance at Jane's accession to the throne and he was promptly seized and his ears severed 'at the root' for his lack of compliance.

That must have hurt.

At this point as the news spread, people were uncertain who to support. Most played a waiting game. On July 12th Mary moved from Kenninghall and set off for Framlington in Suffolk. On the 13th she arrived in Framlington, the ancient seat of the Howards and the strongest castle in the county. Meanwhile Dudley and his men had arrived in Cambridge only to find she'd fled to Sawston Hall. And when they got there it was only to find she'd moved on again.

So they burnt the place down.

Mary was one step ahead in more ways than one.

Dudley had also dispatched six ships containing nearly 1,000 men to Yarmouth in an attempt to arrest Mary but few of them had any naval experience.

There was a bit of a storm so the largest ship, ‘The Greyhound’, lay at anchor off East Anglia whilst the ship’s master received enticements from both sides to arrest or support Mary.

If they could find her.

In the end he tried to play hard ball and, desperate for wages, food, water and strong leadership the mariners broke open the war chest and distributed the money amongst themselves. The ships’ crews defected to Mary.

News got through to Dudley.

Anyone who has played sport knows that there is a moment in every game that real competitors absolutely dread. It’s the moment when they feel they’re about to lose. There’s a certain mental tipping point which comes to all people in competition, but the real winners react to it differently. And it’s the same when pitching for business too. Just like a boxing match, there’s a feeling that happens at some time in the bout when the competitor feels that he is about to lose; a feeling that today is not going to be his day - a feeling that whatever they’re doing right now just isn’t enough. It’s effectively the crux of almost every fight when the adrenalin is still pumping but the strength seems to be draining out of the boxer.

It's arguably the time when sensible people quit. It could also be argued it's when the quitters quit and the losers lose. Surrender seems like a good bet. Few boxers who find themselves with that feeling manage to turn what seems to be certain defeat into victory. I've seen it so often in football matches where a team is two nil down at half time but most of the losing players still believe they can not only get something out of the game but actually win it. But as the time goes quickly away, so much quicker than the time for the winner, you can actually see the mental belief drain out of the players' faces. As the final whistle approaches only the real winners still believe they can get something out of it. It is arguably chasing a lost cause but for me it is the sign of a real competitor and sometimes it can be turned around.

And ironically just at the time when the losers are beginning to feel there is no hope is just at the time where the winners become complacent and think the match is won. And sporting history is absolutely full of such events. And so it is in life and business. The successful people still believe they can win when the moment comes; when the realisation that you are *about to lose* comes.

Fact is Dudley has played for high stakes and he's lost.

Mary and her followers rode into London and imprisoned Jane and her supporters. Mary was the next Queen of England.

Jane had been Queen for nine days.

Hell hath no fury like a woman scorned. Once Mary became Queen in July 1553 Jane and her husband were thrown in the Tower of London. John Dudley was executed for treason at Tower Hill on August 22nd 1553.

Power corrupts.

Absolute power corrupts absolutely.

There is something rather ridiculous really about the monarch. He or she is shut off from the rest of the world, cosseted, fated and lauded. Yet the business of a King or Queen requires them to know their country and its people. And it is the pride of Kings and Queens that has created so many wars.

To the incongruous farce that is monarchy we have then added hereditary succession. Or, rather, *they* did. No one by birth should have a right to set up his own family in perpetual preference to all others for ever.

But in 1553 you were strung up on a strong length of rope for saying things like that.

Dudley and all the other people around Edward VI were far more concerned with their own personal futures. It was very important to them but the actions taken were not in the best interests of the country or the throne. The actions were in the best interests solely of Dudley and his court. And, as I see it, so it is in most people's lives.

So who was this young man? Edward VI became King in January 1547 and died in July 1553 at the age of fifteen, never more than a puppet king who was beaten by his tutors and had to beg his uncle for pocket money whilst the adult Protestant adults were profiting economically from the dissolution of the monasteries. Edward's body lay unburied until August 8th, when it was interred in Westminster Abbey under Protestant rites by his eventual successor, his sister Mary. The Protestant service was carried out by his godfather, Thomas Cranmer, whilst Mary had masses said for the soul of her young brother at the Tower.

Even in death they were sticking to their fervently held religious beliefs that, in time, would lead to many more untimely deaths.

It's time for chapter 14 and The Fourth Golden Rule.

Chapter 14 ~ The Fourth Golden Rule

People often ask me the secret of good time management and I always reply with the same words. 'Ask me another time when I'm not running late.'

Only kidding.

Good time management lies in the ability to distinguish between the important and the urgent. For instance a leaking roof requires urgent attention, whilst it's merely important to fix a loose roof tile.

Once you've made the distinction, you then need to allocate time to do the important things. That's the 'secret' of good time management. If you fail to allocate time for things that are 'important but not urgent' then one of two things usually happens. Either the roof eventually leaks and the problem becomes urgent or the roof doesn't leak and the problem doesn't get fixed at all. And, of course, if you wait until something becomes urgent, it's usually more difficult and costly to fix.

There are exceptions, of course. lastminute.com can offer some great deals if you put off your decision to the last minute. But the trade-off is that you might not get exactly what you want. And, in life, we usually know what we want. My wife is still fuming about that sky-diving package I bought her. It was an absolute bargain.

Once things become important and urgent they have to be done in a hurry. But when you allocate time for things that are important but not urgent you are forward planning.

So fix your roof when the sun is shining. Creosote that fence before the bad weather comes. Pack your suitcase before leaving home. I know that last one doesn't quite fit but I was struggling for a third and it's still reasonably sound advice.

But what if you fail to allocate time and things don't get done at all? You never do get to see Naples or take that African safari. Those Salsa lessons you promised yourself are now a distant dream thanks to your arthritic hip. And imagine if your family never has the pleasure of hearing you play the tuba. Actually, that's probably a good thing.

If you don't allocate time for things that are 'important but not urgent' then you run the risk of never doing them at all. And you may live the rest of your life with regret. Particularly when you get towards the end and can no longer do what was once important but not urgent.

However, distinguishing between things that are important but not urgent is only one part of the task. You also need to be able to prioritise what you do. The best way is often by writing them down in a list. People often complain that they have so much to do they don't know where to start. Well, if you write a list, you will know exactly where to start.

At the top.

Giving things priority over others is how many people enjoy success and happiness. Premier League football managers have long since learned that there are certain trophies that their club can never win. So they prioritise the competitions in order to maximise their chances of picking up some silverware. Even the big clubs know that their superiority in terms of players and depth of squad is unlikely to see them winning every competition they enter. So they prioritise and concentrate on the Premier League, or the Champions League, or the domestic cups.

As you may have experienced, airlines are fond of creating priority services to attract extra revenue. For instance, you can take advantage of priority check-in and priority boarding. You don't take off any sooner, you just get to sit in your seat for longer. And, of course, in the event of an emergency, it's women, children and motivational speakers first.

Well, someone's got to cheer up everyone in the lifeboats.

I recently presented my priority boarding pass at the security gate of Amsterdam's Schipol Airport, a notorious portal for drug and diamond smuggling. Naturally, I was accorded the VIP treatment my priority status deserved. They warmed up the glove and applied extra lube. Ryanair would charge you for that.

If you fail to prioritise it can lead to doing things in a haphazard and inefficient way. In the infamous case of the Yorkshire Ripper in the mid to late seventies, the police team was overwhelmed with information during a five year manhunt. Back then, of course, they didn't have computers to help digest and analyse this information. Everything was kept on thousands of index cards. Nevertheless, it is said that if they had prioritised their lines of enquiry the case may have been solved long before Peter Sutcliffe's eventual arrest. Instead, they were sidetracked by copycat murders and hoax calls, as well as misleading tapes and letters. Sutcliffe himself was interviewed and released no less than twelve times.

It's important to distinguish the urgent things from the important things, and also prioritise how you deal with them. So do that business planning. Fix that meeting with a key potential customer. Make that call that is important but not urgent.

If you are calling an existing client you may well find that complacency has settled into the relationship and that the call can unearth a problem that can be nipped in the bud.

Fix the roof and paint the fence. Spend more time with those closest to you unless it happens to be a stalker when you should walk more quickly and try not to panic. Enjoy your time with elderly parents or grandchildren before it's too late. Above all, have fun. It's important that you do, even though it often doesn't seem the most urgent thing.

The Fourth Golden Rule:

Allocate time for things that are important but not urgent

As I say, if you don't allocate time for things that are important but not urgent one of two things happens. Most often they become important *and* urgent AND DON'T GET DONE AS WELL.

Good planning takes time and it needs a Devil's Advocate. Good planning means adhering to The Second Golden Rule too; thinking about how you are going to treat people and the implications for both of you. Spending time doing things that are important but not urgent also means that you are thinking about the future more.

Good planning also means adhering to The First Golden Rule. What have you learned from what you have done right and what have you learned from what you have done badly?

It's almost as though these Golden Rules have been thought about...

Arguably the human being is the only animal that actually thinks about the future and it is this aspect that distinguishes happy and successful people from those who are not. They do things and make decisions based on what will happen not just now but also in the future.

If you don't allocate time for things that are important but not urgent and you never get to do them, you live your life with regret. So allocate time to spend with your children and the ones you love. Remember, having fun with the people who are closest to you is important but often doesn't seem urgent.

We aren't here long. Fun is underrated and under valued. And so we live our 4,000 weeks or so in life without allocating enough time to having fun with our children. And whilst some people do leave a legacy in business, literature and the arts, most people's legacy is quite simply their children.

Allocating time for things that are important but not urgent means that not only do you plan your time better, plan your fun and plan your holidays, but also you plan your own career better. I meet too many people who started life as a plasterer when they were aged sixteen or started working for a car hire company when they were seventeen and they are still doing that fifty years later.

And wished they had made different decisions many years ago. And rightly or wrongly they now feel it's too late to change.

If they've enjoyed doing whatever it is they do and fulfilled their potential that's absolutely fine. Indeed, the man who told me that he had the best job in the world - and was extremely happy as a result - was a man who ran a stretch of canal in the North of England for British Waterways. Not everyone's cup of tea, but it was *his*. Unfortunately I meet too many people in their fifties who are just waiting for retirement in their sixties. And all that came about because they didn't know The Fourth Golden Rule; you have to allocate time for things that are important but not urgent.

It's mainly about planning for the future and organising fun.

I am writing this in Paradise Bay in New South Wales, Australia. It is probably one of the most tranquil and pleasant spots on the planet to write about A Golden Rule. As I walk up and down the beach each morning I reflect on the fact that I am here - whilst in England it is snowing - because I decided some years ago that I wanted to change the weather in February. It was important for my wife and I to change the weather in February and to be able to live in a warmer climate. But it was never going to be urgent. So it required a great deal of planning and forethought. Indeed, it took some years to get to the point where I can stroll up and down on a beach on a sunny day in Australia in February every year. And make money whilst I'm here too.

Poor young Edward VI never really got a chance to do very much at all. His reign had lasted from January 1547 to July 1553. Just six years on the throne and never saw his sixteenth birthday. Fact is none of us are here very long and most of us achieve very little that lasts longer than our own life time. Those who do leave a good legacy have usually abided by The Fourth Golden Rule.

The Fourth Golden Rule:

Allocate time for things that are important but not urgent

Back to 1553. Mary is the new Queen of England.

Time for everyone to change horses.

PART FOUR
THE REIGN OF HENRY VIII'S DAUGHTER, MARY I

Chapter 15 ~ 'Make Mine A Bloody Mary'

1553 — 1558

In July 1553 the eldest daughter of King Henry VIII, the Catholic Mary Tudor, became Queen. She was incandescent with rage, ready to change anything and everything her little brother had put in place and no time to sleep on it.

Despite being given new information as she came to the throne she was in a hurry to change things based on what she believed. People were about to die.

Mary's resentment of her younger brother was obvious for all to see when the first Parliament of Mary's reign met in October 1553. They basically dismantled the whole legal framework of the English reformation. In addition to completely taking apart the religious enactments of Edward's short reign it also passed an act invalidating Henry VIII's divorce from Katherine of Aragon thus in one fell swoop making Elizabeth a religious outcast and a bastard to boot. Mary had suffered and it was time to get her own back.

Queen Mary

And the small matter of her successor was immediately brought to the fore. She was, after all, 37 years old, single, a woman and had no children. Mary ignored all the advice around her not to marry a Spaniard but, being half Spanish herself, she saw her nephew as the ideal partner to bring England back into the fold of her Mother's church. Relations between Mary and Elizabeth very quickly became strained and despite Elizabeth's affirmation that she was devoted to the Catholic faith, Mary's hostility was deeply ingrained. On November 16th 1553 there was a deputation from the House of Commons formally requesting the Queen to marry an Englishman but she seemed set to start her reign simply doing as she pleased.

And as so many chief executives find, it's not easy to break up well established factions. Not for the first time in history we reflect that absolute power corrupts and that it could all have been sorted out with a sit down, a cup of tea and asking some decent questions establishing each other's motives.

If you've ever been the new kid on the block, you'll know how difficult it is to have your views accepted by the 'established group'. For instance, imagine you've joined a new company and you're attending a think tank to discuss a problem which is new to them, but old hat to you. Something you experienced and dealt with in your previous job. In theory, your views should be welcomed with open arms. But in practice, it's more likely to be open mouths. Who does this up-start think he is? He's only been here five minutes.

This group behaviour is what Psychologist Matthew Hornsey from the University of Queensland calls 'Unreasoning hostility'. It consists of having your views largely ignored or over-looked.

In my house it's called parenting.

Anyway, to test the theory, Matthew's researchers asked 200 health professionals for their opinions on criticism levelled at their hospital by an independent observer. However, whilst one half were led to believe that the critic was a newcomer who had worked there only three weeks, the other half were told that they were the views of someone who had worked at the hospital for 18 years. Naturally, the criticisms were *identical*, with the only difference being the apparent source.

As suspected, the views of the 'newcomer' were thought to carry less weight than those of the 'old-timer'. What's more, their criticism was also seen as *less* constructive whilst their suggestions were more readily dismissed by the health professionals.

So, as a newcomer, how do you worm your way into a group's affections and begin to generate influence? The answer is to tread carefully and gain acceptance *first.* Once you become part of the group you can begin to make all manner of recommendations, however absurd. Newly appointed cabinet ministers are prime examples. For instance, you wouldn't ask the Minister for Transport for expert advice on a schools matter. You'd wait until the cabinet re-shuffle next week and ask him when he's Minister for Education.

Bottom line is you have to be part of the group. A fully paid-up member of the club. One of them. You see, consciously or otherwise, people want others to value *their* group as much as *they* do. So distancing yourself from an old group or employer increases your perceived allegiance to the new one. And criticism from a committed group member is seen as much more valid. In effect, it sweetens the bitter pill of reality.

Of course, the temptation when joining a new group is to try to make a big splash and impress others with your critical perceptions and new ideas. It's what Queen Mary did; thinking that on the grounds she was Queen she could do as she pleased and ride rough shod over established groups and their ways of thinking.

But this research tells us that toeing the line in the first instance is often the best long-term strategy.

Even if you are a Queen.

Remember, groups are hostile to criticism from newcomers and are likely to resist, dismiss or ignore it. Until you can prove your loyalty.

So if you're a newcomer and want to gain influence and promote change in your new surroundings make sure you get well-established first. Because sometimes being right just isn't enough.

She may have been Queen but she was still effectively a newcomer to the group of people who had been running the country.

Before the end of October 1553 she had agreed to marry.

As a child Mary had been betrothed to various suitors. In 1518, when she was two, she was betrothed to the heir to King Francis I, a little later to her cousin, Charles V, the Holy Roman Emperor and when Queen Claude of France died, King Francis I offered himself as a husband. On her accession English hopes were pinned on the 25 year old great-grandson of Edward IV, Edward Courtney. His mother was a friend and confidant of Mary's and the match had the approval of the Privy Councillor. But Mary quickly made it clear she wanted a Spaniard.

No time to sleep on it. No time to think it through. No time to work out the ramifications.

She married Philip of Spain on July 25th 1554. He was to become King of Spain in 1556.

King Philip II of Spain

And yet another newcomer to the group.

From Philip's point of view he'd married his Portugese cousin as a teenager so why not marry his English aunty? He was 26, Mary was 38. If he didn't marry her then his father would probably get in first.

I am not making that up.

On marrying King Philip of Spain, Mary was first rather grandiosely titled Queen of England, France, Naples, Jerusalem and Ireland.

And Mary was to be the second of Philip's four wives; in chronological order they were a Portugese Princess, an English Queen, a French Princess and finally the daughter of the Roman Emperor. He introduced the Spanish inquisition to the New World. He made it to his 70's too.

Quite impressive really.

So, as Queen, Mary proceeded to undo many of Edward's Protestant reforms. Mary, remember, was the daughter of Katherine of Aragon and a devout Catholic. She earned the sobriquet, 'Bloody Mary' due to the number of Protestant Tudors who were executed during her reign. In 1554 Papal authority was re-established in England and the following year Parliament repealed the antipapal laws of Henry VIII and restored the ecclesiastical courts. They didn't restore the church property funnily enough. So lot's of religious persecutions and hundreds burned at the stake including some big names.

In 1563 John Foxe wrote of Mary's tyranny in his book 'Acts and Monuments' better known as 'The Book of Martyrs'.

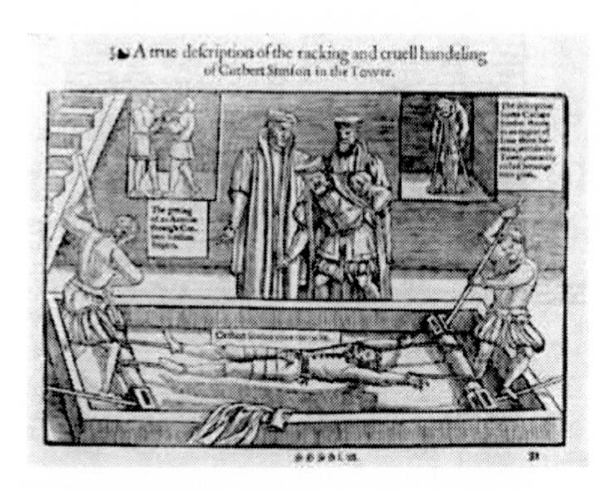

An illustration from John Foxe's Book of Martyrs

At the time it was the second best read book after The Bible. It details the persecutions of people who chose simply to be Catholic rather than Protestant. And that meant that many Protestants came to either fear or hate Catholics. It teaches the lesson we have already learned - that unrestrained power - in this case in the hands of clergy - corrupts both the state and the church.

Those who could read for themselves learned the full details of all the atrocities performed on the Protestant reformers; the illiterate could see the crude illustrations of the various instruments of torture, the rack, the gridiron, the boiling oil and then the holy ones breathing out their souls amid the flames.

Philip the Spaniard got England involved in the existing war between Spain and France and we lost that little bit of Northern France.

Yes, eventually Calais has become French.

There was some interesting literary output during Mary's rule. Just before Mary's death another John, John Knox, wrote 'The first blast of the trumpet against the monstrous regiment of women.'

Great title but slightly dodgy train of thought. As we've discussed before, once people have a view and an opinion and a belief they can find evidence to support it. And he weighed in against women rulers quoting from the ancient fathers and citing various biblical texts to prove that they were incapable of wielding power. To quote from one bit of his book it was 'repugnant to nature, contumely to God, contrarious to his revealed will and approved ordinance' to allow women to have any kind of domination over a nation.

Looking back he must have had an unhappy life as a woman was to be on the throne for a good forty five years after he wrote the book. What is it that possesses people to have such strong views based simply on opinion? What is it that allows someone to spend a lifetime being unhappy because things have changed and they don't like the change?

We live in a world of constant change. It has always been thus. John Knox was not willing to accept a change that was staring him in the face. A woman is your monarch - get over it. It's a lesson we all need to learn:

If you're not part of the steam roller, you're part of the road.

If you had to sum up Mary's rule in one word it would probably be 'strife'. Mary had her younger sister, Elizabeth, imprisoned at Woodstock Palace; saw little of her husband who was eleven years her junior and Queen Mary I of England died in 1558 at the age of 42. Childless, alienated, lonely, despised by her husband and hated by her own people.

Quite a legacy.

A key task if you want to be a leader is to get people to commit to doing things for you; not by getting them to do what you want them to do, but by getting them to *want* to do what you want them to do. Arguably people ask three questions of their leaders and people back in the 1550's were asking those three questions of Mary. Can I trust you, do you know where we are going and do you care about me?

She failed on all three counts. It was her younger sister who was to show the way.

People didn't trust Mary because she made bad, selfish decisions. People thought she didn't care about their rights to choose how to worship and she appeared to not really know where she was going. She appeared to have no real vision for a better England.

Four hundred years later in the movie 'South Pacific' it was another Bloody Mary, this time the philosopher of the South Sea island who sang 'you got to have a dream, if you don't have a dream, how you gonna have a dream come true?'

Juanita Hall - Bloody Mary from the 1958 movie 'South Pacific'

Mary seems to not have had any 'Happy talk'. When she did talk about the things she'd like to do they were destructive and created more factions.

So here is our next lesson; if you don't have a dream how you gonna make a dream come true?

And there's a corollary to this lesson. Mary didn't seem to have a plan other than produce an heir and get the country back to Catholicism. She wanted to turn back the clock and have things as they were. Well, apart from the fact that she and her cohorts quite liked owning more Church land and being Head of The Church. Not easy giving away what you once had. But she appeared not to have a dream of things getting better; for her or her subjects. She probably laughed at those who did. So here's the corollary:

Never laugh at anyone's dreams. People who don't have dreams, don't have much.

But if you really want to be happy you have to turn your dream into a specific goal, then turn that goal into an action plan and then take action. It always starts with a single step.....

Mary's short reign is only now remembered for the murders for which she was responsible; for the bitterness which seems to have been concentrated into her last years. Long an invalid, she had had more than one serious illness during her life. By all accounts she loved her husband but Philip had never returned this affection, and when the hope of her bearing him an heir proved to be a frustrating and embarrassing illusion he treated her with contempt and quit England forever.

She was even responsible for the loss of Calais and this was followed by misunderstandings with the Bishops in Rome for which she had sacrificed so much. No wonder the Queen sank under this accumulated weight of disappointments. Mary died almost piously, as she had always lived. In January 1558 she thought she was six months pregnant. At the end of March she wrote her will making it clear that in the event of her death the crown would be left to 'the heirs, issue and fruit of my body.'

By May most people were doing the maths.

By August she admitted that it was possible she wasn't pregnant. In early November she accepted she was actually near death and not child birth, consented to an agreement that her sister was her rightful heir and asked that Elizabeth keep the Catholic faith.

The word 'forlorn' was quite possibly invented at that time.

In the 12 years from the start of 1547 to the end of 1558 England has had five monarchs, a few wars, burnings at the stake, beheadings and having had a dramatic shift from Catholicism to the Protestant faith under Henry VIII and his young son, we've now had an equally violent move back to Catholicism whilst the monarch rather cynically hangs on to 'The Divine Right of Kings'.

In the 17th century King James's son - Charles I - would go on to famously take his father's struggle with Parliament to unprecedented levels. With his fierce belief in 'The Divine Right of Kings' the last years of Charles's reign were to be marked by the outbreak of the English Civil War, which would see Britain torn apart as the King's Cavalier supporters took on Oliver Cromwell and his Parliamentarian Army. The monarchy would be overthrown and a commonwealth established. The second surviving son of King Charles I, James would be the last Roman Catholic monarch and it would be his religious disposition that would lead to his Protestant son-in-law William of Orange to, in turn, depose him.

How things could have turned out differently if Henry had not created 'The Divine Right of Kings', Mary not been so hell bent on insisting that everyone of her subjects had to practice her preferred religion. Perhaps the events of Bloody Sunday in Derry on January 30th 1972 would not have taken place? Those events effectively marked the end of the non-violent campaign for civil rights in Northern Ireland and the start of decades of hurt. Events that were discussed for 38 years before the British Government formally apologised for the 'unjustified and unjustifiable' killing of 14 civil rights marchers by British soldiers. Lord Saville's inquiry and long-awaited report showed soldiers lied about their involvement in the killings and that all of those who died were innocent.

What ifs, maybes and if onlys.

On the morning of November 17th 1558 the 25 year old daughter of Anne Boleyn, Elizabeth, was strolling the grounds of the estate where she lived in Hatfield. And this is the day she is going to be told she has become the Queen of England.

The last of Henry's children is coming to the throne.

And she's Protestant. And she doesn't like the Spanish.

Here we go again.

At least this time there will be 44 years on the throne; a chance for some valuable stability.

And we all need that. In business and in life. We all need to know what direction we're going in. The more people in business are focused on deciding which horse to back and how best to manouvre politically, the less actually gets done.

Look at the success that football teams like Manchester United and Arsenal have had by sticking with the same manager and the fiascos that are Newcastle United and Leeds United.

People want stability and purpose. And then they can focus on the job.

It's coming up to Christmas 1558 and we have a new Queen. Time for Chapter 16 and The Golden Rule we could and should have learned from Mary's five year tenure.

Chapter 16 ~ The Fifth Golden Rule

Decisions, decisions, decisions. Every day, we all have to make them. Sometimes they have to be 'snap', other times we can afford them more consideration. Occasionally they're hard, sometimes they're easy. The trick, quite obviously, is to get them right more times than you get them wrong.

But how?

Sleep on it. That's right, it really does work. You see, the subconscious mind is brilliant at sorting out all the plusses and minusses associated with making a complex decision. That's because, unlike the conscious mind, it has a greater capacity to process lots of different information and doesn't get sidetracked with pre-conceived ideas or notions. Instead of jumping to a conclusion, it weighs up all the variables and leads you more often than not to the correct solution. That's why so many successful businessmen rely on their instinct or 'gut feel' to tell them what to do.

Of course, there'll always be a place for the rational, conscious mind to make decisions. If there wasn't we wouldn't have to get out of bed in the morning. We'd just have to work out how to get rid of the bed sores. And that's one problem that can't be solved by sleeping on it. For instance, the conscious mind is very good at applying clear, concrete rules. Like figuring out that if we pick up a hot coal it's going to smart a little. But ask it to compute a complex problem with lots of variables and it gets in a bit of a lather. We sweat, we panic, we feel dizzy, we go down the pub, have a few drinks and go home to bed. Then, miraculously the next day, everything becomes clear and we have the answer.

The only problem now is remembering the question.

And here's the proof. Psychologist Ap Dijksterhuis of the University of Amsterdam conducted a series of experiments to compare conscious and subconscious thinking. People were given twelve bits of information about four big topics and asked to make a decision. Each topic had a clear 'best decision' that the researchers were looking for. The first group had to decide immediately, with no time for analysis; the second were asked to reason the problem through before deciding; whilst the third group were given the information and then immediately distracted with another subject before being asked to make a snap decision.

This third group, who had only ever been given the chance to think about the problems subconsciously consistently, arrived at 'the best decision'. So the next time you arrive home in the wee small hours and stay awake half the night concocting a story to tell your partner, don't be surprised when they jump to the right conclusion the next morning having been furnished with only the barest of details. It's a gut thing.

Fact is, the bigger the decision, the more important it is to sleep on it.

It's a lesson our first female Queen to rule outright would have benefited from learning.

Mary Tudor had lived for 42 fairly eventful years. Her hand in marriage had been promised to a variety of Kings with a vow that all the other more interesting bits would soon follow. But it never seemed to work out. *They* liked hunting, shooting and fishing and *she* was into needlecraft. You just don't bridge those sort of gaps.

She had been a pawn in her father's diplomatic intrigues and later a thorn in his side when it came to his divorce from Katherine. Not surprisingly, she remained loyal to her mother as well as to the Roman Catholic Church for whom she knitted endless doilies. All this meant that she spent the entire years of her father's reign in complete misery. She was separated from her mother, denied presence at court, treated as illegitimate, and forced to serve her half-sister, Elizabeth, as a lady in waiting.

On the upside, she did get to spit in her food.

To cap it all, her plans to escape to the continent failed miserably due to a porters' strike at Folkestone. As she said at the time "Of all the friggin' days."

By 1536 she was a beaten woman and finally agreed to acknowledge herself as illegitimate and to repudiate her church, despite never actually believing a word she said.

During the reign of her young half-brother, Teddy, things had got even worse. Protestantism had spread like the Plague only without all the bodies in the streets. It was only when she found enough support to get rid of the usurper, Lady Jane Grey, that she cheered up a little.

After her father's antipapal laws had been torn to shreds she began the religious persecutions that lasted for the rest of her reign.

The number burned at the stake amounted to almost 300 and included such eminent figures as Nicholas Ridley and John Rogers, Hugh Latimer and Thomas Cranmer. The latter reportedly went bravely to his death taunting Mary with an impromptu rendition of 'Come on baby, light my fire' as she bent down with a box of Swan Vestas. Two entrepreneurs, William Bryant and Francis May, were not burned at the stake but it's thought that Mary's arsonistic tendencies inspired them to set up a safety match company in the mid 1800's. But, to be honest, it's only me that thinks that. These acts of vengeance, together with her habit of pricking her finger when needle crafting, gave her the epithet of 'Bloody Mary'.

So what do we learn not only from the bloody pointlessness of Mary's reign but that of her younger brother too? What was gained by this lack of tolerance by one set of worshippers for another? Were the monarch's subjects the better for the cleansing of Catholics from 1547 to 1553 and then Protestants from 1553 to 1558? And who needs rhetorical questions any way?

In a debate we often hear the retort, 'Well, each to his own' as a rather lazy way of bringing an uncomfortable discussion to a close. Sometimes a conclusion is just the place where you got tired of thinking. 'Live and let live' is the sort of phrase that brings informal debates on religion to an end. But they are not just escape hatches for those who either want to leave a debate or to try and water it down.

Bad guys need locking up. We can't just stand aside. In chapter five we commented on how William Wilberforce had emphasised that slavery would not come to an end unless people took action; that all that was necessary for the triumph of evil is that good men do nothing. It isn't always better to pursue peace than justice. Just be careful if you frequently speak your mind. You don't have to go around hating and making others feel your pain.

There are plenty of people telling you how to live your life. You don't have to convert people to *your* way of thinking if their behaviour is legal, decent and fair to others. If people are living their lives by The First Four Golden Rules; if they are learning lessons when they have not done the right thing, treating others well, if they are not omnipotent and have a Devil's Advocate - and if they allocate time for things that are important but not urgent, then you can apply The Fifth Golden Rule:

Ago quod permissum ago, operor non tolerate iniquitas et illigitimi non carborundum.

And remember that life's too short not to smell the flowers along the way.

Allow me to explain.

Ago quod permissum ago is Latin for live and let live.

But life isn't quite that simple. We can't just hang around while the bad guys do their stuff and we have to accept there are things we cannot change. As Reinhold Niebuhr wrote in his now famous 'Serenity Prayer'; God grant me the serenity to accept the things I cannot change; the courage to change the things I can and the wisdom to know the difference.

And maybe that is the real essence of The Fifth Golden Rule; ago quod permissum ago, operor non tolerate iniquitas.

Don't allow injustice.

And illigitimi non carborundum?

That's right, don't let the bastards grind you down.

Many people won't like what you have to say, how you present yourself, or what you do. Accept that the world is not perfect and people don't always see the world as you do. Accept people can have a different view to you.

Queen Mary didn't do any of that. She did a lot of fire-branding and needle craft but the only thing she ever accepted was gifts. If she had accepted that the two religions could live side by side in harmony and embraced her sister as her natural successor we would now live in a better place. The whole of the UK would look like the Cotswolds but with more services. As it was, in 1558, with her health rapidly fading, she wrote a cynical codicil to her will. She stated that she 'would be succeeded by her heir and successor by the laws and statutes of this realm.' She was referring, of course, to her half sister, Elizabeth, but Mary couldn't even bring herself to write her name.

A simple 'Our Liz' would have done it.

To add to her woes in the few years she was on the throne, Mary's husband left her to go to the Netherlands and didn't come back for two years. He'd only popped out for some smokes but got a little disorientated after just a few puffs. As he said, on his return, "That's seriously good gear. Have a bunch of tulips. Now what was it I came back for?"

Once his head was straight he remembered that he'd returned in order to enter England into the existing war raging between Spain and France. The chief result was the loss of Calais - no big deal - and the increasing hostility of the English people towards Mary. Quite a big deal. And then, to top it all, her general ill health meant she died young and childless with just a pin cushion for comfort.

Was there ANY fun in her life? Did she ever stop and smell the flowers along the way? Was she ever appreciative of the little things in life? Was there joy in the family? And who needs rhetori…oh, I've done that one.

Not everyone is cut out for a life in business that has them striving for the next dollar. People have different needs and desires; people have different comfort zones and some will live a happy and successful life if they pretty much stay in them.

And there's nothing wrong with that.

But regardless of whether you are in business or follow a vocation where money is not the main measure of 'success', you need to smell the flowers along the way.

And for more than one just for the joy of doing it. When work's driving you mad, go out and talk to the trees. Trees and fields help you think.

Allow me to explain.

It's often said that a change is as good as a rest. And that's particularly true if you've been sitting at your desk all day working on the same project. Apparently, if you go on for too long without a break your brain simply stops functioning properly. So instead of soldiering on, you need to take a step back.

In fact, better still, take a step outside for a breath of fresh air. Because, according to a study by Berman et al, it really can pay dividends.

The bad news is that if your office is in the middle of a town or city, the benefits of a walk may be somewhat tempered by the distraction of passing traffic. But if you can get to a nice piece of tranquil parkland where you can amble peacefully through the undergrowth, threatened only by the occasional woodland creature foraging for food, then you can really re-set your brain box button.

You see, researchers have concluded that the scenery on your little sojourn is a vital part of re-charging your batteries. And if you want to return to your desk refreshed and revitalised then you need the healing powers of nature. Magnificent trees, pretty flowers, possibly a lake or pond, maybe even a babbling brook – all have the desired soothing affect. Obviously, if you witness someone setting fire to a sleeping tramp or drowning in a boating lake, that's a different matter. Call the emergency services immediately and then head straight to the pub for a stiff drink.

Marc Berman at the University of Michigan studied the effect of scenery on cognitive function. In the first of his two studies, people were given a mentally tiring task to perform that involved repeating lots of random numbers back to the experimenter in reverse order. And then they were sent out for a walk - one group around a pleasant arboretum and the other down a busy city street. On their return they each repeated the memory test.

The results showed that those who went for a wander amongst the trees improved their performance by almost 20%. By comparison, those whose walk took them down a busy street achieved no appreciable improvement in their score. On the upside, they did come back with fizzy pop and fast food to keep them going in the afternoon.

Even just looking at a picture of a tranquil scene as opposed to a busy cityscape can induce a calming effect that improved performance – though not as dramatically as actually going for a walk in the woods.

You're probably wondering why this is. Well, our attention is grabbed by whatever is most immediate to our survival. For instance, the danger posed by oncoming traffic when crossing a road will be foremost in our mind. By comparison natural scenes don't engage our 'involuntary attention' and we can let our minds wander free and relax.

Still can't see the wood for the trees? You need to get out more.

The Fifth Golden Rule:

Live and let live

But don't live with injustice

Smell the flowers along the way

Et illigitimi non carborundum

It's 1558 and we have a new CEO. Time for Chapter 17.

PART FIVE

THE REIGN OF HENRY VIII'S DAUGHTER, ELIZABETH I

Chapter 17 ~ Elizabeth ~ CEO of England Ltd.

1558 — 1559

On November 17th 1558 Elizabeth became Queen of England and Ireland. No one would have predicted that this woman would reign until 1603 when she was 69 years old.

And never marry.

She spoke six languages, could instill as much fear as her father ever could and was ready to fend off other claimants to the throne such as Mary's Spanish husband, Philip and also Mary, Queen of Scots who was Henry VII's undisputed granddaughter. She had sworn to her older sister, Mary, that she was a staunch Catholic to survive being beheaded but she was Protestant and proud to be Head of the Church.

Basically she was 25 years old and ready for the challenge.

We will see that she has learned the First Five Golden Rules and we will learn The Sixth Golden Rule from this remarkable woman's reign. The Sixth Golden Rule is the single most important thing to do in business, life and everything. If you live your life just by this one rule you will have a happier, more fulfilled and happier life.

Guaranteed.

When Elizabeth came to the throne it's important to remember that whilst only 25 years old she came to the position of CEO of England having learned more than most 25 year olds about fear, tragedy, disgrace and performance. Back in March 1554 Elizabeth had been conveyed downriver in pouring rain on Palm Sunday from Whitehall assuming that she was going to meet her end in the Tower. But by all accounts, although disgraced and in danger of her life, she never showed the terror in her eyes. A lifetime in the public eye had instilled in her the instincts of a real performer and she played her part as the victim of a great injustice very well. She even staged her own one woman sit down strike ensuring that one of her gentlemen ushers actually broke down in sobs.

Elizabeth I

She'd learned expediency; she'd learned to go down on her knees in humble obeisance to Mary to save her life and give herself some sort of comfort. Elizabeth had learned to even unceremoniously reject Mary's invitations to court knowing that the supposedly friendly overtures were more motivated by weakness than affection.

At 25 she had already learned how to use power.

By 1558 she had learned the strategy of acquiescence; she had learned to go with the flow and learned the importance of understanding the motives of her enemies. Like many chief executives, at the start of her reign there was someone else who thought they should have had the job.

And that was the Francophile Mary; Queen of Scots.

Elizabeth's cousin.

But at noon on November 17th 1558 Elizabeth was formally proclaimed Queen outside the Palace of Westminster. The English had grown weary of Mary's rule but they knew that the company, England Ltd, had formidable problems and the Kingdom was weak and divided. Conflict with the Scottish on one side, the forever ongoing war with the French on the other; overcharged with debt, the people distracted with different and very strong opinions on religion, and no consort for the Queen.

Even Calais had gone.

Only three days after her sister's death, Elizabeth is known to have said "The burden that has fallen upon me maketh me amazed". Or, in today's language, it's in an even bigger mess than I thought it was.

Whilst Elizabeth was not obviously the first female ruler of the country she was the first one who was untroubled by feelings of inadequacy simply on account of her being female. At a time when women were classed as inferior beings, she didn't try to directly challenge the assumptions that women were weak, frail, impatient and foolish but rather, held that as a sovereign appointed by God the conventions that governed attitudes between the sexes were simply not applicable to her. As we learned from the reign of Henry VIII, everyone needs a good Devil's Advocate. Every CEO needs at least one colleague he or she can rely on, someone to trust, someone to question their decisions but also someone to stand up for him or her in their absence. And the better the choice the more likely the reign of CEO is going to be a good one.

Only three days after she came to the throne and whilst still at Hatfield, she appointed Sir William Cecil her Principle Secretary of State. He was 38 years old and the son of a minor official at Henry VIII's court. He'd been to Saint John's College Cambridge, had a grounding in law and even been briefly imprisoned in the Tower on Protector Somerset's fall.

Cecil had reluctantly endorsed the project to put Lady Jane Grey on the throne but not been punished by Mary for doing so. He'd remained a clear Protestant yet been able to perform some minor tasks for Queen Mary travelling to Brussels at her request in order to escort Cardinal Pole to England.

Elizabeth spotted that this man was loyal to her faith but understood about changing horses.

She had learned one of the lessons that Henry VIII would have done well to learn; don't let a little dispute ruin a great friendship.

Cecil had had regular dealings with Elizabeth and within hours of Mary's death Cecil had already been at work on the new Queen's behalf, making arrangements to ensure European Princes knew of Mary's death, that the accession went smoothly and jockeying himself into position to be seen by Elizabeth in a good light.

And Elizabeth wanted to show to him that she could be trusted too. They were acquaintances but both recognised the benefits of developing a good, business based relationship.

Turning an acquaintance into a business associate is hard. Making them a friend is even harder. There are endless reasons why people fail to connect. And just like a marriage can break down, so too can a business relationship. But how do you prevent it from happening? Well, in a personal relationship you could start by sending more flowers and remembering the kids' birthdays. But in business?

Psychologists tell us that we tend to like those people who disclose intimate secrets more than those who don't. Maybe it's a trust thing. After all, if someone's open enough about their penchant for cross-dressing, surely they wouldn't lie about their business plans? However, when someone you've only just met starts pouring out their heart to you, it's a different story. Rather than lend a sympathetic ear, you're more likely to want to change seats on the train or join another supermarket checkout queue. I mean, you only went out for a pint of milk, right?

However, it's also true that people disclose *more* to those they like. So if that nutter on the train happens to be a major buyer in your industry it's probably best to smile politely and hear him out. Similarly, people tend to prefer those to whom they have made personal disclosures. So again, stick with it.

The trick seems to be not to disclose too much, too soon or too often. Take internet dating. Research suggests that the way internet daters reveal information about themselves provides clues to developing good relationships. Apparently, self-disclosure in terms of earnest conversations about your deepest hopes and fears is to be avoided. So no initial chat about global warming, quantitative easing or social unrest. Stick to your favourite music, food and books and a relationship will be formed more quickly.

Communicating online also gives you more control over the way you present yourself. Webcams excepted, nobody can see the nonverbal communication that a face-to-face conversation reveals. Like your nervous twitch, constant scratching, or lazy eye. Plenty of time for that over a candle-lit dinner. Truth is, it's far easier to construct an online identity with crafted e-mails and retouched photos. A study by Gibbs, Ellison and Heino concluded that successful online daters tended to use large amounts of positive self-disclosure, along with openness about their intent. The very opposite of many people's actual practice in online dating.

The idea that self-disclosure is important in relationships is no big surprise. But while it may be easy to understand in principle, the complexity of the process means it's much harder to do in practice. Generally speaking, it seems best to be open about yourself and honest and clear about your intentions. So don't be afraid to give of yourself if you want to build a good relationship with someone. But remember that the art of self-disclosure is about giving information to others in the *right* way and at the *right* time.

In addition to seemingly knowing when to give information to Elizabeth in the right way and at the right time, William Cecil had both an impressive memory and an impressive capacity for hard work. When faced with a complex problem he would actually write down all considerations relating to it - and it was only after he had meticulously examined all the implications of the various solutions that he would venture an opinion. He looked at the danger England faced from invasion by other countries through to the nation's eating habits.

Important but not urgent.

The Queen and Cecil forged a unique partnership. When she first appointed him, the Queen made it very clear that she wanted to hear his opinions even when they conflicted with her own and for the next forty years she rarely took an important decision without consulting him first.

For Elizabeth, Cecil was the ideal partner; the perfect Devil's Advocate.

William Cecil

He was someone who would stand up to her and give her an alternative opinion but, once Elizabeth had made up her mind, he would then enthusiastically follow her path. And so it was on November 28th 1558 that Elizabeth returned to the Tower in much happier circumstances. For the first public appearance of her reign she was dressed in a striking purple velvet. Before the year was out - and despite having one or two Christmas parties - she had dismissed the majority of her late sister's personal attendants and replaced them with those who had been faithful to her. And she remembered she was a Boleyn too. Her Aunty Mary Boleyn's son, Henry Carey, was given a peerage as Baron Hunsdon and given a nice little manor in Hertfordshire.

Blood runs thicker than water.

She had also developed early on the knack of knowing how much to tell her people what was going on. During her first year on the throne she kept her Council 'in absolute ignorance' of how her marriage negotiations with the Austrian Archduke Charles were progressing.

As Kenny Rogers once famously said 'You got to know when to hold 'em, know when to fold 'em; know when to walk away and know when to run. You never count your money, when you're sittin' at the table. There'll be time enough for countin', when the dealing's done.'

Kenny Rogers

And, again, as is so often the case with incoming new CEO's there was a pressing matter that had to be dealt with if the reign was to be a long one. Since mid November 1558 arrangements for her coronation had been set in motion. It was essential for Elizabeth to have a very public and grand coronation to emphasise that the validity of her title as Queen of England was beyond question. At this point England was still technically at war with France and although peace talks were ongoing there was a concern that the French might put a hold on the talks and argue that Mary Queen of Scots - who had married the French King's oldest son in April earlier that year - was really the rightful Queen of England.

The issue of Elizabeth's legitimacy had hung over her like a heavy cloud since Anne Boleyn had given birth and French diplomats in Rome had already put pressure on the Pope to declare Elizabeth a bastard. Fortunately the Spanish were also at war with the French and they didn't want to see a girl who was half French on the English throne. And so on January 15th 1559 - only two months after Mary had passed away - the arrangements were rushed through and Elizabeth was crowned. In the two months from accession to coronation Elizabeth had been fairly canny in not giving too much public indication of where her religious loyalties lay. Nowadays politicians do focus groups and rely on Mori polls but in those days Elizabeth was savvy enough to test the ground and in the event she was happy to be cast as Protestant and head of the English Church. When she was handed an English Bible by a child she kissed it and plied it to her breast and promised to be a diligent reader of it.

With such gestures going down really well with the spectators, she offered the kind of off the cuff witticisms and repartee that Peter Kay and Billy Connolly would be proud of. Even at this early stage people could see something that was to characterise her reign. She deplored extremists on both sides of the religious divide and for the extremists this meant to them a lack of conviction in spiritual matters. In fact her faith never wavered; it's just that because she was free of fanaticism she was able to steer a steady course. She only attended Chapel once a week and wasn't a big fan of listening to men give her sermons. She didn't see the need to have men of the Church to act as professional mediators between herself and God. And here's a lesson for us all:

Just because someone's not on the same path as you, doesn't mean they're lost.

Don't worry too much when you inevitably compare your life to others. You have no idea what their journey is all about. Sometimes you're ahead, sometimes you're behind.

She could quite rightly see more common ground between Catholicism and the Protestant faith than the differences. And that's what good CEO's do; particularly when bringing together factions within the organisation and the board. She was typically pragmatic in April when the new 'Bill of Supremacy' was given its first reading in the Commons. The original intention that the Queen be appointed 'Supreme Head of the Church' had been amended to be that she should become 'Supreme Governor'. A number of people were unhappy that she should be head of the Church but Elizabeth was happy to take the less controversial alternative which still gave her all the jurisdictional powers she wished but allowed the Archbishop of York and others the feeling that they had contributed.

One of the most offensive things you can do to someone is to ignore them. People hate being ignored and Elizabeth was able to stroke some big egos and get everyone on board. For a slip of a girl she seemed to do well on accommodating all view points. When, in April 1559 the treaty of Cateau-Cambresis had been signed with France, there was peace. And although Elizabeth was unhappy with the loss of Calais there was some sort of honour in that the treaty the French agreed to sign was that after they had occupied Calais for eight years they would either return it to the English or compensate them financially.

All it really did was give us time to get used to the loss. But within six months she'd calmed down the warring religious factions, had a Council who seemed to be singing off the same hymn sheet and made peace with France.

Plus ça change, plus c'est la même chose.

So imagine that, rather like Elizabeth I, you're a CEO charged with turning around a company. If you believe the French, your enthusiasm for the task in hand may be dented somewhat. But don't despair. Because these days, more than at any other time in our history, the only real constant in both life and business is change. Confused?

Let me explain.

For me, the key to success is not how well you change things but how well you adapt to the change. UK businesses now rely more on building good customer relationships than they do on manufacturing. That's because everybody's got access to pretty much the same technology so the only real differentiator is service.

An interesting thing happened the moment I entered my room when I stayed at The Four Seasons hotel in Istanbul. I'd arrived only two minutes earlier and it was almost midnight.

I wrongly assumed it was my wife checking I'd arrived safely in Turkey. Happily I didn't answer it with my customary, 'Hello darling' since it turned out to be the hotel receptionist. She wanted to know if I was happy with the room.

For a second I was tempted to re-enact the scene from Fawlty Towers where the guest demands a view of the Hanging Gardens of Babylon. However, I figured her knowledge of 70's sitcom would probably have only instigated a prolonged silence rather than a belly laugh. Besides the room was perfect and it was very nice to be asked at *the start* of my stay rather than *the end* when they could do nothing about it.

This, I surmised, was a progressive, premium business that took pride in caring for its clientele. And it got me thinking about the service in other hotels and the parallels to be drawn in business generally. As a professional speaker I spend a good percentage of nights in hotels each year. The poorer hotels never ask me what I think of their service. They don't ask if I'm satisfied with the room or if the heating system with a mind of its own caused me to have night sweats again.

Of course, you'd expect things to be different at The Four Seasons since it's a very expensive hotel. After they'd swiped my Gold Card I could actually feel it melting at the edges. And, sure, it would be easy to trot out the old adage 'You get what you pay for' as some kind of excuse. But that, for me, would be missing the point.

They want to improve. They want me to feel valued. They want me to return.

And it's the same for business leaders. Instead of trying to change what people are used to and feel comfortable with, you should concentrate on creating a business environment that makes people feel valued as well as encourages them to flourish and innovate. Leadership is not just about knowledge and intellect but also about wisdom and creativity. Give people room to grow and experiment and more can be achieved because they feel they are making a difference and are appreciated.

So change is going to happen, and with it there can be uncertainty or chaos. So can you influence everything that happens? Well, those who go around saying 'There's nothing I can do.' or 'What's the use of trying?' are effectively disempowering themselves by implying that nothing can be done to change or influence a situation so never run the risk of influencing everything. And potential great leaders don't do that.

Winston Churchill

Churchill didn't promise to fight them on the beaches provided it wasn't too soggy. He might have thought it, but he didn't say it.

Listen to the language you use when conversing with others. Is it positive and encouraging or does it sound sinister and threatening? The style you adopt provides critical clues to your awareness of others and their needs. Good leaders, like Elizabeth I, are aware of other people's feelings and use them to their advantage. In fact, leaders who are often thought to have 'great insight' sometimes have little more than a good understanding of other people's motivations, aspirations, needs and preferences.

When businesses rely more on customer service, perceptiveness is more important than analysis. And when perceptiveness is combined with trust we have a great leader.

And in Elizabeth that's what the country has now got.

Mary Stuart was still waiting in the wings but she'd made a good start.

Chapter 18 ~ 'Someone to make me smile'

1559 — 1566

The end of Elizabeth's honeymoon period as the new monarch was over and it was time for war. In July 1559 Henry II of France had died as a result of injuries in a court tournament and Mary Stuart's fifteen year old husband, despite not yet shaving, had succeeded him as Francis II. Understandably he was somewhat dominated by his Scottish wife and, as she and her family were fanatical Catholics he himself saw himself as Catholic too. Mary Stuart rather fancied the triple crown of Queen of France, Scotland *and England.* Elizabeth gave clandestine financial assistance to her Protestant nobles in Scotland but it was known that the French were preparing to send reinforcements to Mary and it was in October 1559 that Elizabeth realised she'd got a fight on her hands.

Elizabeth had a few problems. England didn't have the armour; England didn't have men experienced in war nor the money for yet another scrap with the French. If she failed in her attempt to eject the French from Scotland it would be likely that the French, still gloating about gaining Calais, would set sail over the channel and deprive her of her throne. But if she didn't fight the Scots then her cousin Mary may well gain confidence and come south. The ideal world for Elizabeth was that the French would withdraw their troops from Scotland and Mary Stuart would renounce all claims to Elizabeth's throne. And with the help of her Devil's Advocate and a bit of luck that's exactly what she achieved.

In February 1560 Elizabeth signed The Treaty of Berwick whereby she promised the Scots that she would 'Send men of war there with all speed' if the French invaded Scotland.

By the end of March 1560 the French had duly arrived in Scotland and eight thousand furious Englishmen under the command of Lord Grey walked up towards Leith in Scotland. In May they made an attempt to take Leith by storm. But the French won this little skirmish with the English not fully equipped and having scaling ladders that were too short.

Not the first time Elizabeth had a decision to make.

Stick or twist? Run for home or send reinforcements? There can be no sitting on the fence.

Despite losing one thousand five hundred men, to cut her losses and have them come home with their tails between their legs could well mean the end of her reign. It was not to be the first time that Elizabeth was to show her tenacious nature and the strong sense of purpose that all CEO's need. Fresh troops were sent to Scotland and the siege of Leith continued. She correctly calculated that the resilience of the French on foreign soil would eventually waiver and that's exactly what happened.

She also got them to measure the scaling ladders properly this time.

As in business it's all the little things that make a difference. Excellence comes from TNTs - Tiny Noticeable Things. Having a good time almost always means somebody has done a lot of work in preparation. The best impromptu events are well planned and someone has taken the trouble to look after all the details.

It's so easy to set off to Scotland with plenty of ladders to scale the walls without checking whether the ladders are the right height. Someone needs to ask these questions when people are planning. That someone is The Devil's Advocate.

And at the same time the English had a stroke of luck. On June 10th 1560 Mary of Guise died and the French lost most of their will to resist. Mary was the Queen Consort of Scotland as the second spouse of King James V of Scotland. She was the mother of Mary, Queen of Scots, and at the time of her death was serving as Regent of Scotland in her daughter's name. Cecil did a grand job negotiating with the French and in early July the treaty of Edinburgh was formally signed.

Ironically, the day after peace had been established Cecil received a letter from Elizabeth saying that she now wanted compensation in the way of Calais. She'd got her tail up and wanted to rub the French's noses in it. Looking back, it's probably good fortune that her letter hadn't arrived in time to stop the peace treaty being signed. Cecil was to show great diplomatic skill in also dealing with the not insignificant issue of the rumours surrounding Elizabeth and the man she loved to be with; Lord Robert Dudley.

Because Elizabeth had also, within the first six months, found someone to make her smile. Attractive, intelligent cultured and with a good, athletic build her Master of The Horse, Lord Robert Dudley was also married, ambitious and flirtatious. He made her laugh.

And we all need someone who makes us laugh.

In September 1560 Dudley's wife Amy was found at the foot of a staircase at Cumnor Hall the Oxfordshire manor house she'd been staying at.

She was dead.

Cumnor Church and the ruins of Cumnor Hall in Oxfordshire

The one thing that was certain was that she'd died of a broken neck but did she fall or was she pushed? Either way, eventually Dudley was cleared of blame but that didn't stop the rumour mongers. Indeed, the rumour mill went into full operation as to whether or not Elizabeth might actually want to marry Dudley. Elizabeth was intelligent enough to know that he was highly unpopular and a marriage with one of her courtiers would give rise to jealously, resentment and infighting. Indeed, it could well plunge the country into civil war. Dudley, remember, had been implicated in his Father's plot to get Lady Jane Grey on the throne but it was Cecil that could read the signs that although Elizabeth was obviously attracted to Dudley, her judgment had not been impaired and she was more in love with the throne than with him.

Cecil understood that everyone needs to save face. Everyone needs acceptance time to come to terms with a difficult decision that has to be made. Just as people need time to accept being made redundant or indeed, grieve, people need time to adjust, reflect and feel that they're making a decision themselves. And in that Cecil did well.

Elisabeth Kübler-Ross did an excellent job of writing about this 'process' of acceptance to change when she first published the Grief Cycle model in 1969. Cecil would have been proud of her. Kübler-Ross argued that we all go through seven distinct phases when we face trauma; at first we are shocked and effectively immobilised, then we deny what has happened, then we have anger, bargaining, depression and before we come to acceptance of the change we have to 'test' for the meaning of it all. Whether it's death and bereavement, divorce, redundancy, enforced relocation, crime and punishment, disability and injury or bankruptcy it helps us understand and deal with (and counsel) personal reaction to trauma.

One person's despair such as a job change or phobia is not at all threatening to someone else. Elisabeth Kübler-Ross, Elizabeth I and William Cecil - and all good managers of people - understand that emotional response, and trauma, must be seen in relative and not absolute terms. We need to appreciate that other people's perspectives are different to our own.

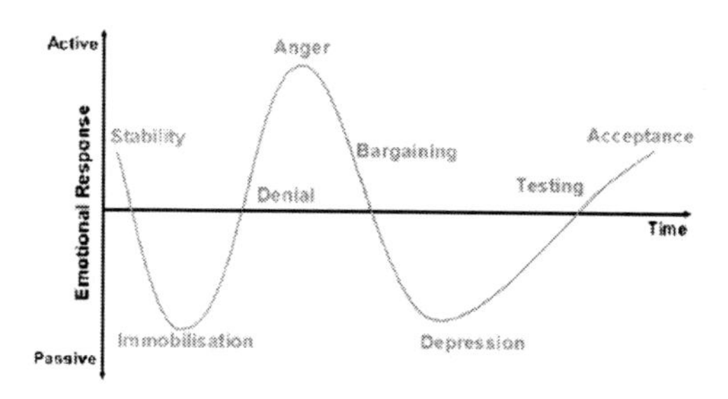

Kübler-Ross was a catalyst. She challenged the 'sweep it under the carpet' and 'don't discuss it' view on dealing with death, bereavement and change. The seven stages are neither linear nor equal in their experience and length. People's reactions to emotional trauma are as individual as a fingerprint.

As people go through the depression phase they need to search for meaning before they can accept things. They need to rationalise and come to terms with why this bad thing has happened to them.

And as a good CEO, Elizabeth I seemed to appreciate that. Certainly she was more sensitive than her brother and sister.

William Cecil could see Elizabeth very clearly resented all criticism of Dudley and she felt duty bound to defend him. Indeed, as Dudley was being badly treated she felt even stronger that she should verbally defend him. Cecil advised people not to make matters worse by badgering the Queen into a decision. Cecil learned how to live with Dudley and his policy of placing subtle and often untraceable obstructions in Dudley's path to husbandry rather than oppose marriage openly, worked well.

Lord Robert Dudley was of course compensated for his love and affection but Dudley spent his life in pursuit of the forbidden fruit. And Elizabeth learned how to handle the whole situation. As she scathingly once famously said to him "I will have here but one mistress and no master." And it was a maxim that Dudley quite simply had to live with.

Her mind was focused on the main job.

And part of that main job was to focus on the economy. Whilst many were focused on the gossip surrounding Dudley and Elizabeth, Cecil had also been looking at the state of coinage in the country. During the time of Elizabeth's father, brother and sister running the country, the English currency had been undermined and in 1559 coins were actually worth less than their nominal value because they contained too high a percentage of alloy. Foreign buyers had started refusing to accept English coinage so English businessmen had to pay for goods in pure gold. This, in turn, caused a shortage of gold at home and that had a disastrous effect on the rate of exchange.

Plus ça change, plus c'est la même chose.

The Queen took a keen interest in these matters and Elizabeth and Cecil eventually issued a proclamation that all base coins in circulation were to be reduced 'as nigh to their value as might be'. This was a huge undertaking at this stage and there were insufficient quantities of silver at The Mint to produce the number of new coins required.

Elizabeth I Shilling from 1561

In the event the crown even made a profit of about £45,000 from the transactions which involved people bringing in old coins and getting new ones in their place. The revaluation helped English merchants and in July 1561 Elizabeth celebrated her remarkable achievement by allowing them to visit her in the Tower of London.

Unfortunately, whilst presiding over this fiscal success, in early December 1560, Francis II suddenly died and that left Mary Queen of Scots a widow at 18 years old. Mary was in France herself at the time and rather fancied coming back to Edinburgh to preside over her people. An envoy was dispatched to ask Elizabeth if Mary might be allowed to pass through England on the way to her own kingdom and Elizabeth probably made her first mistake. Why not be conciliatory? Why not help her on her way to Edinburgh and even meet her in, say, Richmond, for a nice cup of tea and a chat? They were after all cousins and it was an opportunity for Elizabeth to establish the ground rules.

Let Mary rule Scotland and if the French ever come sailing down the Firth or the Clyde with swords at the ready then we would be more than just cousins. But no, Elizabeth refused her that and Mary was able to turn the rebuff to her advantage for she could now suggest it was she rather than Elizabeth who was the injured party. She let it be known she would travel from France to Scotland by sea and by letting the English know of all her plans effectively said 'come and get me'.

In the event Mary sailed to Scotland and on August 19th 1561 she landed at Leith and quickly set about charming the locals. There only appears to be the author and misogynist John Knox who didn't think much of her arrival.

Once installed at Holyrood Palace near Edinburgh she immediately declared she wanted to make peace with England but she had a small condition attached to it. It was conditional on Elizabeth agreeing to reinstate her in the line of succession. And that created an impasse. It's time for either war or a meeting.

Either way it's going to get expensive.

If there was to be a meeting then the nobility accompanying both Mary and Elizabeth would have to have new outfits. There would be substantial transport and accommodation costs and the not insignificant knock-on effect of what people in France would make of it all. People started busying themselves working out how much bread and beer and wine they'd need. Knights started practicing their tilting in preparation for the tournaments which would surely ensue if the Queen of Scotland were to meet the Queen of England.

On July 7th 1562 Elizabeth gave Maitland the formal assurance that Mary would be welcome for a meeting and four days later he left for Scotland bearing a sealed document that stated the two Queens could meet in the North of England; probably somewhere nice like York and sometime in August or September. Unfortunately, the very next day civil war broke out in France and the offer of a meeting was revoked.

Not for the first time the English monarch sensed a bit of disarray in France and thought it was time to declare war again. The Huguenots in France had secretly offered Elizabeth that if she helped them against the Guises they would let her have Le Havre. Not Calais admittedly, but that could be kept as security until they did agree to give Calais back to the English. By the end of August Elizabeth had indicated that the deal was on and by early October the first English troops had landed in Le Havre. Unfortunately that October Elizabeth became so ill with smallpox she actually lost the ability to speak. However, she was soon up and well and appointed Lord Robert Dudley a member of the Council. Mary Stuart wrote the Queen a nice little letter saying how pleased she was she'd got better.

But what this little illness had done was made everyone consider the issue of the inevitability of anarchy and civil war if she was to die without a clear heir. Lord Robert Dudley had shuffled into pole position in Elizabeth's eyes but that would have been disastrously unpopular. And so it was that by the start of 1563 Elizabeth had four plates she was spinning; four issues that were causing great consternation and debate amongst the English people.

They were the war with France, the financial implications of the war with France, the Protestant versus Catholic debate and the matter of her successor; the latter having the added implication of who might father her children.

Interestingly none of these debates and none of these issues made things better for the people in England. Surely the purpose of a monarch and a ruling party is to improve the lot of its people? Just as we've seen when we have disunity and disharmony amongst people, so too we make no progress when we get distractions.

Every year people are killed in accidents all over the world because of one thing; distractions.

Several studies have shown that mobile phones are a leading cause of car crashes. According to a Harvard University study it is estimated that mobile phone distracted drivers are four times more likely to be in a car crash.

People don't keep focused on the most important issue. People lose sight of the real goal and get distracted and begin to concern themselves with issues that affect them rather than pursuing the common goal. So here's our next lesson from 1562:

Always know what the common goal is and keep pursuing it. Don't allow people to get distracted.

But by the end of summer 1563 at least one of her problems had been solved; we'd lost this particular war with France. If it hadn't been for the fact that so many people had died it would be comic. Basically there was an epidemic of plague in June and by the end of the month sixty soldiers a day were dying of the disease. The windmills which ground the corn in the area had all been destroyed by cannon fire so most of the bakers in the town had either died of plague or couldn't produce food. So when Elizabeth sent fresh troops and supplies, the reinforcements themselves promptly fell sick. But even as the English were making their sorry way back to England, Elizabeth was still keen to remind the French that Calais was soon due to be rendered back.

Needless to say there was plenty of laughter in Charles IX's court.

And then, to make things worse the returning soldiers brought plague with them and there were over 20,000 fatalities in London alone and that, in turn, meant a commercial embargo. The cloth trade ground to a virtual standstill and the crown lost revenue in customs duties until the embargo was lifted two years later.

And for what?

A little bit of France.

However, Elizabeth did what all good leaders should do. She accepted her part in the failure. She took responsibility for the unsuccessful adventure against France. She didn't blame Dudley or Cecil but took it on the chin.

She learned a lesson we referred to earlier and that Michael Jackson would go on to make such a big hit of. She wanted to make the world a better place, she took a look at herself and made that change.

Big mistake but top girl.

And she learned her lesson. It's often said that you need to be careful what you wish for and in endeavouring to manipulate both Mary Queen of Scots and Lord Dudley, Elizabeth was to get her comeuppance. Using Dudley as a pawn she conferred the title of Earl of Leicester on him and had her emissaries suggest that Mary marry him. She was probably testing Lord Dudley's affections and toying with her cousin, Mary.

Initially Mary played along saying that she would marry Lord Robert Dudley - now Earl of Leicester - if it also meant the succession to the English throne would pass to her. To confuse things even further Cecil and Queen Elizabeth decided to let Elizabeth's cousin 19 year old Henry Stewart - also called Lord Darnley - go to Scotland to meet Mary.

They were endeavouring to obfuscate and confuse the whole issue of Mary marrying and having a child.

Unfortunately, the 19 year old Darnley was tall, athletic, good looking and a grandchild of Henry VIII's sister Margaret Tudor.

Henry Stewart - Lord Darnley

As was Mary.

Not tall and athletic that is; just a grandchild of Henry VIII's sister.

If Darnley and Mary were to form a real relationship it could be a formidable partnership as their respective claims to the throne of England could be merged. Elizabeth wrongly assumed that even when Darnley was north of the border she would still be in control. Unfortunately for Elizabeth, Mary and Darnley fell in love. And when Darnley had been taken ill by measles, Mary became totally smitten. By the time Darnley had recovered she was besotted and had resolved to marry him; with or without Elizabeth's approval. By May 1565 Mary had conferred a Scots peerage on Darnley. On hearing of this, Elizabeth tried summoning Darnley home but to no avail. Elizabeth even put Darnley's Mother in the Tower in July for having 'encouraged her son in his undutifulness' but by the end of the month Darnley was King of Scotland and Mary was his bride.

Not what Elizabeth had planned.

It was an expensive lesson for Elizabeth to learn:

Not only do you have to be careful what you wish for; you have to be mindful of the consequences if your wish comes true.

Or, as Oliver Hardy was keen on saying to Stan Laurel 'That's another fine mess you've got me into'. In June 1566 Mary, Queen of Scots, gave birth to a son James and Elizabeth was to accept Mary's invitation to be Godmother to the infant. For now, at least, years of tension, war, misunderstanding and scheming, the relationship between the two cousins Elizabeth and Mary seemed to settle down.

Needless to say, it wasn't to last.

Chapter 19 ~ Darnley's Demise and Mary's imprisonment

1566 — 1570

Time for a recap.

Queen Elizabeth of England had fancied herself as a bit of a matchmaker and tried to hook up her friend, Lord Robert Dudley, Earl of Leicester, with her cousin, Mary Queen of Scots. She had also sent her second cousin, 19 year old Henry Stuart, aka Lord Darnley, along for moral support. Unfortunately, being at the peak of his sexual prowess, Henry had other ideas and soon wormed his way into Mary's favour, as she liked to call it. Following a whirlwind romance, the two were married in July 1565.

As Henry said on their wedding night "So, I'm the King of Scotland, right?" and then added rather cheekily, "Love the garter, by the way."

However, before the end of the year, Mary discovered that her new King was pursuing a life of drink and depravity. Thinking he was as a bit of a comedian, he had developed a stand-up routine that bombed desperately at the Edinburgh Fringe and the whole experience seemed to tip him over the edge. He accused a Scottish-Italian guy named Riccio of having an affair with his wife and murdered him in cold blood by boring him to death with roughly four hundred and sixty knock-knock jokes. This shocking news was swiftly followed by the revelation that Mary was expecting. In June 1566 she gave birth to James, a happy healthy boy with suspicious olive skin that nobody much mentioned. Four months later, Mary was discussing with her advisors the possibility of divorcing Darnley and just four months after that he was dead.

He'd been murdered; strangled or suffocated after a bomb went off in the house he was staying at. My money's on suffocation since I've never heard of a bomb strangling anyone. Mary was sleeping somewhere else at the time.

Nod, nod, wink, wink.

By the end of May 1567 Queen Mary had married once more, this time to the Earl of Bothwell.

The Earl of Bothwell

The Earl of Bothwell's other name was James Hepburn. Bit confusing when people have two names.

Suspicions understandably grew that Mary had organised Darnley's death. She refuted this by claiming she couldn't organise a p** up in a brewery and spent the next three months trying to prove it. Maybe she was honest in her protestations; maybe she wasn't. But, just as in business and indeed all relationships, it's not enough to be honest. You have to have verisimilitude; the appearance of honesty. And if your husband has just died, perhaps appear just a little sad. No wearing bright colours, that sort of thing. Lay off the bingo for a while too. Looking back, she didn't try hard enough to find her first husband's killers. And so people talk and gossip. And here's the next lesson for us all:

It's not enough to be honest; people have to believe that you're honest. You must have verisimilitude.

Many Scots were in uproar. They felt that Mary hadn't done enough to find Darnley's killers and now she was marrying someone they didn't approve of. History has a habit of repeating itself.

Time for another fight.

Not surprisingly, Mary Queen of Scots and her new husband had to leave Edinburgh sharpish. However, on June 15th 1567, just as the royal forces were beginning to prepare battle against the dissidents, Mary agreed to surrender. Bothwell literally galloped away, escaping to Denmark where he heard the bacon was especially fine; nice and crispy just the way he liked it. Unfortunately, on his arrival he was imprisoned by the King and died completely insane eleven years later.

No, I am not making that up.

Mary was incarcerated at Loch Leven and that left Elizabeth in a quandary.

Loch Leven Castle

In many respects, Darnley's death and Mary's demise suited Elizabeth as Scotland was now run by a clique of Protestant Lords who were keen to be on good terms with their English neighbours. But at the same time if the Scottish Lords were permitted to bring down their own monarchy then perhaps Elizabeth too could be divested of her regal status?

So, like all good CEOs, she had to make a decision.

Needless to say the French felt duty bound to get involved. King Charles IX of France tried to ingratiate himself with the Scottish Lords and on July 24th 1567 Mary was forced into signing an abdication statement. Her thirteen month old son, Prince James, was crowned King of Scotland. He cried continuously throughout the ceremony and filled his nappy at least twice.

I'm just reporting the facts.

Elizabeth knew that there was a good middle ground between war and apathy. She still withheld official recognition of the new regime in Scotland but had overseen constructive talks between the English and Scots on border security and had written to the King of Denmark asking if Bothwell could be sent back to Scotland so he could stand trial, unaware that he was now insane, wearing pretty floral smocks, and answering only to the name of Brenda. Just as things seemed to be getting back on an even keel, Mary escaped from Loch Leven. The Douglas family was responsible for both security *and* the plot to allow her to escape.

Tidy.

There was a window in Mary's tower looking out over the water. A window of opportunity, you might say. George Douglas's cunning plan was to bring a boat up to the window in the night and take Mary down the wall into it. Early on the Sunday evening he'd signalled to Mary across the loch and was duly ready with his boat. When it was dark, he rowed cautiously across the water, and took his position under Mary's window. Meanwhile William Douglas was having his supper in the great square tower with his father and mother.

The keys were lying upon the table. He quietly slipped them into his trouser pocket and then cautiously stole away. He locked the tower as he came out, went across the court to Mary's room, sneaked her out through the postern window, and descended with her into the boat. One of her maids, Jane Kennedy, was to have accompanied her, but in their excitement they forgot her and she had to leap down after them.

It sounds more like a panto than a prison escape.

They threw the keys of the castle into the lake, as if that would mean the rest of the Douglases would be holed up in Loch Leven Castle forever.

They rowed hard all night and landed safely on the south side of the Loch, far from Kinross. Several of the Hamilton Lords were waiting for her, put her on the back of a horse and galloped away. By the end of the week Mary found herself at the head of an army of six thousand men.

Wondering what to do with them.

She rode further south shaving off her hair to avoid recognition and intended to throw herself at the mercy of Queen Elizabeth. A fortnight after her escape Mary crossed the Solway Firth and landed at Workington in Cumbria. So now Elizabeth is faced with a dilemma.

If she refuses to help Mary, Mary may well go to France. And if the French were to help her she would feel indebted to them and the French would be in league with the Scots against the English. "This is just like the Six Nations" she said to herself without really knowing why.

Elizabeth could hardly detain Mary in England against her will as she'd consistently said that a monarch should be allowed to reign. And you have to do what you say you are going to do if you want to maintain your reputation.

The Scots were claiming that Mary was guilty of her first husband's murder so they put pressure on Elizabeth to have her deported back to Scotland. However, Elizabeth decided to buy herself some time by arranging for Mary to be holed up in Lord Scrope's castle at Carlisle.

That really was his name.

He was a small chap, difficult to spot with the naked eye. A sort of micro scrope.

Elizabeth let it be known to Mary that she was sorry for her predicament but unable to meet her personally on account of the murder charge which she assumed was without foundation. Elizabeth even sent her a fresh supply of clothes; her cast offs. Elizabeth had learned one of The Golden Rules; always have a Devil's Advocate. And it was Cecil yet again who was able to outline in detail the various options that Elizabeth now had. So

Elizabeth reverted to one of the basic laws of negotiation; don't give anything away without getting something in return.

Mary was told that if she was cleared of Darnley's murder, Elizabeth would do all that she could to allow her to regain her royal status. However, there were conditions. In return she was to sign an alliance with England precluding her from making a claim on the throne during Elizabeth's lifetime. She was also to give up Catholicism and revert to The Book of Common Prayer. Plus, if she could do anything to stop that damn Tattoo every year, that would be a bonus. With Mary having agreed to all points but the latter, there was to be a trial at York with Lord Herries and the Bishop of Ross representing her.

In January 1569 proceedings came to a stalemate. Mary couldn't be found guilty unless she had put forward a defence which she refused to do. Elizabeth had played the game well. She'd achieved her aim of disgracing Mary without actually passing judgement on her as a Queen and had avoided formally labelling Mary as an adulteress and a murderer. She was moved to Tutbury castle in Staffordshire where Elizabeth hoped the security arrangements were better than those at Loch Leven.

Needless to say Mary Stuart's incarceration in an English castle heightened the tension between France and England and gave the French a ready-made grievance if they fancied declaring war again. And whilst relations with France were not in a particularly friendly state, things with Spain were about to get a little bit hairy too.

In November 1568 several Spanish ships carrying treasure towards The Netherlands were forced to take refuge in various English harbours as there were a number of ill meaning pirates in the English Channel at the time. Elizabeth issued a permit for the goods to be carried from Plymouth and Southampton over to Dover where they could then be transported to The Netherlands.

But then she discovered that it wasn't actually the property of King Philip at all; he was being lent it by some merchants from Genoa.

Naturally, she did the only decent thing a monarch could do and kept the treasure for herself. Spain was pretty much at war with Holland and Elizabeth didn't think this would hamper the war effort. However, for every action there is an equal opposite reaction and several English ships were seized. So in a tit for tat manoeuvre all Dutch and Spanish ships in English harbours were stopped from sailing in January 1569.

Mary Queen of Scots

And Mary Queen of Scots was obviously still putting her oar in too.

Fortunately, not literally. There was no man in a boat but she did have access to pen and plenty of paper. In September 1568 she had written to the wife of King Philip of Spain saying that if they were to help her she would, in turn, ensure that her son James would marry Philip's daughter and that Catholicism would be returned to England. She also enquired if that apartment on Majorca was still available for the last two weeks of August?

Thomas Percy, 7th Earl of Northumberland, secretly visited the Spanish Ambassador in January 1569 and suggested that the recently widowed Philip II should take Mary Stuart as his wife. Thomas himself having an axe to grind as he felt the Queen's confident, Cecil, had too much power and had converted to Catholicism himself two years earlier.

As is the way with office politics, Percy's three allies; the Earl of Westmoreland, the Duke of Norfolk and Lord Lumley plotted against Cecil but were reluctant to actually speak to the CEO herself. The members of the cabal deluded themselves that they were all powerful and busied themselves with politics rather than getting on with their jobs.

The Queen tackled the problem head on.

Elizabeth wasn't prepared to discard her loyal servant and Devil's Advocate simply to appease her rivals. She spoke to them directly and explained that Cecil was to stay but did take on board some of their misgivings about certain issues. She also spoke directly to Norfolk when she found out that he was planning to be Mary Stuart's new husband. Word spread and he himself became an outcast at court.

In September 1569 he left London for Kenning Hall, his house in Norfolk, and on October 3rd he was stopped en route to Windsor and put in the Tower by order of the Queen. Good CEO's know when to appease and when to be direct. They need to know when to quell a rebellion and when to let things run their natural course and go with the flow.

Kenny Rogers was pretty prophetic when he wrote 'The Gambler.'

But for every action there's an equal and opposite reaction and in November 1569 Northumberland, Westmoreland and the Sheriff of Yorkshire, Richard Norton went in to Durham Cathedral, tore down the communion table, ripped up the English prayer books and set off south. They assumed that they would be next after

Norfolk to be put in the Tower. On November 22nd Elizabeth ordered that the Earl of Shrewsbury should move Mary Stuart to Coventry so that she wouldn't be liberated by the Northern rebels and proclaimed Queen.

That's right; she was sent to Coventry.

Meanwhile the Northern rebels had reached Clifford Moor in Yorkshire; not to be confused with the big shopping centre, Clifton Moor in York.

And then they began to have second thoughts. The Earls of Cumberland and Derby hadn't come on board as they'd anticipated and when they looked behind them their army consisted of a few ill-disciplined farmers who were terribly excited but didn't have any weapons; just pitch forks. They'd heard Mary had been sent south, they were getting short of money, winter was coming and by the end of November they'd got cold feet.

Literally and metaphorically.

Before Christmas they'd told their rag tag and bob tail assortment of supporters to 'make shift for themselves' and they went back north to Scotland. By the end of 1569 Elizabeth had seen off the rebellion.

A lot had happened in the five years since Elizabeth had sent her friend and confidant Robert Dudley to Scotland with the plan to have him marry her cousin Mary Stuart. Mary had married a different cousin, then married a fruit cake who had probably killed her first husband, had given birth to a son who had become King, been imprisoned and was now, under Elizabeth's jurisdiction, holed up in a castle in Coventry where nobody would talk to her.

If only the head of security at Loch Leven had done his job properly. If only Norfolk hadn't desired power so much that he wanted to marry Mary and become King. If only Henry VIII had stayed with his wife and not met Anne Boleyn. If only Henry VIII hadn't married Anne Boleyn. If only Anne Boleyn had been content with the Catholic religion?

If only Sid Smith hadn't been late for that Physics exam.

What ifs, maybes and if onlys.

It's 1570 and at the start of the new decade the only thing that's constant is change. Mary is to remain in prison for another seventeen years and destined never to meet the Queen of England.

Elizabeth has other fish to fry.

Chapter 20 ~ Juggling balls, procrastination and succession.

1570 1580

The 1570's were a difficult time for Elizabeth. At any point there seemed to be a good chance of a war against Scotland, The Netherlands, Spain or, of course, France. As early as January 1570 the Earl of Moray was assassinated which left the Protestant party in Scotland without a leader. Mary Queen of Scots was in prison and there was a huge dilemma as to whether or not she should get involved and run the risk of the French siding with the Scottish. It seemed an unlikely alliance; haute cuisine on the one hand, battered Mars bars on the other. But as the saying goes, stranger things happen in deep fat friers.

In May 1570, Elizabeth dined with the French Ambassador, and over the main course hinted - without really making a promise - that she would start discussions aimed at putting her cousin back on the throne. And then, looking down at her plate, added, "Crikey, is that all you get?".

And that perhaps was one of her great attributes. Speaking the truth, I mean. Not dissing French cuisine. Probably more so than any other monarch, Queen Elizabeth told the truth and did what she said she was going to do. And if you're going to live your life by that mantra, then you don't make false promises, empty threats or commitments that are going to be difficult to fulfill.

By July 1572 the breach between England and France was wide enough to consider completely breaking off diplomatic relations. Consideration was even given to passing a law making it illegal to eat a croissant in public. However, shock horror, by the end of the decade she very nearly married a Frenchman. It seems to be the decade for either marrying a Frenchie or going to war with them. Of course, if you really want to inflict suffering and misery, marriage is really the only sensible option.

Or you could do both.

Again, throughout the decade, she stuck to one of The Golden Rules of always having a good Devil's Advocate. In fact, she now had two. Naturally, Cecil was still there - newly promoted to Lord Burghley of Horse Trials. But now there was also Walsingham, who offered opinions which she didn't necessarily like. "But that's the idea of a Devil's Advocate, isn't it?" he would protest, as he was carried kicking and screaming from the room. Secretly though, Elizabeth seemed to admire his incisive mind and was consistently willing to listen to information she didn't want to hear. He just had to shout a bit louder from the ante room.

Like all good CEO's she would listen and give the impression she was at least taking the other person's concerns seriously.

In addition to the presence of Mary Queen of Scots, the threat of war from neighbouring countries and the matter of the succession, she also presided over a fairly impressive cost cutting exercise. By 1572 she really had turned the monarchy's economy around. Elizabeth's net annual income from feudal and ecclesiastical dues, customs duties and crown lands had dropped from over £200,000 a year to less than £135,000 a year. She'd started with a debt inherited from her sister Mary, had to finance various expeditions to Scotland and France but still managed to get the economy back on an even keel.

Full marks.

So by 1572 things were going quite well with France. At least they agreed to stick to their side of the channel and we agreed to stick to ours. Charles IX had asked Elizabeth to be godmother to his daughter, which was nice, but then upon his death two years later things seemed to go downhill again. You see, his successor was Henry III who had been King of Poland for the previous few years and, more importantly, was anti Protestant. Apparently, Elizabeth had been given the opportunity to marry him but had given him the brush off. So at the end of that year, Lord North led a small group to France to try and establish whether the new French King's intentions towards England were as hostile as they might have feared.

And that made things worse.

Elizabeth even thought about taking an army to France and the thorny subject of Calais came up again.

Back in September 1572, she'd sent Sir Henry Killigrew up to Scotland to suggest to them that it was quite a good idea to take Mary back, stage a trial, and then execute her for crimes she'd committed when she was on the throne there. But the Scots weren't happy at the idea of doing Elizabeth's dirty work and were far too busy with their own civil war which was really starting to hot up. By 1575 the Spaniards were ready to repossess The Netherlands - something to do with late payments - but the French were keen on having it too since they'd heard about the wacky backy and how everyone there was really chilled and laid back. Meanwhile, the Queen was getting older.

Perhaps the single most pressing issue for most people at court at that time was the matter of succession. On the one hand, there was Mary Queen of Scots and her son James. On the other, there was Elizabeth whom most people felt still had time to marry and produce an heir. For the thick end of thirty years she'd had various suitors put in front of her starting with Thomas, Lord Seymour of Sudeley, when she was only fifteen. And probably the last great attempt for her to marry was towards the end of the decade. None had thus far measured up. And then she met the Duke of Alencon.

Francis, Duke of Alencon, later Duke of Anjou, was the son of Catherine de Medici, Queen Mother of France, and a brother to the French King. Having been born in March 1555 he was 24 to Elizabeth's 45 years of age.

I'm saying nothing.

Duke of Alencon

The negotiations were based on the mutual needs of England and France to make an ally of each other, with a few of Elizabeth's personal needs thrown in for good measure. The traditional European alliance system whereby England was united with Spain was rapidly deteriorating, and England needed the support of France if she was to protect herself against Spain.

The Duke had sent his man Jean de Simier to England to present his case. De Simier had the rather grand title of 'Chief Darling to Monsieur' and seemed to do a pretty good job with Elizabeth. It's worthwhile reminding ourselves that Elizabeth's biological clock is ticking and maybe time has actually run out. She's still trying to find a husband and she's still fussy about how negotiations take place. As always Elizabeth was absolutely insistent that she must *see* her possible suitor before she could agree to a betrothal. Women, eh…there's always something.

However, the French being a canny lot were reluctant to have Alencon come over and risk the embarrassment of him being turned down. Plus, there was the question of expenses. Ferries weren't cheap in those days. Then there was the small matter of Alencon being a Catholic and one of their conditions was that Alencon would be crowned King of England immediately after the wedding and endowed with a large pension payable for the remainder of his life regardless of whether he remained King. His ancestors were later to run several British banks and had a similar clause written in.

All this made it very tough for Elizabeth to agree to his terms, particularly, when all she requested was that he wore carpet slippers in the house and gave up garlic.

The alliance might stop a war with France but we'd never get Calais back.

Alencon and Elizabeth eventually met in August 1579. And what the Queen found standing in front of her was a disfigured young man under five feet tall. She referred to him as 'my little frog'

Not a good start.

And so by the end of the decade Elizabeth was 46 years old and still unmarried.

Was it procrastination over tough negotiations or was it a good decision? Well, the finances were in better shape; we're not actually at war with anyone; Mary's still banged up in jail and a little bearded man from Devon called Francis Drake has been plundering, sailing the globe and generally getting up the noses of the Spanish.

Procrastination is probably the most popular criticism of Elizabeth. And you'll not be surprised to know that there has been quite a bit of psychological research done on the impact procrastination and the incompletion of tasks has on us all. It dates back to the 1920's when the Russian psychologist Bluma Zeigarnik gave some children puzzle and arithmetic tasks to do. She then interrupted one-half of them in mid-task and allowed the other half to complete the tasks. Shortly after only about one in ten recalled the completed tasks and slightly less than that remembered the same number of each.

But 80% remembered the interrupted tasks.

And a whole body of research has repeatedly found that individuals of all ages tend to remember uncompleted tasks far better than completed ones. We also tend to remember negative experiences and feelings longer than positive ones. Basically, there seems to be little motivation to recall jobs we've finished, whilst there's a strong investment of interest in unfinished projects. If you collect things you probably know the items you still want, and don't remember as well what you've already found.

We tend to think more about the rooms in our house that need decorating rather than the rooms we have taken several weeks to paint. So given we are more likely to remember what we don't complete, especially the negative, while we tend to not remember what we have completed, the 'Zeigarnik Effect' - as it's now known - impacts on our lives every day. The stress you have from everyday hassles and frustrations often stems from incomplete tasks.

Procrastination is not good for you. So finish tasks, take satisfaction from making a productive difference, savour your successful completions and you will have greater inner peace.

Perhaps if Elizabeth had dealt with the matter of succession and what to do with Mary Queen of Scots, she might have had a happier life.

Either way, at the start of 1580 the King of Portugal died suddenly with no heir. Bizarrely, his last words were "I can't breath, I can't breath, there's no air…" Philip of Spain took this opportunity to send an army across the Portuguese border and England could do nothing but watch helplessly as he absorbed the rich Portuguese empire into what was already a pretty extensive organisation.

Alencon had taken up the offer of becoming Prince and Lord of The Netherlands and power was shifting yet again.

But before we pick up the story again in 1580 it's worthwhile outlining the careers and achievements of the three best known names of Elizabeth's era and how it was she who invented what we now know as The National Lottery.

Time for Chapter 21.

Chapter 21 ~ Francis, Walter and William

During Elizabeth's reign, it's fair to say that her subjects included a number of great talents that served her well. However, those destined to leave the most memorable and lasting legacy were William the Writer, Walter the Explorer, Francis the Pirate, and Mike the Masseuse. Okay, perhaps not Mike. But certainly the other three. And like all good CEO's, she allowed each of them the freedom to do what they did best. So Francis would spend his days plundering the high seas, Walter would explore far and wide, William would churn out one blockbuster after another, and Mike would just let his fingers do the walking. And sometimes not just his fingers.

So before we return to the thorny issue of how Elizabeth deals with her cousin Mary and her tiresome plots - she was a keen gardener - here's a brief pen picture of the three main men in Elizabeth's life. Plus a brief introduction to the National Lottery. Don't worry, all will become clear.

Francis Drake

Francis Drake was born in Devon in 1540 and went to sea at an early age. He didn't particularly want to but his parents didn't like him hanging around the house. At the age of 27, he made one of the first English slaving voyages as part of a fleet led by his cousin John Hawkins, bringing African slaves to work in 'The New World'. However, on the return journey, the expedition was attacked by a Spanish squadron who were out looking for target practice. The bad news for Drake was that only two ships survived the attack. The good news was that he was on one of them. From this day on, Drake became a lifelong enemy of the Spanish and was put right off tapas. They, in turn, considered him a pirate and, for a brief moment, he considered hosting an off-shore radio show.

Francis Drake

In the 1570/71 pirate season, Drake made two profitable trading voyages to the West Indies. In return for slaves, he exchanged anything the locals couldn't get enough of. A year later, he commanded two vessels in a marauding expedition against Spanish ports in the Caribbean. They retaliated by beating us in a hastily arranged re-match. In later years, Drake went on to see action in the Pacific Ocean and captured the port of Nombre de Dios on the Isthmus of Panama. He returned to England with a cargo of Spanish treasure, six hundred Panama hats, plus a reputation as a brilliant privateer.

In 1577, Drake was commissioned by Elizabeth to set off on an expedition against the Spanish colonies on the American Pacific coast with the specific instruction to bring back no hats, just treasure. He sailed with five ships, but by the time he reached the Pacific Ocean only Drake's flagship, 'The Pelican', was left. Slightly shocked when he turned around to see nobody alongside him, he quickly scaled down his plans from major league marauding and pillaging and plumped for a spot of petty pilfering instead. His ship was later renamed 'The Golden Hind'.

Among his many achievements, Drake became the first Englishman to navigate the Straits of Magellan and sailed further up the west coast of America than any European. Unable to find a passage, he turned south and then in July 1579, west across the Pacific. His travels took him to the Moluccas, Celebes, Java and then round the Cape of Good Hope. He'd successfully completed a circumnavigation of the globe and ensured that the Spanish and the Portuguese were not having it all their own way.

During the 1570's, he sailed to Panama, led raids on treasure houses and ambushed mule trains in Peru. He robbed towns and vessels along the South American coast and, in particular, the Casa Fuego. He claimed a bit of California for the Queen and generally ingratiated himself with her whilst making himself enemy number one with the Spaniards. In September 1580, he sailed triumphantly into Plymouth harbour with a boat full of Spanish goods. Castanets, pot matadors, wicker place mats, stuffed donkeys etc. With 'The Golden Hind' neatly docked on the South Coast, he headed up to London to personally present Elizabeth with his piece-de-resistance: a crown studded with emeralds plus a diamond cross. Slightly suspicious, the Queen tested it with her teeth before paying Drake handsomely and declaring, "Crikey, it's real." And then added, "You can keep the castanets."

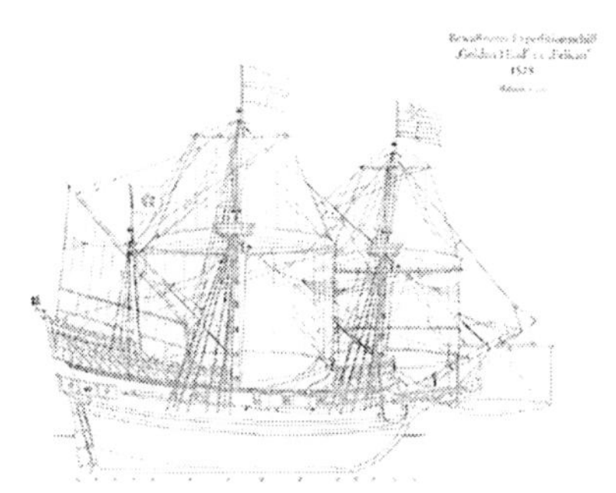

The Golden Hind

Elizabeth knighted him aboard 'The Golden Hind' much to the annoyance of the King of Spain.

In 1585, Drake sailed to the West Indies and the coast of Florida where he sacked and plundered Spanish cities. On his return voyage, he picked up the unsuccessful colonists of Roanoke Island off the coast of the Carolinas, which was the first English colony in the New World.

In 1587, with war against the Spanish imminent, Drake entered the port of Cadiz and destroyed 30 of the ships the Spanish were assembling against the British. A year later, he was a vice admiral in the fleet that defeated the Armada. Drake's last expedition, with John Hawkins, was to the West Indies. This time the Spanish were ready for him and the venture ended in disaster when he was struck on the head by a series of well-aimed cricket balls. Drifting in and out of consciousness, suffering from dysentery, and occasionally muttering 'no ball' and 'surely, that's a wide' Drake passed away on January 28th 1596 off the coast of Puerto Rico. His body was buried at sea.

Quite a guy.

A bad one.

But good for his CEO.

Walter Raleigh

Drake's relative, Walter Raleigh was also born in Devon - fourteen years after Drake - in 1552. He studied law at Oriel College, Oxford, just so that in later life he could be sure of what he was flouting. In 1578 he sailed for America and in 1585 he created the first English colony now known as North Carolina. It was whilst exploring North America looking for gold that he discovered both potatoes and tobacco. Given that neither looked very attractive hanging from a chain around your neck or fashioned into a brooch, it was a while before their true worth was realised.

Walter Raleigh

Raleigh had first come to the attention of Elizabeth in 1580 when he went to Ireland to help suppress an uprising in Munster. "Who's the guy on the bike?" she was heard to say. Later, using his newly discovered root vegetable as a substitute for a tennis ball, he invented the chipped potato when it went straight through the strings of his racket. Knighted in 1587 for his services to road transport and the potato snack market, Raleigh became an MP in 1584 and received extensive estates in Ireland.

However, things started to go wrong for Raleigh when he embarked on an affair with Bess Frockmorton, the Queen's Maid of Honour. I say embarked, because it was a bit like a cross channel ferry. Roll on, roll off, and you're there before you know it. Anyway, by the following summer, Bess was well and truly pregnant with Walter's child. Raleigh was caught between a rock and a hard place. He could stay and do the decent thing or high tail it out of town in the dead of night. After much soul searching he announced to Bess that he had a flat and would be staying. She thought he meant a place to live but he was referring to a puncture. They secretly married in the autumn and she secretly gave birth in the March. It was all very hush hush, apart from the birth which was punctuated with a few muffled groans. Although he constantly denied to Elizabeth that he was both married and a father, it was only a matter of time before she discovered the truth.

And here's the next lesson. Don't leave your benefits book lying around. And also, be sure your sins will find you out.

Moses said it. If you commit a crime, you run the risk that it will haunt you forever, even if you aren't found out. If you ignore The Second Golden Rule and don't treat people as you would like to be treated yourself, it can only lead to misery and regret. The ultimate result of all ambition is to be happy at home. If you aren't happy in your own skin, you aren't happy.

Raleigh couldn't keep up the deceit forever and by May the secret was out and he was under house arrest. He had committed the fundamental sin of making Elizabeth look stupid and, understandably, she took exception. Raleigh failed to appreciate the gravity of what he'd done and assumed he could sweet talk her round. But in August 1592 he and his wife were sent to the Tower. Being a simple girl, Bess thought they were spending a weekend in Blackpool, so incarceration in a small cell came as a bit of a shock. Despite being released before the end of the year, neither was readmitted to court.

Not for the first time, a man who had power had become greedy and complacent which started the infighting. He'd alienated too many people with his arrogant ways and there was no sympathy for his plight. To use Raleigh's own eloquent words he was "like a fish cast on dry land, gasping for breath with lame legs and lamer lungs". Then he ruined it by adding, "like maybe a carp or some bream."

In an attempt to regain favour with the Queen, Raleigh set off to discover El Dorado; the fabled 'Golden Land' thought to be somewhere near Venezuela. It ended in disappointment but it got him out of the house for a while.

When Elizabeth died and James VI of Scotland became James I of England, Raleigh was accused of plotting against the King and sentenced to death. This was ultimately reduced to life imprisonment of which he served just twelve years. During his time in the Tower he wrote the first volume of his history of the world. In 1616 he was released to lead another expedition to search for El Dorado but the expedition again ended in failure. The last straw came when Raleigh defied the King's orders to attack Spain and instead spent a fortnight in Benidorm sunning himself. On his return to England the death sentence was reinstated and Raleigh's execution took place in October 1618. Some people gasped as his limp body was taken away, others couldn't help but admire his tan. Even in death he managed to appear healthier than most of the onlookers.

Raleigh crossed the CEO and paid the price.

William Shakespeare

William Shakespeare was born in April 1564 and was but a young man when Drake and Raleigh were strutting their stuff. His father, John Shakespeare, was a member of the local government in Stratford. By trade, he was a money lender and once appeared in court when it was discovered he was charging interest rates in excess of 20%. Not uncommon then. In fact, not uncommon now. At his trial the judge gave a stern warning of the perils of money lending. "Neither a borrower nor a lender be; for loan oft loses both itself and friend, and borrowing dulls the edge of husbandry". "That's genius" said young William, eagerly scribbling it down. "I can use that beauty."

During his own life time, William Shakespeare was better known as an actor rather than a playwright. He didn't go to University and there are great gaps in his whereabouts for chunks of his life. When he was just 18, he married 26 year-old Anne Hathaway. His plays are racist, sexist; regularly include incest, half truths about former monarchs and have women dressed as men and men dressed as women.

William Shakespeare

Although Elizabeth was an active and generous patron of the theatre and Shakespeare's company was selected several times, there was probably little or no relationship between them. His fame and popularity would come a long time after they were both dead.

Shakespeare once wrote that all the world's a stage and all the men and women merely players. Not bad for someone who never left England. Of course what he was really saying is that life is all about relationships. And that's obviously just as true today.

However, the question is not whether it is nobler to suffer slings and arrows. That's an easy one; avoid them at all cost. The real question is do we act our part simply to achieve our objectives, or are we influenced by how we think others view us?

This idea that other people's expectations about us directly affect how we behave was examined by Dr Mark Snyder from the University of Minnesota. Acknowledging that one of the quickest ways people stereotype each other is by appearance, he set up a series of 'blind dates' whereby couples chatted to one another via headsets but didn't actually meet.

Having read this far, you will now know that most good psychological experiments involve a certain amount of sleight of hand. Two fistfuls in this case. You see, psychologists know that it's human nature to assume that people who are very attractive are also more sociable, humorous and intelligent. Think Peter and Katie.

So, men were given a photograph of the woman they were going to chat to. Except, of course, the photograph wasn't genuine. Half were given pictures of real stunners and half of women who were somewhat more challenged in the looks department. So, would the women pick up on the vibe given off by the men and unconsciously fit into the stereotype they had been randomly assigned? That's to say, would the 'beautiful' women actually be more friendly and sociable, and would the 'less attractive women' be dull and uninteresting?

On analysing the audio tapes, independent observers concluded that the 'attractive' women did indeed exhibit more of the behaviours stereotypically associated with attractive people: they talked more animatedly and seemed to be enjoying the chat more. In short, they conformed to the stereotype the men projected on to them. It seems people really do sense how they are viewed by others and change their behaviour to match this expectation.

The world is a stage. Expect your fellow players to like you and think well of you. It really could help the relationship.

So how does that help us to get on with people better? Well, understanding that other people's expectations about us directly affects our own behaviour means we have to be very careful when meeting someone new. Particularly if we think they don't like us. Because that negative vibe will influence their behaviour in a negative way.

On the upside, it also means that we can exert influence over the behaviour of others simply by changing our expectations of them. So if we think that they are going to place a big order, then that's exactly what they are most likely to do.

Elizabeth happened to have three great talents in her company when she was CEO of England Ltd. And she did what all good leaders do; she let them do what they were good at. She allowed them freedom to express themselves and only stepped in when they were either out of line, not on brief or deceived her.

And there was one other thing that Elizabeth should be given credit for too - our National Lottery. It can be traced back to the 16th century when a jackpot of £5,000 was up for grabs. Back then, of course, there was no mass media to publicise the event and no lottery machines in newsagents. Which is why it took three years to sell all the tickets and announce the winners. However, by a strange quirk of fate, the Voice of The Balls back then, like now, was also called Alan.

Because there was no Camelot to organise the draw, Queen Elizabeth did it herself. She wrote a letter to Sir John Spencer giving instructions for collecting money, commanding that 'persons of good trust' be entrusted with the prizes. She suggested 400,000 lots be sold, each costing 10 shillings, with prizes to be paid in a combination of gold and merchandise, including tapestries, linens and fine fabrics.

The jackpot of £5,000 is equivalent to £850,000 in today's money and part of the funds raised also went to good causes, just like today. Not surprisingly, since it took so long to organise, the 16th century lottery pretty soon died out but there were similar ones held between 1750 and 1826. I've actually got a ticket for the latter and the results are due in any decade now.

Fingers crossed.

Time for Chapter 22 and Elizabeth to deal with her troublesome cousin, Mary, Queen of Scots.

Chapter 22 ~ Mary's boy child

1580 1587

Whilst Mary Queen of Scots had been incarcerated in some luxury in England and Elizabeth was busy spinning plates, Mary's son James, of course, was growing up. Born on June 19th 1566 he was twelve when an ambassador from France went to Queen Elizabeth to speak on behalf of Mary and Elizabeth replied that Mary was "the worst woman in the world whose head should have been cut off years ago." She also added for good measure that Mary would never be free as long as she lived. James had had twelve years of being brought up as a Protestant but knowing he had a Catholic mother who had a right to the throne and was being kept at an English prison.

He'd spent his life living with criticism so he'd learnt to condemn. He'd been brought up with hostility so he was prepared to fight. As we discussed in chapter 3 you reap what you sow as far as bringing children up is concerned. And our next lesson comes from Dorothy Louise Law Nolte who wrote on her 83rd birthday 'if a child lives with security he learns to have faith in himself and those about him'.

Fact is James's somewhat loveless, confusing and strict upbringing had left him marked; as all childhoods leave us marked.

Harry Harlow would have had a field day studying James's childhood.

No father, didn't know his mother but was always expected to behave; he'd learned duplicity at a very young age. And so just short of his fifteenth birthday he started flexing his own muscles. He organised that the anglophile Earl of Morton - who had acted as Regent during the early part of James's reign - was arrested and charged with the murder of his father. No real evidence but this is 1581 and you don't really need much evidence.

James ruthlessly had Morton executed on June 2nd 1581. He was fourteen and had just put down his first marker.

Word spread and not for the first time Elizabeth deferred taking action.

Was Elizabeth guilty of procrastination in dealing with Mary Queen of Scots or did she make the right decision by waiting and thinking it through? Certainly it must be one of the longest periods of time that any CEO has ever taken to make a big decision. Fact is there was a quick, easy, ready made solution to the problem of Mary Queen of Scots and that was to have her executed when she first entered England.

But like so many other knee jerk reaction decisions that haven't been thought through it would have been the wrong decision. It's a lesson for us all. There is a quick, easy, ready-made solution to every problem. Unfortunately it's usually the wrong solution.

Kenny Rogers knew about that.

People fall into one of two categories when it comes to getting things done. There are those who draw up to-do lists and manage their time efficiently, and there are those who never have enough time. The former tend to get things done whilst the latter are busy procrastinating. Putting off today what they'll probably also put off tomorrow.

This issue of procrastination is such a big one hanging over Elizabeth's legacy - indeed, one that so many people struggle with - it's worth further examination.We all have an item or two of unanswered correspondence in our in-tray. Things we don't really want to deal with like writs and summonses, parking fine demands and county court judgments. (It's never dull in my office, I'll tell you.) Two weeks later and the unanswered correspondence is officially a 'pile'. Two weeks after that and it's become a hillock. Wait further and it's a mountain. You get the idea.

In chapter 20 we looked at how and why procrastination is bad for your general health and well being. So how *do* we stop procrastinating and start getting things done? Well, a psychological study by McCrea, Liberman, Trope & Sherman appears to demonstrate that how quickly we act depends upon how we construe the issue. Apparently, there are two kinds of construal: abstract and concrete. Suppose you have a major presentation that you are putting off planning. An 'abstract construal' is one where you imagine the audience laughing along and clapping rapturously at the end. Whereas a 'concrete construal' is where you imagine specific feedback on your performance such as a flattering e-mail from your boss.

So researchers devised a study to get participants into one of these two modes of thinking. Half of them were shown a painting and told it was a good example of neo-impressionism in which the artist was using order and colour to invoke emotion and harmony. This is a good example of an 'abstract construal'. Meanwhile, the other half were just shown the detail of the painting and told that it demonstrated a particular technique of using contrasting points of colour to build up an image. This is a concrete construal.

Both groups were then asked to complete a survey and return it within three weeks. Their answers were irrelevant - the only thing the researchers wanted to discover was how long participants took to return the questionnaire. This was their measure of procrastination. Those thinking about abstract issues such as emotion and harmony took almost twice as long to return the survey as those who were thinking about specific techniques and details. Taking on board findings from other research in this area the answer is clear: to avoid procrastinating on a task, you should keep the ultimate abstract goal in mind but also focus on its details and use self-imposed deadlines.

If you can be bothered.

Elizabeth was very definitely bothered. But she also understood the ramifications of making a 'final' decision as far as Mary's life was concerned.

James intimated that he would declare war - probably along with France too - if Elizabeth went ahead with the execution but he didn't actually say that in so many words. What he did do was suggest very clearly that they would only resort to hostilities if Elizabeth excluded him from the succession.

Not for the first time we see that potential monarchs look after themselves even when their mother's life is at stake.

Mary was eventually put on trial in October of 1586.

19 years after Elizabeth ordered her arrest.

She was alleged to have conspired to kill Elizabeth. The Queen of England had asked her advisors if they could not arrange for the 'natural' death of the Queen of Scotland and as those requests consistently fell on deaf ears she eventually pulled the trigger.

Mary Stuart's Trial

Or, to be more specific, ordered the axe to be wielded.

On February 7th 1587 Mary was informed that she was to be executed the very next day. Mary didn't lose her composure before the execution. She made her will on the dawn of the day of her execution. She was executed in the Great Hall of Fotheringhay Castle at 8 o'clock on February 8th.

She was 44 years old when her head was struck off with two blows of the axe. She was 24 when she'd been first imprisoned by the Protestants in Scotland so she'd been held captive for nearly half her life. James was not yet 21 and although many of his subjects were up for a fight with the English he could see that he could become the first King of England and Scotland.

And that would come to pass before he would reach his Mother's age at her death.

Mary Queen of Scots had actually been betrothed to Edward VI in 1543 when he was six years old.

It might have turned out so differently.

What Ifs, If Onlys and Maybes.

Chapter 23 ~ 'Pass me something light'

1587 — 1599

In the spring of 1587 Mary Queen of Scots was no longer a thorn in Elizabeth's side. Instead, the French and the Scots were an ever-present threat and the rumours from Spain suggested they were preparing for war. To make matters worse, Elizabeth's army in the Netherlands hadn't been paid for several months and were growing restless. Even the delights of the local nightlife were beginning to wear thin.

King Philip of Spain hadn't been happy with the treatment of the English Catholics and even less impressed when Elizabeth killed his sister-in-law. On top of this, Francis Drake was getting right up his nose with his exploits in what was described as 'The New World'. He also believed that he had a claim to the English throne. His minions trawled through the genealogy and reminded him that Edward III's son, John of Gaunt, had married Constance of Castille. "And your point is?" he replied impatiently. "Well, your mum was their daughter which makes you the grandson and rightful heir. And you never shut up about the weather." Few could argue with their logic.

Not for the first time when people have an opinion they look for evidence to support it - and they can usually find it. That summer Philip signed a treaty with the Pope which stated that after he had conquered England he could crown whoever he wished as King or Queen provided that the new ruler converted the country to Catholicism. The Pontiff also offered the thick end of a quarter of a million pounds towards Philip's expenses, payable only after Spanish troops had landed in England.

It would have been best if this plan had been kept a secret. However, Pope Sixtus V was an old man and, a little worried he might pop his clogs at any time, he decided to let the cardinals in on the top secret plan. And, naturally, they told everyone else.

Eventually, the Queen found out and sent Francis Drake to Spain to have a good look at what they were plotting. She advised him to attack as many Spanish ships as possible and to apply sun cream liberally. Not one to drag his feet, Drake was soon in Cadiz harbour causing mayhem. He burnt or captured nearly forty ships and was clearly loving his work. Within a short time he had sunk around a hundred Spanish ships and burnt all their precious cargo. Still a Guinness World Record.

Sensing that he was on a roll, Drake left his base at Cape St. Vincent and sailed for the Azores where he captured the San Felipe and brought it back in some triumph to Plymouth. His navy somewhat depleted, King Philip was forced to revise his plans. He decided to sail right up the English Channel and anchor at the picturesque seaside town of Margate.

Who said war can't be fun?

And so, as 1588 drew nearer, more and more English people were worried what the New Year might bring and began hastily changing their holiday plans. Margate was out, Blackpool was in. A 15th century mathematician, Regiomontanus, had read the heavens and concluded that in 1588 there would be either a universal consummation and a final dissolution of the world, or at best, a general alteration of principalities, kingdoms, monarchies and empires.

Naturally, people started to worry and wish they were better educated. So many long words.

Still, it didn't sound good.

Regiomontanus was the stage name of Johannes Müller von Königsberg. He'd built a portable sundial for Pope Paul II in 1465, gained favour with the Pontiff and his reputation as an astronomer grew and grew even after his death.

Johannes Müller von Königsberg

In response to Regiomontanus's forecast, the Privy Council ordered Dr. John Harvey to write a book saying it was all nonsense and there was no need to panic. He even took the trouble to explain that although there would be two lunar eclipses, the position of Mars within the solar system suggested that there would be no negative issues to trouble them.

People really did believe this stuff in those days.

Some still do.

A psychologist by the name of Leon Festinger came up with the theory of cognitive dissonance in the 1950's. It helped explain why people of strong convictions are so resistant to changing their beliefs even in the face of undeniable contradictory evidence. I myself have some strong convictions but mainly just for motoring offences.

Festinger and his associates at Stanford University heard about a housewife called Marion Keech who had mysteriously been given messages from aliens on the planet 'Clarion' that the world would end in a great flood before midnight on December 20th. Convinced that the aliens would come to their rescue, a group of believers had gone as far as quitting their jobs and leaving their spouses in order to prepare for the evacuation via flying saucer at one minute to midnight. So strong was their conviction that none had sent Christmas cards or bought presents.

Festinger and his colleagues infiltrated the group of nutters - I mean believers - and were probably a little disappointed that, as dawn was on the horizon, there had been no flood, no visits from extraterrestrials, and no free trip on a flying saucer.

But at 4.45am Mrs. Keech had a new vision. Apparently, the world had been spared because of the impressive faith of her little band. "And mighty is the word of God," she told her followers, "and by his word have you been saved - for from the mouth of death have you been delivered and at no time has there been such a force loosed upon the Earth." And then she added, "Have we missed the last Christmas post?"

Fruitcake.

In early 1588 Elizabeth prepared for war. Defence preparations were made on land, men were trained, merchant ships were requisitioned and a list was drawn up of likely landing spots by the invading Spanish. By the spring, the Spanish still hadn't shown up and Elizabeth, itching for a fight - though some say it was her cotton sack underwear - was thinking about going on the attack. Wishing to seize the initiative, Francis Drake was first to volunteer. "I knew you'd be well up for it, Franny" the Queen said.

Well, something like that, anyway.

Perhaps, like all pugilists she wanted to keep fighting even though it was probably best to retire. However, she was well off retirement age. Plus, she'd spent a lifetime stabilising the country. But despite all her successes, and the fact that England Limited was in much better shape when she left it than when she arrived, there was still a simmering cauldron of problems left for her successor to ladle.

Although an English fleet set sail for Spain from Plymouth at the end of May the weather was so bad they were driven back and Elizabeth changed her mind on the attack. "Do people really come here for their holidays?" she was heard to muse. However, she was worried that the Spanish would sneak up and get England while they were away.

She was probably right.

In July 1588, the Spanish Armada finally left Spain and made for England. A week later it was spotted off the Cornish coast refuelling with pasties. The Spanish had adopted a very complicated defensive formation where the slow and less well armed supply ships were screened by rows of war ships. To the English it must have looked quite daunting, but when you've got Francis Drake on your side you don't fear much.

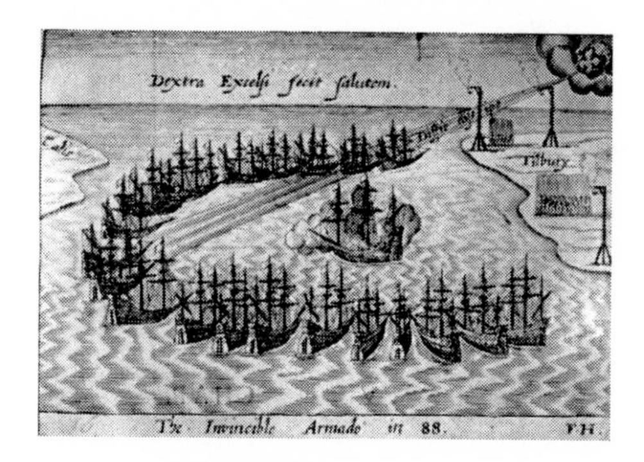

For several days the English fleet trailed the Armada as they made a little progress around the Isle of Wight. It was Cowes week and the traffic was shocking. The Spanish were weighed down with all the supplies and ammunition necessary for a long campaign and needed to get alongside the English ships. However, the English knew this and wouldn't let it happen, taunting their Spanish foes with renditions of 'Who ate all the pies' long into the night. Eventually Drake calmed them down. "Alright boys, enough's enough."

At midnight on July 28th, eight English ships were selected and turned into mobile incendiary boats by stuffing them with combustible materials. They were sent towards the Spanish hoping to dislodge them from their anchorage in Calais. It worked. As dislodgements go, this was pretty spectacular. The Spanish were thrown into confusion. They assumed that the English fire ships were packed with explosives and so cut themselves loose and sailed out to sea. By now the English had the numerical and tactical advantage, plus all the pies.

Fresh ships were called for. In the fog and mayhem of war this order was misheard and two hundred bags of chips were delivered. Drake almost blew a gasket and screamed, "I said ships, not chips!" and then added sheepishly, "Pass me some sea salt." With the wind behind them, the English finished up chasing the Spanish armada all the way to the Firth of Forth.

The Spanish were stuck north of Scotland, low on fuel, low on provisions and low on morale. The tourist board there told locals just to ignore them. You can't please everyone. Meanwhile, James VI had assured Elizabeth he would not befriend the Spanish as he had his eyes on the main prize of the English throne. In August 1558 Queen Elizabeth sailed to Tilbury to review her troops and give her most famous speech:

"I know I have the body of a weak and feeble woman but I have the heart and stomach of a King; and a King of England too. I myself will take up arms. Now, pass me something light."

Elizabeth gave people the belief that the tipping point that losers see had not arrived. The English would win. The motivational speech over, and no sign of the Armada returning, she took cheese and crackers with her good friend and cohort, Leicester. His penchant for cheese and habit of blushing uncontrollably in the presence of royalty, gave rise to his nick name of Red Leicester.

Still popular today.

By the end of August the camp at Tilbury was dissolved and Elizabeth made dramatic reductions in her armed forces with the carefully chosen words, "Thanks boys.You're all fired".

The act of a good CEO but a little tactless, perhaps.

Elizabeth had learned one of the great lessons. Namely, that you need to finish off your opponents when you're in a position to do so. So, following victory over the Armada, she was intent on putting Spain to the sword. In September 1588 she had plans for an expedition under Francis Drake and Sir John Norris but costs escalated.

They finally agreed to ditch the onboard cabaret and make do with deck quoits.

Six months later, the fleet set sail but was back with its tail between its legs within a month. Money had been wasted and estimates of English losses stood at 11,000. Drake and Norris were asked to justify their conduct before the Privy Council and it was some years before Elizabeth entrusted Drake with further military responsibility.

And so the war with Spain was not really finished. Over the next few years the French had their own civil war and Elizabeth actually sent troops to help Henry IV on the understanding that they would side together against Spain. But the men and the money that Elizabeth had poured into her campaign in Normandy had pretty much been squandered and no ground gained.

Elizabeth was incensed at the way the French had deceived her and Henry had not done what he said he was going to do.

In September 1592, the French King presented her with a love token in the shape of an elephant. Elizabeth jumped up and down and clapped her hands excitedly at the thought of what this wondrous gift might be that was shaped like an elephant. And then she realised. "It *is* a f***ing elephant!"

And then she fainted.

If you were to draw up a list of the very last thing she wanted to concern herself with at that moment, looking after an animal that was very big, very grey, and growing at an alarming rate would be at the very top of it.

Meanwhile, King Philip of Spain had no time for pachyderms. We don't know that for sure, it's just a hunch. Instead, he was putting pressure on anybody who might be interested to declare his daughter the Queen of France. However, for Frenchmen, the idea of a foreign female on the throne was too much to bear. In the autumn of 1594 Elizabeth sent troops to Brittany which helped rid the Spaniards from their base near Brest.

And all this, of course, was costing England money. Elizabeth's financial position was poor. The cost of the victory over the Armada, the cost of the Portuguese expedition, and financing operations in The Netherlands and France, meant she was spending a prohibitive amount of money. And in 1590 she sold crown lands and also frequently participated in privateering ventures. In 1592 Elizabeth was part of a syndicate that captured 'The Madre de Dios', a great merchant ship loaded with carpets, silk, jewels, and spices from the East Indies. Losing men, losing money and a sequence of poor harvests in the 1590's meant that the Queen was in trouble. There's also the ongoing matter of unrest in religious terms. And she'd had to have Sir Walter Raleigh arrested too for marrying Bess Frockmorton. Although she did approve of his plans for a Spud-U-Like franchise throughout Europe.

In December 1595, preparations began for another major offensive against Spain. This one was to be a joint Anglo Dutch affair with eighteen of the Queen's warships being matched by eighteen from the Dutch navy. With additional ships from private individuals, the fleet eventually numbered one hundred and fifty sails. Times had changed since the days when Drake had first preyed on outposts of the Spanish empire. Back then they weren't so well defended. Now ports were much more strongly fortified. With Drake having died early in 1596 the Queen announced the command of the new expedition was to be entrusted to Robert Devereux, the Earl of Essex and Charles Howard - better known as Lord Howard of Effingham.

You can make your own joke up there.

By April, all the preparations were complete but things changed when news arrived that a troop of Spanish boats were unexpectedly laying siege to Calais. Henry IV of France was unable to defend it and it was clear that unless Elizabeth did something to help, Calais would fall. She agreed, on condition that we could keep it.

What is it about Calais? There's got to be more than just cheap beer and fags.

However, Elizabeth acted too slowly. By the end of the month, Calais had been taken by the Spanish and her dreams of repossessing it had gone. The Spaniards were literally perched on our doorstep whilst the people on the south coast scratched their head in bemusement.

In June 1597 an expedition eventually left Plymouth led by Robert Devereux, 2nd Earl of Essex with Sir Walter Raleigh as his right hand man. The fleet was in Cadiz before the end of the month. Two of Philip's largest warships were destroyed and others captured. The 'Islands Voyage' was an English campaign against the Portuguese colonies in the Azores and was a key part of the Anglo–Spanish War.

However the voyage was doomed to failure when Essex, defying the orders of Elizabeth, pursued the ships carrying the treasure without first defeating the Spanish battle fleet. It turned out to be the last major expedition sent to sea by Elizabeth and contributed to Essex's decline in her favour. It was also to be her last real attempt to win a decisive victory over Spain.

The Crown's resources were overstretched and the Queen had no new ways of raising additional money. Although she had her failings as a leader, in particular cancelling possible exhibitions and changing the men in charge, in the final analysis it must be said she never withdrew her support from a naval venture to which she had earlier committed herself.

The only serious consequence of her actions was when Calais fell to the Spaniards in 1596. In truth, her main problem was people embezzling the loot she had paid them to seize, and her commanders being reluctant to carry out her instructions to the letter.

Men. We just never listen.

Chapter 24 ~ Past Pensionable age

1599 — 1603

By the end of the 16th Century the Queen was 67. And the war mongering with Spain Portugal, Ireland, France and Holland had consistently swallowed up resources. She'd pretty much been at war for all of her time on the throne and for what? During the last years of her reign she attempted to cut down on court expenditure and that created a negative atmosphere both at court and in the country.

As we enter the 17th Century there are still various rival claimants to the throne and although Elizabeth never formally endorsed it, it seemed to be James VI of Scotland who would succeed her.

Her father, Henry VIII, had made it clear in his will that should all his children die without having children themselves then the crown should pass to his sister Mary's children.

But they were the Greys.

Henry VIII's sister Mary, if you recall, after a desperately unhappy but short lived marriage to The King of France, had married Charles Brandon. And only the middle one of their three children, Frances, had given Mary grandchildren. Firstly Jane, the nine day Queen, then Catherine and finally Mary.

Elizabeth had always hated the Grey family. When Lady Jane Grey was forced onto the throne in 1553 Elizabeth had been officially branded a bastard and banned from the succession. And that's not the sort of thing you forgive and forget easily.

You reap what you sow.

In 1560 the middle daughter, Lady Catherine Grey, secretly married Edward Seymour who had been created Baron Beauchamp and Earl of Hertford by Elizabeth I in January 1559. Catherine's new husband was a nephew of Henry VIII's third wife, Jane Seymour, and son of Edward Seymour, Lord Protector under Henry VIII and Edward VI, who was executed by the Duke of Northumberland in 1552.

When Queen Elizabeth discovered the marriage of Lady Catherine Grey and Edward Seymour, she imprisoned both Catherine and Edward from 1561 until 1563. During Catherine's time in the Tower she gave birth to her first son.

Lady Catherine Grey died in 1568 and Elizabeth refused to recognise Catherine's two sons as legitimate so the elder, Edward Seymour, could be passed over for succession by Elizabeth.

And the youngest sister Mary was not to learn from Catherine's and, indeed, her grandmother's mistakes in marrying without the permission of the monarch. She made an ill advised marriage in June 1565 and her chosen bridegroom could not have been a worse choice, as she married the royal gatekeeper, Thomas Keyes. He was twice her age and called 'the largest man in the kingdom.' A particularly bad match if the reports of Mary's appearance are true and that she was 'very small, crooked and deformed'. Mary and her husband were both imprisoned although Mary was released in 1572, following her husband's death months earlier. By then Mary was not only small, crooked and deformed but also an old and disgraced princess. She died in 1578.

Elizabeth's brother and sister had also tried to challenge their father's will and failed. So Elizabeth had the will locked up in an iron casket and threw away the key. No photocopiers in those days.

In February 1603 Elizabeth gave an audience to the Venetian ambassador and was in good health. But she died on March 24th 1603 of blood poisoning. She was nearly 70 years old. She had never made a will but by this stage everyone knew who would succeed her.

To make a will and name names would, in her mind, create factions and the successor would probably gather forces and rise against the Queen.

Before March 24th was out James VI of Scotland had been proclaimed King James I of England.

King James VI of Scotland

When Elizabeth had ascended her kingdom it was weak, poor, demoralised and suffering great internal strife. Under her tutelage the nation regained its self confidence, sense of direction and sense of purpose. Despite the ups and downs the reign was fundamentally stable and united and the company 'England Limited' was left in a better state than when she joined it.

Her country hadn't been invaded and she had died a natural death. Not something that could be said for a lot of monarchs in those days. She'd shown tolerance to Catholics and was regarded as a popular and strong monarch.

As is always the case with good CEO's and good football managers she'd been given a long enough period of time to see her plans come to fruition. She was consistently well advised and she used her Devil's Advocates well. She did what she said she was going to do and that enhanced her reputation.

She had learned The Golden Rules.

When she died, King James of Scotland came to Westminster to be crowned King of a united Britain. And although the Kingdom of Great Britain would not be formalised until the Act of Union in 1707 under Queen Anne, the two would never declare war on each other as they had done for centuries before.

Like Henry VII all those years before he had brought together warring factions - in this case Scotland and England - by uniting the crown. Unlike Henry he'd married a nice Norwegian girl.

When James the VI of Scotland became King of England on March 24th 1603 he was thirty six years old and had already been married for twelve years to Anne of Denmark, the second daughter of King Frederick II of Denmark and Norway. The marriage had been in Oslo.

When he was crowned King of England he had a two year old son who would go on to become Charles I and marry the daughter of King Henry IV of France.

Plus ça change.

This book started with English princes having a penchant for young French girls and despite all the warring with France, all the disagreements, all the broken pacts and promises, we leave the story just before the gunpowder plot and the development of 'The New Land' with the English Kings likely to declare war on France or marry a young French girl.

Elizabeth, of course, had already left her mark on 'The New Land' with Virginia being named after her.

And we also leave the story with, for the first time, the King of England, Scotland and Ireland being the same person. But despite all these changes, his son Charles would go on to marry a French princess just as Edward I, Edward II and Richard II had done in the 14th Century.

Within a few years of the end of Elizabeth's reign the English set sail for America and many men were lost in the hopeless attempt to keep control of what would become the USA. Within the same time frame Guy Fawkes and his pals would be responsible for an event that we still celebrate every November to this day. Within 100 years the crown itself would be usurped. Did they learn the lessons that we have outlined in this book? An emphatic 'no' to that one. Have we, in the 21st century, learned what we could and should have from this remarkable period in history?

Make your own mind up.

Chapter 25 ~ The Sixth Golden Rule

Elizabeth seemed to understand the importance of not losing the lesson when she lost. She had learned what *not* to do from her siblings. She had also shown a tolerance not exhibited by her sister, brother, father and ancestors. She had been tough on dissidents but even with her biggest rival, Mary Queen of Scots, she had spent years treating her as she would have liked Mary to treat her if the roles had been reversed.

Well, at least she let her live.

In Cecil she had found the perfect Devil's Advocate. She had listened to his counsel before taking the big decisions. And she ruled the better for it.

She had understood the importance of taking her time over decisions that would cost lives and have long term repercussions for the country. Unlike her mother. She allocated time for things that were important but not urgent. Such as what to do with Mary Queen of Scots.

And she had been mindful of The Fifth Golden Rule too. With the burning (literally in her sister's day) issue of religion she had encouraged people to live and let live. Only the fanatics and bigots hated her for that. She had sought justice and didn't let her detractors at court get her down.

And she lived her life by The Sixth Golden Rule.

The Sixth Golden Rule:

Do what you say you are going to do

I hear people say that the essence of great customer service is to 'under-promise and over deliver'. I understand the sentiment but I have a problem with that. It's not easy to *over* deliver every day. Day in and day out.

Just promise.

And then deliver.

Just do what you say you're going to do. If you sign a contract, abide by your commitments.

Elizabeth I's Signature

That's what Elizabeth did.

If you make a promise that you will be at a certain place at a certain time then be there. If you are not there it's almost always because you didn't set off early enough. And that, in turn, usually means because you didn't think it was important enough to be there. You had other, more important things to do.

Or, of course, you just don't care.

Or are just plain lazy.

Looking back on running a business I would say that the root of the vast majority of problems with clients, staff and suppliers was that somebody had not done what they said they were going to do or someone had misunderstood what, when and how someone was going to do something. If you say you're going to deliver a product or a service to a customer by a certain date and you don't deliver it, the customer draws the conclusion you either forgot, you are lazy or you had more important things to do.

What other conclusion could they draw?

Do what you say you're going to do. How hard is this? Apparently very hard.

I am writing this two days after I did a talk for a fine firm of jewellers by the name of Rudell's. As always, I had agreed a fee with the client and turned up on time. As always I didn't ask for any kind of deposit. My guarantee is that if I don't do what is expected of me - if the client doesn't think that what I deliver is worth it - then they don't have to pay the bill.

I don't do credit control. I aspire to be as good as I can possibly be when I am presenting. Because all that matters right now is now. I don't take phone calls and don't allow myself to be distracted by other events in my life. Because when you are working all that matters is now.

Be 'in the moment' and focus on what you are doing.

So, as I sit here two days after speaking to the good people of Rudell's, I get a nice surprise from the post man. Anthony 'Roundy' Rudell - the CEO - has sent me a gift and a hand written note. In it he thanks me for the 'great job you did for us last night' and makes reference to the fact that his staff are talking very positively about our time together. The gift is a Cartier writing instrument.

Which is nice.

Very nice.

He asks me if I will return.

You bet.

I did what I said I would do and he has exceeded my expectations in terms of gratitude. Oh if business were always this simple. The only other person who sends me hand written personalised cards is Jonathan Wild. He runs Bettys.

It's our next lesson.

Everyone wants to be treated as an individual. Everyone wants to be treated in a special way.

So why don't institutions honour their moral obligations? Why don't politicians live up to their promises?

We crave consistency. We want reliability. We don't want tiresome excuses. We enjoy more relationships with people who care; people who do what they say they are going to do.

'Success' is, of course, different things to different people. It has many meanings depending on what each person is seeking for in his or her life, relationship and career. And it would be easy to conclude that for an athlete success is winning that gold medal but it would be to miss the point. For many athletes success is getting to 'the next stage' and achieving their full potential. Each individual has to determine the true meaning of success in his or her own life.

In my view it is doing what you want to do.

But whatever your definition is, the one over riding factor that affects people's opinions of you - and therefore the reputation you have - is whether you are reliable; whether you do what you say you are going to do. Of course there are many examples of people in the arts who are successful and reliably unreliable. But people don't trust them. They know they can't rely on them.

Are they successful in what really matters in life - the relationships we have with the people who are closest to us? If we aren't trusted by the people we love we are surely not successful. And it's difficult to keep loving someone who is unreliable and doesn't do what they say they are going to do.

The things that really count in your life can't be counted.

It's a lesson too many people take too long to learn.

When I ask people all over the world what is the most important thing to them I almost always get 'family' as the answer; particularly those who have their own children. And if your own children don't see you as reliable - if you don't do what you say you are going to do - you are unsuccessful in the most important thing in your life.

One measure of success is how close one comes to accomplishing one's pre-determined, self-set goals. Nothing in life occurs just by chance. You have the power to control your life, to control your success and your failure.

We get set backs of course. But people are there to help us when we do; the closest people to us. But if we are unreliable those people are less likely to want to help. If you haven't shown you care by doing what you say you are going to do, why should they?

You reap what you sow.

Success is about working at something, progressing and having a 'purpose'. It is doing exactly what you want to do with your life providing it's worthwhile, you are happy within yourself and happy with the thought of the future.

Expectation, belief and desire are the three powerful forces that come together to help us be 'successful'. If you really want something to happen you have to desire for it to happen first, and you have to not only believe deeply that it will happen but that you actually expect that it will happen.

Your subconscious mind works on the information and messages you send to it. So not only is it critical that you do what you say you are going to do because it enhances your reputation and makes you happier (because people don't criticise you for being unreliable) it also means you are more likely to achieve your goals and aims in life because you have told your subconscious brain that you do what you say you are going to do. And if that means you are going to win the metaphorical gold medal it's more likely you will be on the podium.

It's natural.

Elizabeth I is one of our best known and most respected monarchs. She took over the running of the country after her father, brother and sister, in turn, had caused strife and deep divisions not only amongst their own people but amongst families. She treated other people - particularly her cousin Mary - as she would wish to be treated. She used Cecil - and others - as a

Devil's Advocate and listened to their sage advice. She made sure she spent time doing things that were important but not urgent and she was tolerant of other people's religious beliefs. She had a 'live and let live' attitude but didn't tolerate fools. Nor those people who ignored her or threatened her realm. And she lived her life by The Sixth Golden Rule.

Starting in chapter 1 with Edward III we have seen fourteen monarchs in this book. We have seen the throne switch from white rose to red and back again. We have seen the Plantagenets give way to the Tudors and we leave it as we enter the House of Stuart. The longest reign is that of a woman.

And the most successful.

The Sixth Golden Rule:

Do what you say you are going to do
When you said you were going to do it
How you said you were going to do it
And with who you said you were going to do it
Always

Postscript and The Final Golden Rule

Well, we're almost at the end of our journey. We've had a little romp through English history, a whistle-stop tour through major events in world commerce, and hopefully learned more than a few lessons along the way. If you've got this far and absorbed even a tenth of all the facts and figures I've thrown at you then you deserve a big pat on the back. Not of the bovine variety, of course, that would be silly. But what has studying all these incidents of 'What Ifs, If Onlys and Maybes' actually taught us?

Should Richard have been happy with his lot and let the boy King rule? And did he miss out big style in the luxury ice cream market? The truth is we'll never know.

Should Arthur have plumped for a fortnight in Benidorm rather than a wet weekend in Wales and avoided catching his death? If so, he would surely have been crowned King and Henry VIII would never have ascended to the throne.

And how should we judge the lasting legacy of Sir Walter Raleigh's exploits? Sure enough, chips *are* very popular but with a fat content heavily outweighing their nutritional value it's not for nothing that health experts have coined the phrase 'Couch Potato'. On the upside, he did have a hand in the bicycle which does help to burn off the calories.

Or maybe I'm mixing him up with another Raleigh.

Very definitely on the downside was his discovery of tobacco. Of course, it was only ever a matter of time before it reached our shores and then spread throughout the world, but Raleigh had the distinction of setting in motion an industry that has both made billions for its distributors and cost a great deal more for its users. During Elizabeth's reign, few could have foreseen the dangers of taking up the habit beyond possibly setting your head on fire when trying to cadge a light from an open fire. Even throughout much of the 20th century, few people had any qualms about the potential health risks of smoking, which was given the thumbs up by Dresden's Fritz Lickint in his scientific paper on the subject. To prove his point, he then rolled up the paper, filled it with tobacco and smoked it. Or maybe I'm just making that bit up.

It's what I would have done.

Elizabeth's successor, King James I, was less enthusiastic about Raleigh's discovery. He described the habit as 'a custom loathsome to the eye, hateful to the nose, harmful to the brain and dangerous to the lungs'. But then he was trying to shove a potato in his pipe.

Not the brightest, that one.

In fact, it wasn't until the 1950's that a scientific consensus on the dangers of smoking emerged. By then, of course, it was big business, earning billions for companies and governments alike. Despite knowing its harmful effects, American Tobacco handed out huge amounts of cash to popular Hollywood stars as part of a massive strategy that ran for nearly a quarter of a century. The intention was to make smoking a symbol of virility for young men and femininity and freedom for young women. Almost 200 stars, including two thirds of the Top 50 box office actors took the Big Tobacco Shilling, praising brands for their taste, smoothness and ability to provide relaxation.

One of the biggest stars, John Wayne, even told the public that smoking helped to define his distinctive voice. Unfortunately, he had to have a lung removed when he developed cancer.

And all for the money.

Enron boss Andy Fastow knew that his elaborate hiding of the figures would lead to ordinary people losing their pensions. When he pleaded guilty in 2004 and accepted a jail term of ten years, he did so in order to reduce his sentence and name others. In the same year, Enron ex-chairman Kenneth Lay was still pleading 'not guilty' to eleven criminal charges including bank fraud, share trading fraud and making false statements.

He died before sentence was passed.

On April 10th 1912 'The Titanic' set sail from Southampton with 2,200 passengers and crew. Although J. Bruce Ismay, chairman and managing director of the White Star Line, had had a proposal for the ship to be fitted with 48 lifeboats, he regarded the ship as being unsinkable. She was actually certified to carry over 3,500 passengers and crew.

J. Bruce Ismay

The safety regulations at the time only required vessels over 10,000 tons to carry 16 life-boats; sufficient to carry 962 people. In simple terms the British government's Board of Trade allowed 'The Titanic' to sail with insufficient lifeboat accommodation. And Ismay was complicit in the complacency. On April 14th 1912 it collided with an iceberg and sank. Over 1,500 people died and 700 survived.

Commissions of enquiry into the disaster were subsequently held in both Britain and America. The Report of the British Commission blamed the disaster on excessive speed and a failure to maintain a proper watch. It recommended that an international conference be held about safety at sea. The conference concluded that there were not enough lifeboats on board to hold all the passengers and crew.

Well, we knew that.

When the lifeboats were launched they were not filled to capacity. At the British Inquiry into 'The Titanic' disaster Sir Alfred Chalmers of the Board of Trade was asked why regulations governing the number of lifeboats required on passenger ships had not been updated since 1896. Sir Alfred gave a number of reasons for this but they can be summed up in one word; hubris.

Here's what E. J. Smith, the Captain of 'The Titanic' said before the voyage: "In all my experience, I have never been in any accident of any sort worth speaking about. I have seen but one vessel in distress in all my years at sea. I never saw a wreck and never have been wrecked nor was I ever in any predicament that threatened to end in disaster of any sort."

He went down with the ship.

'The Titanic' is symbolic not only of disunity and hubris but also greed. They are the ever-presents when things go wrong.

And let's revisit Tennyson's poem about The Charge of the Light Brigade in 1854. Let me tell you more of what he wrote:

'Into the Valley of Death rode the six hundred; cannon to the right of them, cannon to the left of them' as though it were not only heroic but also the right thing to do. The Charge of the Light Brigade has long held its place in the public imagination. It seems to me it is a symbol of heroic failure, a high-Victorian icon of self-sacrifice and devotion to duty. But it was actually a rather stupid thing to do and an event that caught a world about to change. It showed that chivalric cavalry charges and officers in their nice, bright, full-dress uniforms were no match for modern fire-power.

Basically it was the most lethal costume party in history; a few hundred cavalrymen mounted a doomed charge against the Russian artillery. The aristocratic, self-centered generals, who appeared to have little concern for casualties but who decided on the charge should have known better. At the heart of the decision was the upper-class rivalry of Lord Lucan and Lord Cardigan.

In the 20th Century the image of military sacrifice acquired a very different character but the decisions were made with the same reckless attitude towards the people who lost their lives. In 1916, the Battle of the Somme saw 60,000 British casualties in a single day - and the poets of the First World War saw nothing heroic about such an appalling loss of life.

The threads that run through the MPs' expenses scandal, 'The Titanic', The Charge of the Light Brigade, The Battle of the Somme, The Herald of Free Enterprise, Enron and, of course, the period of history we have covered in this book, are arrogance that eventually manifests itself as hubris and then disaster.

And then the ordinary man's need for the truth and for accountability.

People want the truth. They need to know why things have gone wrong and what steps will be taken to ensure it won't happen again. They want a sincere apology and a promise that someone will take action.

Despite the fact that J. Bruce Ismay's coat of arms carried the motto 'Be Mindful' he allowed 'The Titanic' to sail with too few lifeboats. He also turned a blind eye to the antics of wireless operators who were more concerned with making money from sending passengers' telegrams than conveying messages about icebergs. But he did have a marvellous staircase at the heart of the ship that only sailed for four days.

'Be mindful' eh?

This pattern of wealthy and powerful people misusing their influence and becoming complacent is a recurring theme throughout *all* periods of history.

Following the seizure of Catholic lands and properties during the Tudor period, the Protestant landed gentry flatly refused to return any money or possessions when the country later converted back to Catholicism. When Dudley became Master of the Household, Duke of Northumberland and Earl Marshall of England, he wasn't content with having the longest title of anybody in the room at any one time. He demonstrated his appreciation to the boy King, Edward VI, by stealing Church land. "There's gratitude for you" said a bemused Edward when spotting a dozen or so freshly replanted gravestones on Dudley's front lawn.

Henry VIII fared little better with his close companions. Cardinal Wolsey, his right hand man for many years, embezzled money to fund his colleges at Oxford University and only handed his ill gotten gains back when his number was well and truly up.

Anne Boleyn's father was open to bribery and corruption too. He not only thrust his wife and daughters into the King's favour but stood aside as his own son was wrongly accused of having sexual relations with his youngest daughter. "You'll find him in his bedroom on the PlayStation" he suggested helpfully as soldiers burst into his home.

He also stood aside as Henry VIII had carnal relations with his wife and both his daughters. He may have even left the room. And why? All so that he could progress his political career and personal power base.

Talking of which, why do you suppose Peter Mandelson's memoirs in 2010 criticised the very people he had been working with for so many years? Even acknowledging that Mandy is a lightning conductor for criticism, he did it for himself; for the power and the glory; not forgetting the money.

Plus a few more days in the spotlight.

Here is a man who openly admits that he adores pimps and celibacy.

To be fair, I think he said pomp and ceremony and was woefully misquoted. He had already been rewarded with the bauble of an honorific title that, to him, meant so much. The Baron of Hartlepool and Foy rather coyly said that he was happy to be just plain 'Lord Mandelson'. When his title was formally conferred he appeared just like a Tudor courtier, stooping under the weight of his gold chains and medallions. Think Peter Stringfellow in a fur coat.

Plus ça change, plus c'est la même chose.

The thread that has run through history is that human greed, hubris and disunity bring about the fall.

In 1470 the Yorkists became complacent and King Edward IV released Henry VI from prison and rued the day he did.

In 1485 Richard III had become complacent when he arrived in Bosworth for what he thought would be a walk over with a rag-tag and bobtail assortment of a few dozen disenchanted Lancastrian supporters and promptly lost the fight.

When Sir Walter Raleigh embarked on his affair with Queen Elizabeth's maid of honour he thought he could get away with marrying her without the Queen's permission. He became complacent. He and his wife were sent to the Tower in 1592.

If, in 1569, the head of security at Loch Leven had not become complacent, Mary Queen of Scots would never have made it to England.

You get the idea.

So here is The Seventh Golden Rule for you to live a happy and successful life.

The Seventh Golden Rule:
Beware Hubris

That's it. We have seen too many monarchs and their cohorts rise and then fall because they became complacent. Although I have usually limited myself to using just one company, battle or downfall as an example, the sinking of 'The Titanic' was such a spectacularly avoidable mess that it warranted more than one appearance in this book.

And it all came down to hubris.

I see it in all divorces, in sporting teams that hit the heights and then slump. I see it in politicians, business people and organisations. I see a rise and then a fall.

Live your life being always mindful of The Final Golden Rule and you will be happier and more successful.

Because once you become complacent not only are you heading for an inevitable fall but you will be living your life with less joy. Once the thrill of the chase is gone and you take things for granted there is little chance of happiness.

The first secret to happiness is acceptance.

In Kübler-Ross's studies on grief and great trauma she concluded that people cannot be happy until they first accept the way things are. And the second secret to happiness is that it's all in the *journey* and not the destination. And if the journey you are on does not thrill you with a sense of purpose; if you become complacent and insouciant you give off those negative energies to the people around you.

If you're bored, you're boring.

We all need a sense of purpose. We all need to be on a journey. With its ups and downs of course. But it's the unpredictability that creates the uncertainty that keeps hubris at bay.

Thomas Gilovich is Professor of Psychology at Cornell University in Ithaca, New York. He has been studying the psychology of regret for over a decade. He has asked hundreds of people to look back on their lives and describe their biggest regrets. His work is consistent with others in the field and my own interviews with octogenarians. Most people regret the things they *didn't* do rather than the things they *did*. Along with not studying hard enough at school and not taking full advantage of opportunities that came their way, up there in the top three of regrets for most people is not spending enough time with their friends and family.

Of course we all have some regrets; we all leave the odd stain on life's carpet. Henry VIII probably reflected ruefully on Anne Boleyn. He may even have been remorseful.

He certainly should have been.

It's easy to reflect on your life and notice the things you've done which you didn't value or enjoy. And you can come to terms with them. But when you miss out on something you *could* have done but never did; when you've missed the pleasure and positive benefits of missed chances you are left with the question 'What if…?'

What Ifs, If Onlys and Maybes.

It's where we came in.

You only get one chance at life and we all become complacent about how things are *now*. We take for granted what we have. We take for granted the most important people in our lives. As we said in chapter 2, you don't know what you got 'til it's gone.

If you become complacent and don't go for change, you leave your life to chance.

I guess the final lesson is that life is always going to be a series of choices. And the price you have to pay for making a choice is wondering what would have happened if you had made a different one. Some good, some bad.

Your place in the world, your meaningfulness, is something you must create for yourself.

Too many people live for no reason and don't see their purpose in life. Some see it as making lots of money, others to make themselves famous, or to become powerful; sometimes all three. And whether or not they attain these objectives, they often find their lives empty and meaningless. If you don't decide what is worth doing, someone will decide for you.

What you are doing right now is the thing that you most want to do. Of course, you may be thinking that you would rather be on a beach. But if you really wanted to be, you'd be there. The reason you're not is because you have chosen other priorities in life; probably good choices like your family, your job and your education.

Even bad consequences are mainly a matter of choice.

When Denis Pratt reinvented himself as Quentin Crisp it was no surprise that he was to subsequently comment that life was 'a mad dash between the cradle and the grave across open country under heavy fire.' Well, Quentin, when you set yourself apart from the crowd, you set yourself up to be shot down.

So here are The Golden Rules for a happy and successful life. Live your life with these rules as your constant companion and you will be more liked by more people, enhance your reputation, be happier and be more successful in what you choose to do. Because success is doing what you want to do.

And then you can leave this planet the better for you having being here.

For that is the purpose of life; to develop loving relationships and make a meaningful, positive contribution.

The Seven Golden Rules:

When you lose, don't lose the lesson

Treat others as you would like them to treat you

Always Have a Devil's Advocate

Allocate time for things that are important but not urgent

Live and let live, but don't live with injustice

Do what you say you are going to do

Beware Hubris

According to many experts you should be able to remember *Seven* Golden Rules. Seven is thought to be the maximum number of items that our short-term memory can hold.

That's probably why there are only seven days in a week. Any more and we'd lose track. The same goes for the wonders of the world, the seven seas and, of course, the deadly sins. There are possibly more but we just can't recall them. Throw in seven colours in a rainbow, Snow White and her vertically challenged helpers, the seven ages of man and S Club Seven you can see that the number seven is pretty special.

Well maybe not the last one but you get the idea.

It was many, many years later that I returned to Bath. I never did get to be a Civil Engineer nor gaze expertly through a theodolite.

Exactly forty years after the incident with Sid Smith outside the Physics exam I was asked to speak at a conference for MultiYork in that fine Somerset town. I was drawn to walk around the town and wonder what might have been if I had studied there.

What Ifs, If Onlys and Maybes.

Incidentally, Susan Garlick and I did have a brief relationship.

She dumped me.

A bit like when Pete Best was told to leave The Beatles by Brian Epstein but without the drum roll. They already had another drummer lined up and, for all I know, Susan may have had another suitor waiting in the wings.

Many years later, Best famously said that he was very happy living a quiet life with his wife and two daughters. That he was happier than he would have been if he had stayed with the Beatles.

Unlike Pete Best I *know* that, for me, it turned out for the better. I could not have asked for more in terms of joy from my darling wife and three wonderful sons.

And I hope the decisions you make mean that your life turns out for the better too.

I *have* wondered what might have happened if Sid had not spoken to Susan Garlick on that particular day in 1971. I've also wondered what might have happened if the future King Arthur and his new bride, Katherine of Aragon, had not gone to Ludlow Castle in 1502. But you can't rewrite history. Though, as you may have gathered from this book, there's nothing to stop anyone from having a go.

The truth is, this is how it is. We are where we are. We need to accept it and face the future whilst learning from the past.

And as for history itself?

Well it's a bit like life really; it's just one bloody thing after another.

Appendix:

The Seven Golden Rules:

The First Golden Rule:

When you lose, don't lose the lesson

The Second Golden Rule:

Treat others as you would like them to treat you.

Always

Because you reap what you sow

Eventually

The Third Golden Rule:

Always Have a Devils' Advocate

Someone has to check the checker

Always

Have a good Devil's Advocate

Have a good, conscientious checker

Listen properly

The Fourth Golden Rule:

Allocate time for things that are important but not urgent

The Fifth Golden Rule:

Live and let live but don't live with injustice

Smell the flowers along the way

Et illigitimi non carborundum

The Sixth Golden Rule:

Do what you say you are going to do

The Seventh Golden Rule:

Beware Hubris

Lightning Source UK Ltd.
Milton Keynes UK
UKOW03n0603160414

230053UK00002B/19/P

9 780956 759801